THE VICTORIA HISTORY OF LEICESTERSHIRE

LUTTERWORTH

Pamela J. Fisher and Andrew Watkins

VICTORIA
COUNTY
HISTORY

First published 2022

A Victoria County History publication

© The University of London, 2022

ISBN 978-1-912702-82-4

Typeset in Minion pro
Published by the University of London Press
Senate House, Malet Street, London WC1E 7HU
https://london.ac.uk/press

Cover image: Church Street, from an original painting by Sue Browne,
by courtesy of the artist.
Back cover image: Bust of Sir Frank Whittle in Lutterworth Memorial Gardens
(photograph by Pamela J. Fisher).

CONTENTS

LIST OF ILLUSTRATIONS

We are grateful to Sue Browne for allowing us to use her painting of Church Street for the front cover, to the Record Office for Leicestershire, Leicester and Rutland (Figures 3, 10, 17 and 24 and Map 1) and to Geoff Smith and Lutterworth Museum (Figures 11, 14, 15, 16 and 27) for permission to publish these images. The other photographs were taken by Pamela J. Fisher. Map 2 is published with permission of the Ordnance Survey, licence no. CS-253662-L8P9W1. Maps 3 and 5 were digitised by the National Library of Scotland and are reproduced under a CC BY-NC-SA licence.

Maps

FOREWORD

THIS HISTORY OF LUTTERWORTH IS the latest in a series of books on towns and villages in Leicestershire being published by the Victoria County History. This is a great national project, begun at the end of the reign of Queen Victoria, and has been rededicated to Queen Elizabeth II. The Leicestershire Victoria County History aims to write the history of every place in the county; good progress was made in the 1950s and 1960s, and the work resumed in 2011.

As mayor of Lutterworth, I am pleased to welcome this informative and attractively illustrated book, which shows the town's widely known associations with John Wyclif, the church reformer, and Sir Frank Whittle, who developed the jet engine. Lutterworth was also important as one of six well-established market towns in Leicestershire. It was a centre of the timber trade and a home to important wool merchants in the Middle Ages, and a communications hub in the days of the stagecoaches. The town's prosperity in the early 19th century is demonstrated by its distinguished town hall, designed by Joseph Hansom, while in the 20th century factories such as the Vedonis Works and Alfred Herbert Ltd employed many townspeople.

Lutterworth is a town with a long and fascinating history, ably described within these pages, and local residents will enjoy the many stories of the town's past that have been uncovered and are explained here, while reflecting on how their town has changed over the years. The research has been carried out mainly by Pamela Fisher and Andrew Watkins, assisted by local volunteers and by undergraduate students from the University of Leicester.

The timing of this book is particularly appropriate, as it coincides closely with the move of the Lutterworth Museum to its new town-centre location. I am especially pleased that it has been published by a national organisation with overseas connections, which means that it will circulate outside Leicestershire and spread the news about Lutterworth's interesting history and heritage to a wider audience.

Richard Nunn
Mayor of Lutterworth, 2021–2

ACKNOWLEDGEMENTS

THE VICTORIA COUNTY HISTORY (VCH) series was established in 1899 with the aim of researching and publishing the history of every city, town, village and hamlet in England. Leicestershire has lagged behind the progress seen in many other counties but, after a long period in which the project was dormant in this county, we are delighted to be able now to share our research into the history of Lutterworth. This is the fourth paperback history for a Leicestershire parish to have been published in the VCH series since 2016, and the first for one of the county's major market towns.

A full chronological history of any place requires substantial research and the involvement of many people. We gratefully acknowledge the generous support received from Leicestershire Archaeological and Historical Society, Lutterworth Area Community Fund and GLP, Lutterworth Town Council, the University of Leicester and many individual donors and supporters of Leicestershire Victoria County History Trust, who have patiently seen us through the research, writing and publication stages of this book. Particular thanks are tendered to Chris Dyer for his warm support, encouragement and advice on interpreting historic documents and landscape features, extended over several years; to John Goodacre, who generously shared his detailed knowledge of the history of the town, the surrounding area and the surviving original source material; and to Terry Slater for his helpful comments on the development of the medieval town. We are also very grateful to Richard Nunn, Mayor of Lutterworth, 2021–2, for kindly agreeing to provide the Foreword.

Illustrations and maps are important for any history. We thank Sue Browne for the cover image; Geoff Smith, Lutterworth Museum and the Record Office for Leicestershire, Leicester and Rutland for allowing us to reproduce old photographs from their collections; St Mary's church for their permission to use the photographs we took inside the church; and our cartographers Cath D'Alton and Simon Hayfield not only for their maps but also for their patience when alterations were requested.

We acknowledge with thanks the help given by Miriam Gill, Susan Tebby, John Thornton and Tony West, who kindly shared their own research with us, by Helen Wells at Leicestershire County Hall and by Sarah Finch-Crisp of the Friends of Lydiard Park. We are also grateful to Magnus Williamson and Louise Rayment, who helped with information about early choral music when we tried to figure out what a common *cantibilum* might once have been. Other volunteer researchers and undergraduate student historians have collected information for us from sources in The National Archives, local record offices and online, have identified and spoken to those with specific knowledge of aspects of Lutterworth's history in the late 20th and 21st centuries, and have helped to produce draft text. Our thanks are therefore also extended to Anne Bryan, Carol Cambers, Sam Daisley, Emily Danaher, Niamh Deane, Helen Edwards, Ellie Ferguson, Estevan Fortin, Mick Gamble, Jamie Harris, Lynda Hill, Amy Hopes, Molly Juckes, Sean Lane, Peter Langworth,

Huw Mabe, John Martin, Courtney Mower, Lauren Rowe, Sarah Taylor, Sue Turner, Anne Watson and Harry Wilkinson. Those who provided information from their own knowledge are acknowledged within the relevant footnotes. Any omissions from this list are inadvertent, and our apologies are offered to anyone we have failed to mention.

This book could not have been produced without the help and support of staff in record offices, libraries and museums, and especially those in the Record Office for Leicestershire, Leicester and Rutland and The National Archives. Both produced numerous documents for us and advised about other sources we might otherwise have overlooked. We are indebted to the volunteers in Lutterworth Museum, which we visited on many occasions, as well as staff at the British Library, the Bodleian Library, Lambeth Palace Library (and the former Church of England Record Centre), the David Wilson Library at the University of Leicester, Dr Williams's Library and the Principal Probate Registry. The archives and record offices for Buckinghamshire, Coventry, Gloucestershire, Lichfield, Lincolnshire, Northamptonshire and Warwickshire, Cotesbach Educational Trust and the Shakespeare Birthplace Trust have been unfailingly helpful to us, and we thank them all. We also thank those involved with major digitisation projects, including the British Newspaper Archive, FindMyPast and ProQuest (for parliamentary papers), who have made research so much easier, especially during pandemic lockdowns.

Finally, but just as importantly, we would like to thank members of the public and the anonymous peer reviewer for their helpful comments on our draft text, our colleagues at VCH Central Office in London, especially Adam Chapman, who has spent many hours reading and providing helpful comments on earlier drafts of this text, to Karen Francis for her meticulous proofreading, to Robert Davies and to Jamie Bowman at the University of London Press for all their help turning the text into this attractive book.

INTRODUCTION

THE MARKET TOWN OF LUTTERWORTH, 13 miles south of Leicester, occupies a prominent raised plateau above the valley of the river Swift. The town may have begun in embryo before the Norman Conquest, in association with a minster church, but its later growth was connected to the grant of a market charter in 1214. The market prospered because of its relatively early foundation and its favourable position linking two distinct *pays*: the open-field villages of south-west Leicestershire and the Warwickshire Arden with its natural resources of wood and coal. Within the Leicestershire hundreds of Guthlaxton and Sparkenhoe, only Hinckley (11 miles away) had more taxpayers in 1377.[1] Beyond the county, medieval Lutterworth enjoyed regional links with Coventry (14 miles to its west) and Northampton (21 miles to the south east). These enabled trade between the East and West Midlands. Watling Street, the Roman road that linked London and Chester, formed the south-western boundary of the parish and county (Map 1) and facilitated trade between Lutterworth and London in the Middle Ages. This road remained an important arterial route in the early 21st century.

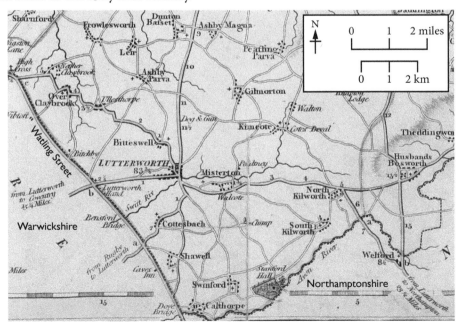

Map 1 *Lutterworth and surrounding villages, from Charles Smith's county map of 1801.*

---

1   Fenwick (ed.), *Poll Taxes*, I, 487–9.

Figure 1 *The Wyclif memorial (1897) and Wycliffe Memorial Methodist Church (1905).*

Lutterworth is perhaps best known for its association with John Wyclif, the noted dissident theologian, who became its rector in 1374. Wyclif lived in the parish between his exile from Oxford in 1381 and his death in Lutterworth in 1384. His teachings became an inspiration for Lollardy, and in later centuries his connection to the town became a source of pride to many residents. Visitors to St Mary's church in the late 18th century were shown 'Wyclif's pulpit', 'his table', 'his chair', 'his candlestick' and part of 'his vestment'.[2] Although these attributions were comprehensively discredited in 1861, unsuccessful attempts were made in the early 1880s to build a museum where these items could be displayed to mark the five-hundredth anniversary of Wyclif's death.[3] There was already a monument to Wyclif in the church, and it was decided to erect an obelisk of Aberdeen granite to him on a prominent site at a road junction, which would also mark Queen Victoria's Diamond Jubilee in 1897 (Figure 1). Two large tablets describe Wyclif as 'the Morning Star of the Reformation' and 'the first translator of the Bible into the English Language', claims that have not withstood later scrutiny, with inscriptions beneath commemorating the Queen's anniversary.[4]

2   J. Throsby, *The Memoirs of the Town and County of Leicester* (Leicester, 1777), II, 113–16; Nichols, *Hist.*, IV, 264.
3   M.H. Bloxham, 'Lutterworth church and the Wycliffe relics', *Trans. LAHS* 2 (1860–4), 72–80; J. Crompton, 'John Wyclif: a study in mythology', *Trans. LAHS* 42 (1966–7), 7–8; J. Goodacre, 'Wyclif in Lutterworth: myths and monuments', *Leics. Historian* 3 (1983–4), 30.
4   *ODNB*, s.v. Wyclif [Wycliffe], John [called Doctor Evangelicus] (d. 1384), accessed 28 Nov. 2017.

Figure 2 *Lutterworth High Street in 2020, looking south towards the much lower river valley. The town hall occupies a small but prominent site on the southern edge of the market place. The large building opposite was the Hind Inn, one of the town's two main coaching inns.*

Medieval Lutterworth displayed many of the characteristic features of market towns: a planned layout, specialised trading areas, civic and commercial buildings, permanent shops and stalls, diverse occupations and a hospital on the edge of the town. Lutterworth never obtained a charter of incorporation, but by the 16th century at least some of the assets that had been owned by a fraternal religious guild had been diverted to a secular trust. The trust was able to collect the rents on the lands and properties, and to apply these in ways that benefited the town and its mercantile interests, including the upkeep of the town's roads and bridges and a school. The trust became known as the Town Estate, and its assets continued to benefit the community in later centuries.

Land around Lutterworth, in Leicestershire and Warwickshire, had been enclosed for pasture by the late 15th century. Three Lutterworth residents were members of the Company of the Staple in the 15th and early 16th centuries, buying the wool clip from farmers, monastic houses and middlemen and exporting it to Calais. The wealth generated by this trade probably benefited the guild and Town Estate as well as individuals, and enabled the Feilding family to increase its landholding in the town prior to its purchase of Lutterworth manor in 1629. The town's market thrived in the early 16th century, with a vibrant trade in manufactured goods, livestock and timber.

From the late 18th century, as new routes and modes of transport were developed, Lutterworth's prosperity became dependent upon decisions made by coach and rail companies and, from the 1950s, by district and national government. Coaches on four cross-country routes stopped in Lutterworth from the late 18th century. Growing prosperity led to the building, extension or refashioning of many properties, mostly in the Greek Revival style. This created a visual harmony that continued to be an attractive feature of the town in the early 21st century (Figure 2). In part this was because building activity came to an abrupt halt in 1840, as the railway replaced coach travel but bypassed the town. This resulted in a period of economic stagnation that continued until the end of the 19th century.

The completion of the 'London extension' of the Manchester, Sheffield and Lincolnshire Railway in 1899 (by then the Great Central Railway), with a station in Lutterworth, led the way to recovery. George Spencer, a native of Old Basford (Notts.), opened a hosiery factory in 1902 which became a major employer. The first of two iron foundries opened alongside the railway in 1906. The relocation of the toolmaker Alfred Herbert Ltd to Lutterworth following the Coventry blitz of 1940 brought further employment. Between 1937 and 1942, Frank Whittle developed his jet engine at Ladywood Works. A replica of the Gloster E.28/39 aircraft in which the engine made its maiden flight in 1941 rises above a traffic island on the main approach to the town, and a commemorative bust of Whittle stands in the town's memorial gardens (back cover).

Changes to national transport networks in the 1960s included the extension of the M1 motorway north to reach Lutterworth in 1964 and the closure of Lutterworth's station in 1969. The thought expressed in 1961 that Lutterworth's proximity to the anticipated motorway network would 'safeguard the town's continued progress – and its reputation as a welcome resting place for the weary traveller' proved optimistic, as the weary traveller often chose to stop at a motorway service station.[5] By the late 1980s, Lutterworth's position on the A5 (Watling Street) and within a triangle created by the M1, M6 and M69 motorways led to the opening of a major logistics estate (Magna Park) on the edge of the parish, although many of the jobs created were filled by people who lived, and shopped, elsewhere. Since 2011 the A5 Partnership, a consortium of county and district councils, enterprise partnerships (between councils and businesses) and Highways England (from 2021, National Highways) took responsibility for determining a strategy for economic growth along the Watling Street corridor between Northamptonshire and Staffordshire. This partnership recognised the importance of this part of the Midlands to the national economy, and the need to consider the local impact of individual developments.

Lutterworth was given early prominence by its minster church and, while its later fortunes fluctuated, the town has proved resilient. Its weekly market lost its regional importance but continued to be held on a more modest scale in the early 21st century. As traditional British industries declined in the late 20th century, smaller commercial units took the place of the factories and foundries, attracting a range of independent businesses and continuing Lutterworth's role as a provider of services to a wider area. Two large coaching inns (the Denbigh Arms and the Hind) retained their impressive façades, while their interiors have found new uses as flats and retail units. Independent shops, inns and cafes occupy other historic buildings in the town centre. The return of Lutterworth Museum to town-centre premises in 2021 will enable the town to build further on its connections with Wyclif and Whittle, and its important links to early religious reform and industrial innovation.

---

5   Lutterworth RDC, *The Rural District of Lutterworth Official Guide* (London, 1961), 11; https://motorwayservicesonline.co.uk/History:Leicester_Forest_East (accessed 1 Sept. 2021).

LANDSCAPE AND SETTLEMENT

Boundaries and Extent

LUTTERWORTH'S PARISH BOUNDARY (MAP 2) was largely defined by the Roman Watling Street (the county boundary with Warwickshire), the river Swift (a tributary of the Warwickshire Avon) and three brooks. At the southernmost point of the parish, Bransford bridge carries Watling Street over the river Swift. From here, the parish boundary originally ran north west along the centre of the Roman road, but was moved to the sides of the road in 1935 for administrative convenience.[1] It then turned away from the road at a high ridge of land, initially following this ridge to the north east, then east, along a well-defined track (later part of Bitteswell airfield) towards Leicester Road, then north along Bitteswell brook, following this upstream for nearly 2 miles to its source.

The northern boundary is poorly defined. From the source of the brook it extended north east for *c.*750 yd., crossing Leicester Road, then south east across open country for *c.*900 yd. to meet the source of another brook. It followed this downstream to its confluence with a slightly larger brook, and continued along this watercourse to meet the river Swift.

From this point the ancient boundary probably continued along the Swift to Watling Street. If so, the boundary had moved south, away from the river, by *c.*1216, when St John's hospital (south of the river) was founded in Lutterworth.[2] The boundary in 1884 turned away from the river at the Spital mill dam, and crossed the roads to Market Harborough and Rugby before turning south west across fields for *c.*600 yd., then north west for *c.*400 yd., to rejoin the Swift.[3] This section of the boundary was altered in 1993.[4] From a point where the former mill leat was crossed by the motorway embankment created in 1964, the revised boundary ran south along the centre of the motorway for nearly 1 mile, then turned north west to cross fields for *c.*1,300 yd., to meet the river at the point where the 1884 boundary rejoined the Swift. This transferred 124 a. from Misterton parish to Lutterworth. It then followed the course of the river downstream for *c.*1½ miles to Bransford bridge, where this perambulation began. The civil parish contained 2,589 a. in 1891[5] and 1,102 ha. (2,722 a.) in 2011.[6]

1   Ministry of Health Provisional Order Confirmation (Leicester and Warwick Act), 1935.
2   *VCH Leics*. II, 42–3.
3   OS Map 25", Leics. XLIX.13 (1884 edn).
4   The Harborough (Parishes) Order, 1993.
5   Census, 1891, http://www.visionofbritain.org.uk (accessed 25 Jan. 2020).
6   https://www.nomisweb.co.uk/reports/localarea?compare=E04005452 (accessed 25 Jan. 2020).

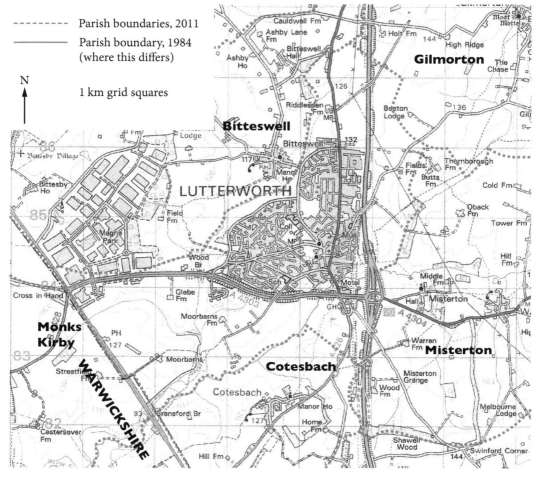

Map 2 *The Civil Parish of Lutterworth in 2009.*

Landscape and Soils

The town occupies a prominent plateau on a tongue of high land that rises sharply above the valley of the river Swift, which flows south west, and that of the Bitteswell brook to its west. The Swift valley lies *c.*100 m. above Ordnance Datum (OD), the parish church is *c.*130 m. above OD, and the highest point in the parish, on the north-eastern parish boundary, is *c.*140 m. above OD.[7] The river and its valley would have been striking features of the early landscape. The first element of Lutterworth's place name may be derived from *hlūtre*, an Old English word meaning pure, clear or bright, which might be the original river name.[8] The river name is recorded as the Swift in 1577, probably from the verb *swīfan*, to wend or sweep, describing its winding course through the valley.[9]

---

7   OS Map 1:25000, Landranger sheet 140 (2009 edn).
8   B. Cox, *The Place-Names of Leicestershire*, V (Nottingham, 2011), xiv, 137.
9   E. Ekwall, *English River-names* (Oxford, 1928), 387.

The parish sits on the western edge of the blue lias mudstone. Across most of the parish this is overlain by diamicton (boulder clay) of moderate fertility, with alluvial deposits alongside the river and brooks.[10] The riverside meadows are prone to flooding, but excess water soon subsides into the alluvium.[11] No woodland was recorded in Lutterworth or any of the surrounding parishes in 1086,[12] and there was no suitable stone for quarrying. The need for timber for domestic and agricultural buildings established Lutterworth's importance as a market centre linking south Leicestershire and the neighbouring part of Northamptonshire with the woodlands of north Warwickshire.

Communication

Roads

Watling Street, the Roman road from London to Chester, may be a restatement of an ancient route. It passes over only the headwaters of rivers, with those to its west flowing towards the Severn and Bristol Channel and those to its east discharging into the Humber estuary.[13] The road was carried over the Swift by Bransford bridge, a crossing that does not appear on Christopher Saxton's county map of 1576.[14] William Camden noted in 1586 that although this bridge had been 'of long time broken downe', it had 'now' been repaired 'at the common charge of the country', suggesting the road was being used more heavily than before. This bridge appears in John Speed's map of 1610.[15] It was repaired again in 1649 by the counties of Leicestershire and Warwickshire.[16]

The most important road for Lutterworth's medieval economy was probably the approach from Coventry and the west, known to the east of Watling Street as 'The Coalpit Lane', and in Lutterworth as 'the king's highway called Colespitts'.[17] After entering the parish, this crossed Bitteswell brook at Wood bridge, which had been rebuilt in stone by at least 1601.[18] This bridge was briefly removed in 1667, giving rise to protests from the inhabitants of ten Warwickshire towns and villages up to 12 miles away, indicating the extent of Lutterworth's regular trade in this period.[19] The north–south route through the town crosses the river Swift at Spital bridge, immediately south of Lutterworth's market place and adjacent to the town's medieval hospital. This bridge may have been built by Nicholas de Verdun when he obtained the market charter in 1214, to replace a

10 http://mapapps.bgs.ac.uk/geologyofbritain/home.html (accessed 24 Feb. 2019); M.J. Simms, N. Chidlaw, N. Morton and K.N. Page, *British Lower Jurassic Stratigraphy* (Peterborough, 2004), 4; Cranfield Soil and Agrifood Institute, http://www.landis.org.uk/soilscapes (accessed 24 Feb. 2019).

11 Warws. RO, CR 2017/L/5/8; *Northampton Merc.*, 16 Oct. 1875.

12 H.C. Darby and I.B. Terrett, *The Domesday Geography of Midland England* (Cambridge, 1954), 338.

13 I.D. Margary, *Roman Roads in Britain* (1973), 186; *VCH Leics.* III, 62–3.

14 C. Saxton, *Warws. and Leics.* (1576).

15 Camden, *Britannia*, 517; J. Speed, *Theatre of Great Britain* (1610).

16 *VCH Leics.* III, 90; S.C. Ratcliff and H.C. Johnson, *Warwick County Records*, II (Warwick, 1936), 198, 225–6.

17 OS Map 1" (1834–5), in Cassini, *Past and Present Maps: Rugby and Lutterworth* (London, 2007); Warws. RO, CR 2017/E42, f. 1.

18 Warws. RO, CR 2017/L5/8.

19 Warws. RO, CR 2017/L5/1–12.

ford.[20] Perhaps originally of timber, it had probably been rebuilt in stone by 1576, when it appeared on Saxton's map.[21] Minor roads into Lutterworth from the north west through Bitteswell and the north east through Gilmorton would have been important for local villagers attending the market. Spital bridge was rebuilt by subscription in 1778 and widened in 1910.[22]

Almost all the roads converging on Lutterworth became turnpikes (subject to tolls for their upkeep) in the 18th century. The road from Market Harborough through Lutterworth to Coventry became a turnpike in 1755. Toll gates were built south of Spital bridge and at Cross in Hand on Watling Street.[23] In 1762 the road from Hinckley to 'Lutterworth Town's End' was turnpiked. This left Watling Street at High Cross to pass through the Claybrookes, Ullesthorpe and Bitteswell, entering Lutterworth on Bitteswell Road and terminating at a toll gate at the parish boundary.[24] The Leicester to Lutterworth road was turnpiked in 1764, with a toll gate on Leicester Road at 'Bitteswell Gate', immediately north of the junction with Hall Lane, Bitteswell.[25] This ended free passage into the town from every direction except the rural route from Gilmorton and the north east. A road from Banbury through Cotesbach to 'the South End of Mill Field' in Lutterworth became a turnpike in 1765.[26] From 1785 this connected with the turnpike road to Rugby from 'the Gibbet or Lutterworth Hand' on Watling Street.[27] A toll gate south of Spital bridge charged travellers who were not crossing the bridge into Lutterworth.[28]

The section of Watling Street that formed Lutterworth's parish boundary never became a turnpike road. It may not have been an attractive proposition financially, as much of the traffic turned off the road at High Cross, Cross in Hand or Gibbet Hill. Through traffic not wishing to stop at Lutterworth had an alternative route on improved road surfaces from 1724 if it took the turnpike linking Weedon Bec (Northants.), on Watling Street, 18 miles south of Lutterworth, to Dunchurch (Warws.), and another from Dunchurch through Coventry to Meriden (Warws.). From 1744 another turnpike linked Coleshill (Warws.), 6 miles north of Meriden, to Watling Street at a point near Lichfield (Staffs.).[29] These created financial interests opposing any improvements to the stretch of Watling Street alongside Lutterworth. Petitions presented to parliament in 1734, 1760 and 1809 in favour of a trust for the Lutterworth section failed, leaving this free of tolls.[30] The Turnpike Acts expired during the 1870s: Banbury to Lutterworth in 1871,[31] Leicester

20 D. Harrison, *The Bridges of Medieval England* (Oxford, 2004), 57–8.
21 Saxton, *Warws.*
22 White, *Hist.* (Sheffield, 1846), 401; *Leic. Daily Post*, 16 Mar. 1910.
23 ROLLR, DE 115/1.
24 2 Geo. III, c. 54; *VCH Leics.* III, 91; ROLLR, DE 115/1; A. Cossons, *The Turnpike Roads of Leicestershire and Rutland* (Newtown Linford, 2003), 58; OS Map 25", Leics. XLVIII.12 (1887 edn).
25 4 Geo. III, c. 84; *CJ* 29, 1051; *VCH Leics.* III, 81, 91; Cossons, *Turnpike Roads*, 62; *Leic. Jnl*, 12 Feb. 1875; OS Map 25", Leics. XLIX.5 (1904 edn).
26 5 Geo. III, c. 105; Cossons, *Turnpike Roads*, 63.
27 25 Geo. III, c. 115; Cossons, *Turnpike Roads*, 67.
28 ROLLR, DE 115/1.
29 W. Albert, *The Turnpike Road System in England, 1663–1840* (Cambridge, 1972), 227.
30 *CJ* 22, 387, 388–9; *CJ* 28, 705, 742, 744, 760, 766, 778, 779, 781, 789; ROLLR, QS 71/3; Northants. Arch., QS 2A; Cossons, *Turnpike Roads*, 59–61.
31 33 & 34 Vic., c. 73.

to Lutterworth in 1872,[32] Market Harborough to Coventry in 1874,[33] Hinckley to Lutterworth in 1876,[34] and from Rugby to the road which linked Lutterworth and Market Harborough in 1878.[35]

The M1 motorway reached Lutterworth in 1964, when a junction (J20) was constructed for the town.[36] The extension of the M6 southwards in 1971, with a junction midway between Lutterworth and the centre of Rugby,[37] and the M69 motorway between Coventry and Leicester, which opened in 1976–7, crossing Watling Street to the south east of Hinckley, were significant.[38] These three motorways form a triangle that is bisected by Watling Street, which remained a key arterial route through the Midlands, with heavy goods vehicles comprising more than 20 per cent of the traffic on this road in 2015.[39] A road linking the M1 junction to Watling Street, which also serves the Magna Park logistics estate, opened c.1994, creating a southern bypass to the town.[40] Within the town centre, the demolition of properties on High Street (The Narrows) in 1960, which stood on the site of early market encroachment, removed a tight bend from a busy road, which continued to be well used in 2021.[41]

Road Transport

Carriers and Logistics

William Perkins provided a weekly carrier service by wagon between Lutterworth and London in 1681.[42] A weekly service to London from the Denbigh Arms in 1794 took three days in each direction.[43] In 1822 carriers operated weekly services between Lutterworth and 14 towns and villages, including Birmingham, Coventry, Northampton and Rugby, and twice-weekly services to Leicester and Market Harborough. Weekly services in 1835 went to London, Leicester, Hinckley, Market Harborough, Coventry, Rugby and Stretton Wharf on the Oxford canal, near Brinklow (Warws.).[44] A further 23 destinations had been added by 1846, including North Kilworth and Welford, where there were wharfs on the Grand Union canal and its Welford branch. Only the Leicester

---

32   34 & 35 Vic., c. 115; 35 & 36 Vic., c. 85.

33   35 & 36 Vic., c. 85.

34   39 & 40 Vic., c. 39.

35   36 & 37 Vic., c. 90.

36   *Coventry Eve. Telegraph*, 30 Sept. 1964.

37   The Motorway Archive: Midlands, https://web.archive.org/web/20080126114511/http://www.iht.org/motorway/m5m6midlink.htm (accessed 19 Jan. 2022).

38   *Coventry Eve. Telegraph*, 8 Dec. 1976.

39   A5 Partnership, *The A5: Draft: A Strategy for Growth, 2018–2031*, 209, http://politics.leics.gov.uk/documents/s136054/A5%20Strategy%20Appx%20B%20-%20Current%20working%20draft%20of%20revised%20A5%20Strategy.pdf (accessed 20 Feb. 2021).

40   OS Map 1:10000, SP58SW (1993); https://lutterworth.magnapark.co.uk (accessed 9 Oct. 2020).

41   *Leic. Eve. Mail*, 1 Jan. 1960.

42   T. Delaune, *The Present State of London* (1681), 418; T. Delaune (ed. Anon), *Angliae Metropolis: or, the Present State of London* (1691), 423.

43   *Universal Dir.* (1794), 604.

44   Pigot, *Dir. of Leics.* (1822), 227; (1835), 150.

services (on Wednesdays and Saturdays) were noted in 1877.[45] Most packages were presumably then carried by train from Ullesthorpe or Welford stations.

Magna Park, situated at the junction between Watling Street and Lutterworth's southern bypass, was developed from 1988 on the former Bitteswell airfield. Described by the site's owners in 2020 as 'Europe's largest dedicated distribution location', it then comprised over 8 million sq. ft. of warehousing and office space.[46] Heavy goods vehicles from Magna Park have added substantially to the volume of traffic passing across the parish.

Coaches and Buses

The earliest passenger stagecoaches between London and Chester did not pass near Lutterworth, but in 1788 the London to Chester mail coach was rerouted to run through Northampton, Lutterworth and Hinckley.[47] A 'New Commercial Post Coach' service between Manchester and London had been introduced the previous year. This travelled along the Lutterworth to Hinckley turnpike (through Bitteswell), and passengers 'supped' at Lutterworth. One of its five proprietors was William Mash, the tenant at the Denbigh Arms and Lutterworth's postmaster. Trade goods and small parcels were also carried.[48] Mash was also a proprietor of the 'Cambridge and Birmingham Sociable Post-Coach', a one-day service between those towns for passengers and goods that called at Lutterworth, where passengers could transfer to the Chester and Holyhead Mail, or to 'heavy coaches'. The latter offered a slower twice-weekly service from Lutterworth to Chester and Holyhead, probably on carriers' wagons adapted for passengers.[49]

The 'Umpire', a stagecoach service between London and Liverpool, called at Lutterworth in 1822, also using the turnpike road between Lutterworth and Hinckley. It travelled through the night, with the northbound service arriving at Lutterworth at 3 a.m., and the southbound at 5 a.m. The mail coach and the London to Liverpool service both continued to call at Lutterworth until 1835, when there was a further service, the 'Regulator', which operated between Leicester and Oxford, calling at Lutterworth.[50]

The London to Chester mail coach was withdrawn in 1838, with the mail transferred to the railway.[51] The stagecoaches also ceased, with the exception of the service from Oxford through Lutterworth to Leicester, which still ran in 1841, although travellers were advised that the train service from Aylesbury to Leicester would be faster.[52] No coaches passed through Lutterworth in 1846.[53]

The Midland Counties Railway appointed William Veers of the Denbigh Arms the sole agent for the transport of passengers and goods to the railway station at Ullesthorpe

45   White, *Hist.* (Sheffield, 1846), 411; (Sheffield, 1877), 526.
46   https://lutterworth.magnapark.co.uk; https://lutterworth.magnapark.co.uk/site-information/about-site (accessed 9 Oct. 2020).
47   D. Gerhold, *Carriers and Coachmasters: Trade and Travel before the Turnpikes* (Chichester, 2005), 119–22; J. Soer, *The Royal Mail in Leicestershire and Rutland* (Midland (GB) Postal Hist. Society, 1997), 10–11.
48   *Manchester Merc.*, 17 July 1787; 21 Oct. 1788; 10 Feb. 1789; *Universal Dir.* (1794), 605.
49   *Northampton Merc.*, 15 Sept. 1792; 8 June 1793; *Universal Dir.* (1794), 604; Gerhold, *Carriers*, 80–3.
50   Pigot, *Dir. of Leics.* (1822), 227; (1835), 150.
51   Soer, *Royal Mail*, 182.
52   Pigot, *Dir. of Leics.* (1841), 41.
53   White, *Hist.* (Sheffield, 1846), 400–11.

when it opened in 1840.[54] This was a popular service, with complaints made in 1858 and 1874 that there were more passengers than the six seats available.[55] Edward Voss of the Fox Inn began a service in a 20-seat omnibus in 1875.[56] Services were infrequent in 1890.[57] Omnibus services between Lutterworth and Welford station, which opened in 1850 on the London and North Western Railway (L&NWR), appear to have been infrequent, but a 'new omnibus connection' was introduced in 1887, which took 40 minutes.[58] These services probably ceased when the Great Central Railway opened a station in Lutterworth in 1899.

Fred Gee relocated his bus business from Swinford to Lutterworth in 1953, and ran five buses until 1969, when the business was taken over by Woods Coaches, and later by Lutterworth Coaches Ltd.[59] The company was dissolved in 2015.[60] Following the closure of Lutterworth station in 1969, Midland Red provided a bus service between Rugby and Leicester, calling at Lutterworth. A service from Leicester to Coventry via Lutterworth was introduced in 1974 but redirected along the M69 in 1977, bypassing the town.[61] A postbus service between Lutterworth and six local villages, which also collected and delivered post to village post offices, was introduced and subsidised by the Royal Mail for five years from 1996.[62] A daytime service between Rugby and Leicester, through Lutterworth, continued to operate in 2020, with stops in many local villages.[63] Buses also ran between Hinckley and the Magna Park logistics estate with connections into the town, and between Lutterworth and Market Harborough, although the last afternoon buses would be too early for most employees.[64]

Railways

The Midland Counties Railway opened a line in 1840 from Derby through Leicester to meet the London and Birmingham Railway at Rugby, with a station at Ullesthorpe, 3 miles north west of Lutterworth.[65] Presumably in a bid to attract more custom, the station's name was changed to 'Ullesthorpe for Lutterworth' in 1879, then 'Ullesthorpe and Lutterworth' in 1897. It was renamed Ullesthorpe in 1930.[66] The line was closed in 1962.[67]

The Stamford and Rugby branch line of the L&NWR opened between Rugby and Rockingham (Northants.) in 1850 with a station 5½ miles east of Lutterworth, between North Kilworth and Husbands Bosworth, which was named Welford, where there was

54 *Northampton Merc.*, 27 June 1840.
55 *Leic. Jnl*, 24 Dec. 1858; *Rugby Advertiser*, 12 Dec. 1874.
56 *Leic. Jnl*, 11 June 1875.
57 *Leic. Chron.*, 13 Sept. 1890.
58 R.V.J. Butt, *Dir. of Railway Stations* (Sparkford, 1995), 243; *Northampton Merc.*, 26 Nov. 1887.
59 Lutterworth Local Hist. Group, *Jnl* (2002), 8–9.
60 Companies House.
61 *Coventry Eve. Telegraph*, 28 Jan. 1969; 12 Dec. 1973; 9 Nov. 1977.
62 https://www.independent.co.uk/money/spend-save/post-bus-delivers-a-rural-lifeline-1341797.html (accessed 20 Aug. 2020).
63 https://lutterworth.magnapark.co.uk (accessed 20 Aug. 2020).
64 Ibid.; https://bustimes.org/services/58-market-harborough-lutterworth (accessed 20 Aug. 2020).
65 *VCH Leics.* III, 116; R. Williams, *The Midland Railway: A New Hist.* (Newton Abbot, 1988), 18.
66 *Leic. Chron.*, 13 Sept. 1890; Butt, *Dir.*, 237, 243.
67 Butt, *Dir.*, 237.

Figure 3 *The bridge under the Great Central Railway at the east end of Station Road in Lutterworth, c.1897 (west elevation). The steps to the island platform were to the side of the northern abutment. The wagon on the rails had seats for navvies.*

a wharf on a branch of the Grand Union canal.[68] The station was renamed 'Welford, Kilworth' in 1853, 'Welford and Kilworth' in 1855, 'Welford and Lutterworth' in 1897, and back to 'Welford and Kilworth' in 1913. The line closed in 1966.[69]

A public meeting was called in Lutterworth in 1861, with the 7th earl of Denbigh in the chair, to discuss the possibility of a branch line linking Lutterworth to the railway network. Some of those attending lived in local villages, and sought an option that would also favour their needs. It was resolved that a deputation of 13 people would wait upon the directors of the L&NWR, but nothing came of this.[70] A crowded public meeting in Lutterworth's town hall in 1890, with Marston Buszard, QC, in the chair, listened to the proposals of the Manchester, Sheffield and Lincolnshire Railway (renamed the Great Central Railway in 1897) for a line from Liverpool to London. Their engineer advised that the route would probably pass close to Lutterworth town centre. Although absent, Lord Denbigh (the 8th earl) was said to be a firm supporter, and a resolution welcoming the proposal was carried 'with the greatest enthusiasm'.[71] Construction began in 1894 (Figure 3).[72] The line opened to coal traffic in 1898 to bed down the track, and Lutterworth station opened to passengers and goods in 1899.[73]

68   *VCH Leics.* III, 120–1; Butt, *Dir.*, 243; Gerhold, *Carriers*, 7.
69   Butt, *Dir.*, 243; A. Moore, *Leicestershire's Stations: An Historical Perspective* (Narborough, 1998), 98–101.
70   *Leic. Jnl*, 25 Jan. 1861; 8 Mar. 1861; *VCH Leics.* III, 121–2.
71   *Leic. Chron.*, 13 Sept. 1890.
72   G. Boyd-Hope and A. Sargent, *Railways and Rural Life: S.W.A. Newton and the Great Central Railway* (Swindon, 2007), 8, 54.
73   *Leic. Chron.*, 30 July 1898; *Rugby Advertiser*, 18 Mar. 1899.

The line was recommended for closure under the Beeching proposals in 1963.[74] Goods services ceased in 1965, and the line closed as a through route to London in 1966. The section between Rugby and Nottingham remained open to passengers until 1969, with Lutterworth station becoming an unstaffed halt.[75] The track between Leicester and Rugby was lifted in 1970.[76]

Post and Telecommunications

Lutterworth received its post from Market Harborough in 1669. Henry Tilley of Lutterworth made payments to the Post Office between 1713 and 1739, suggesting that he may have offered a postal service. His place was taken by Thomas Wyatt, and in 1750 Thomas's widow Susanna was named as postmistress.[77] Lord Denbigh asked for John Smith to be appointed in 1767.[78] William Mash, innkeeper of the Denbigh Arms, was postmaster in 1783. He died in 1829 and was succeeded by his son Stephen.[79] Stephen Mash left the Denbigh Arms in 1833, retaining the post office business until 1835, when William Veers of the Denbigh Arms was appointed and the office returned to the inn. He remained postmaster until his death in 1862.[80] The post office has occupied several different premises since then. It became a sub-post office under Rugby in 1914, and under Leicester from 1973. A delivery office serving Lutterworth and surrounding villages was opened on Bilton Way in 1992.[81]

There were plans to install a telephone exchange at the post office in 1908, and there were 11 subscribers in 1911.[82] A new exchange was built on Lower Leicester Road in the mid 1960s. Fibre broadband was available from 2011.[83]

Population

The 28 people listed in 1086, including three slaves, suggests a well-established settlement, with a population of *c*.125.[84] The 42 tenants and 25 burgesses in 1279 imply that the number of residents had grown to *c*.300.[85] The poll tax of 1377 recorded 225 people over the age of 14, suggesting *c*.450 inhabitants.[86] Little more is known about the size of Lutterworth until 1509, when 116 dwellings were listed (perhaps 520 people), a figure that appears to have hardly changed over the next century, with 106 households

74 House of Commons Debate, 13 Mar. 1961, vol. 636, 1151–60; ROLLR, DE 1379/517/69b; *Reshaping Britain's Railways* (HMSO, London, 1963).
75 Moore, *Leicestershire's Stations*, 177, 189.
76 http://www.disused-stations.org.uk/l/lutterworth (accessed 29 June 2021).
77 Soer, *Royal Mail*, 8, 181.
78 Warws. RO, CR 2017/C243, p. 64.
79 Soer, *Royal Mail*, 181; ROLLR, DE 2094/11.
80 Soer, *Royal Mail*, 181–2; ROLLR, DE 2094/12; White, *Hist.* (Sheffield, 1863), 759.
81 Soer, *Royal Mail*, 181–2.
82 *Rugby Advertiser*, 21 Mar. 1908; 6 Jan. 1912.
83 Harborough District Council, *Settlement Profile: Lutterworth* (2015), 8.
84 *Domesday*, 645.
85 Nichols, *Hist.*, IV, 247; *Rot. Hund.*, 239.
86 Fenwick (ed.), *Poll Taxes*, I, 491.

recorded in 1563 and 117 homes in 1607.[87] Rapid subsequent growth is suggested by the 225 properties listed in the Hearth Tax of 1670, but contemporaries recalled that the period of rapid population growth occurred in the late 16th century, when houses began to be occupied by several families.[88] This helps to account for a lower rate of increase in the recorded number of communicants in the 17th century, from 564 in 1603 to 644 in 1676.[89] Many of the new arrivals would have been migrants from local open-field villages then being enclosed, such as Cotesbach in 1607 and Catthorpe in 1656.[90]

It was estimated in 1709 that there were 310 families and 1,000 residents in the town.[91] A census in 1781 found 353 houses and 1,484 inhabitants.[92] By 1801, the resident population had increased to 1,652. This grew steadily to reach 2,531 in 1841, but then declined each decade until 1901, when the population was just 1,734, fewer than in 'industrial villages' such as Barwell and Enderby.[93] Steady growth then returned, but Lutterworth in the 20th and early 21st centuries never exceeded the size of a large village. There were 3,197 residents in 1951, before modern housing development driven by county plans provided homes for a population of 9,353 in 2011.[94]

Settlement

Settlement before the Market Charter

Many worked flints have been found through extensive archaeological fieldwalking across the parish,[95] with the quantity near Thornborough spinney suggesting a significant site.[96] A cinerary urn was found within a 'tumulus' noted by the Ordnance Survey in Moorbarns, which is believed to be an early Bronze Age round barrow.[97] Another possible barrow, identified from aerial photographs, was partly destroyed by the construction of the M1.[98] Iron Age discoveries have been concentrated in the Leaders Farm area in the

87   Warws. RO, CR 2017/E42; A. Dyer and D.M. Palliser (eds), *The Diocesan Population Returns for 1563 and 1603* (Oxford, 2005), 216; TNA, LR 2/255.

88   *VCH Leics.* III, 172; TNA, E 179/240/279; E 134/1658–9/Hil16, m. 5; J. Goodacre, *The Transformation of a Peasant Economy: Townspeople and Villagers in the Lutterworth Area, 1500–1700* (Aldershot, 1994), 60–1, 72–3.

89   Dyer and Palliser (eds), *Diocesan Population*, 381; A. Whiteman, *The Compton Census of 1676: A Critical Edition* (Oxford, 1986), 336.

90   L.A. Parker, 'The agrarian revolution at Cotesbach, 1501–1612', *Trans. LAHS* 24 (1948), 41–76; J. Lee, *A Vindication of a Regulated Inclosure* (1656).

91   J. Broad (ed.), *Bishop Wake's Summary of Visitation Returns from the Diocese of Lincoln, 1705–15*, II (Oxford, 2012), 857.

92   Nichols, *Hist.*, IV, 257.

93   *VCH Leics.* III, 192.

94   Ibid.; https://www.nomisweb.co.uk/reports/localarea?compare=E04005452 (accessed 25 Jan. 2020).

95   Leics. & Rutl. HER, MLE 1941, 1943, 2078, 2143, 2144, 6010, 6052, 6438, 6440, 7031, 7032, 7034, 7117, 7199, 7200, 7500, 7666, 10412, 10413, 10427–31, 10455, 15846, 21679, 21680, 22472.

96   Leics. & Rutl. HER, MLE 1905 (Mesolithic), 1906 (Neolithic) (OS SP 551 846).

97   Leics. & Rutl. HER, MLE 1920 (OS SP 531 834).

98   Leics. & Rutl. HER, MLE 1903 (OS SP 550 845).

west of the parish, where a small settlement site has been found.[99] A field system of the late Iron Age or Roman period has been identified on adjacent land.[100]

A total of 318 Roman coins have been recorded in Lutterworth, including hoards of 46 coins (from AD 69 to 161) found in 1725, and 254 bronze coins (from AD 251 to 270) discovered in 1869.[101] There is little sign of any Roman settlement in Lutterworth's fields other than an oven and possible smithy between the former railway line and the motorway,[102] and a possible Roman field system on the west of the town.[103] A fragment of a possible Roman column 32 cm. in diameter and part of a moulded cornice were found in Regent Street in the 1960s; it is possible that a villa or a larger Roman settlement lies beneath the modern town centre.[104]

The second element of Lutterworth's place name is derived from an Old English word meaning an enclosure. This enclosure may have been prehistoric in origin or constructed in the 7th or 8th century. Part of its boundary may survive as the sweeping curve at the south end of High Street, leading into Regent Street. The land to the north west of this arc rises sharply to a plateau of higher ground, with St Mary's parish church occupying a prominent site at the centre of what may have been an elliptical enclosure of c.20 a. (Map 3). The church may have been built on the site of a pre-Conquest minster endowed with the land within this enclosure together with further land in the neighbouring village of Misterton.[105] Minster churches often stimulated the growth of a town, as the provisioning needs of a religious community and visits from the pious on Sundays and feast days would have encouraged trade.[106] This may suggest that Lutterworth's origins as a centre of trade, at least in embryo, date from before the Norman Conquest.

Seven sherds of early Anglo-Saxon pottery were found in a pit 240 m. south west of the motorway junction, and a similar quantity of late Anglo-Saxon pottery was found in a ditch at what became Station Road.[107] While not conclusive, these may indicate a settlement between the 7th and 10th centuries in the vicinity of the present town, with any pottery scatters from that period subsequently covered by modern residential development.

Development of the Medieval Town

The beginnings of the market town lay in the charter obtained in 1214 by Lutterworth's lord Nicholas de Verdun.[108] The triangular market place was laid out 200 yd. east of the church, and burgage plots were created to its south, possibly concurrently, along both sides of what became High Street (Figure 4). These plots were regular in width, and those

99 Leics. & Rutl. HER, MLE 19881 (OS SP 531 842).

100 Leics. & Rutl. HER, MLE 19883 (OS SP 530 841).

101 Leics. & Rutl. HER, MLE 7867, 7868, 7871, 7873, 7874; VCH Leics. I, 180; A. Pownall, 'On a recent find of Roman coins in Leicestershire', Trans. LAHS 4 (1869–75), 36–47; M.J. Winter, 'A survey of Romano-British coin hoards in Leicestershire', Trans. LAHS 53 (1977–8), 3, 5.

102 Leics. & Rutl. HER, MLE 2141 (OS SP 548 836); PAS, IARCH-3D95E1 (1725); IARCH-CE93EB (1869).

103 Leics. & Rutl. HER, MLE 18332 (OS SP 522 839), 20570 (OS SP 530 842).

104 Leics. & Rutl. HER, MLE 7870 (OS SP 543 843).

105 Below, Religious Hist. (Church Origins and Parochial Organisation).

106 J. Blair, 'Small towns, 600–1270', in D.M. Palliser (ed.), The Cambridge Urban Hist. of Britain (Cambridge, 2000), I, 251.

107 Leics. & Rutl. HER, MLE 23244 (OS SP 548 830), 21783 (OS SP 545 844).

108 Rot. Chart., 1199–1216, 201.

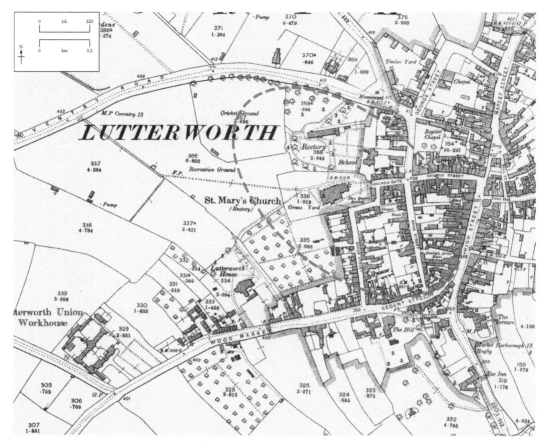

Map 3 *The possible boundary of the 'worth' within Lutterworth's place name, an enclosure that may have contained a pre-Conquest minster church and its precinct.*

on the east side of the road were of uniform length, while those on the west extended back to Small Lane (later Bank Street), and differed in length (Map 4 insert, labelled A). Nicholas de Verdun also endowed a hospital *c.*1216, dedicated to St John. Like most medieval hospitals, this was located on the edge of the town near a river crossing, in this case immediately south of the river, on the east side of the approach to the town, channelling visitors past the institution to encourage the giving of alms.[109]

There may have been difficulties in attracting permanent residents to the town, as 43 burgage plots were recorded in 1279 with only 25 burgesses.[110] The burgage plots did not extend the whole length of High Street, as in 1365 Thomas Feilding conveyed to John Feilding, his wife Agnes and son John a half burgage on High Street, between the burgage of John Feilding and the messuage of William Milner.[111] These burgages may have

---

109 C. Rawcliffe, 'The earthly and spiritual topography of suburban hospitals', in K. Giles and C. Dyer (eds), *Town and Country in the Middle Ages: Contrasts, Contacts and Interconnections, 1100–1500* (Leeds, 2007), 251–5, 263–7.
110 Nichols, *Hist.*, IV, 247–8.
111 Ibid., 256; A.H. Dyson, *Lutterworth: The Story of John Wycliffe's Town* (London, 1913), 25.

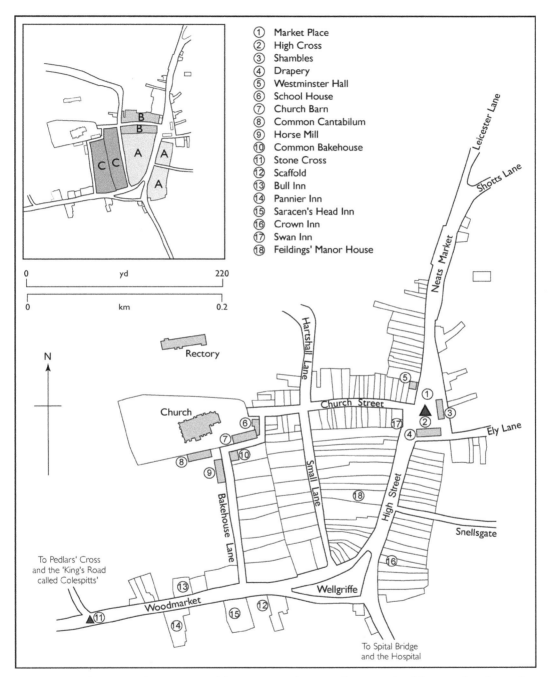

1. Market Place
2. High Cross
3. Shambles
4. Drapery
5. Westminster Hall
6. School House
7. Church Barn
8. Common Cantabilum
9. Horse Mill
10. Common Bakehouse
11. Stone Cross
12. Scaffold
13. Bull Inn
14. Pannier Inn
15. Saracen's Head Inn
16. Crown Inn
17. Swan Inn
18. Feildings' Manor House

Map 4 *Medieval Lutterworth, reconstructed from a terrier of 1509, with topographical features plotted onto the boundaries of 1887.*

Figure 4 *This group of three shops on High Street, rebuilt in the early 19th century, may occupy three of the burgage plots laid out by Nicholas de Verdun. The pilasters and their capitals were inspired by the Greek Revival movement, as were many other properties in the town.*

become the Feilding's manor house (later the Denbigh Arms). The division of some plots into half burgages suggests a high demand, at least occasionally. A burgage conveyed in 1362 by Thomas Feilding to William, son of Thomas Pulteney, the lord of Misterton, may be the plot 'next the Swanne' on the west side of High Street, which was still described as a burgage in a lease of 1595 from Gabriel Pulteney of Misterton to his son John.[112]

The Shambles ('Fleshamills') and the Drapery, both permanent buildings by 1509, stood on two sides of the market place, which was dominated by the High Cross.[113] Other stalls were occupied in 1512–13 by merchants, shoemakers, tanners, bakers and glovers.[114] Part of the main market area may have been cobbled with fieldstones by

112 Nichols, *Hist.*, IV, 256; TNA, E 40/13463.
113 Warws. RO, CR 2017/E42, ff. 2, 3; The plan of the town was first set out diagrammatically by John Goodacre and the Lutterworth Town Study Group: 'Lutterworth in 1509', *Leics. Historian* 2 (1975), 17–25; Goodacre, *Transformation*, 10–11.
114 TNA, SC 6/HENVIII/1824.

1520, when John Paybody left money for repairs to the town's pavements.[115] The Neats Market, where cattle were sold, was immediately north of the market place, along the road towards Leicester. A cottage in Neats Market near the High Cross was known as Westminster Hall in 1509, when it was held by Sir Everard Feilding.[116] Named with a fine sense of irony, or self-importance, this might have been a courthouse or a market hall. Other market areas in 1512 included the Sheep Market, Horse Market and Swine Market, the latter in Shottes Lane (Snellsgate in 1509, later Misterton Way).[117] Parallel to this lane, to its north, Ely Lane (later Station Road) led away from the eastern side of the market place. There were four shops at the west end of Ely Lane in 1509.[118]

To the west of the market place, the broadly regular-sized plots on either side of Church Street and to the east of Small Lane (Map 4, inset, labelled B) are also indicative of planning rather than of organic growth, and may have been laid out at the same time as those on High Street, or represent a later extension of the trading area. To the west of Small Lane, the houses on the north side of Church Gate belonged to the church in 1509 and were described as five tenements in 1601.[119] These have been substantially rebuilt, and their original date of construction is unclear. All the cottages that stood opposite these in 1509 were then owned by St John's hospital. This land may have been part of the hospital's original endowment, and possibly laid out at its foundation, c.1216.[120] Some of these houses were rebuilt in the late 16th century as a jettied timber-framed row (front cover), which was restored between 1968 and 1976.[121]

Bakehouse Lane (later Baker Street) skirted the churchyard before turning south to join Woodmarket. Three buildings stood in 'the corner of Bakehouse Lane' in 1509: a schoolhouse, a cottage held 'to the use of the town' and a church barn, presumably to store tithe corn or hay. All these buildings may once have been connected to the church, a chantry or a guild. Round the corner and near the churchyard was a 'common *cantabilum*'.[122] The word *cantabilum* is not recorded elsewhere, but it is from a document that is a 17th-century copy of the original and may be a transcription error. This building, considered to be a 'common' asset of the community in 1509, housed the town bull in 1607,[123] but its location and the stem of its name suggest an earlier musical use, possibly related to the church. Nearby and facing each other on Bakehouse Lane were a horse-mill, owned by the manor, and the common bakehouse, most likely also manorial in its origin.[124]

Between Bakehouse Lane and Small Lane there is evidence of a further planned layout (Map 4 inset, labelled C). The properties on both lanes have a common back boundary, and the land between them is arranged in uniform plots much wider than those along High Street. This may have been laid out in the late 13th or early 14th century, perhaps as

115 ROLLR, Will register 1515–26, f. 374–374v.
116 Warws. RO, CR 2017/E42, f. 1.
117 TNA, SC 6/HENVIII/1824.
118 Warws. RO, CR 2017/E42, f. 2.
119 Warws. RO, CR 2017/E42, f. 1; Lincs. Arch., DIOC/TER/5, f. 450.
120 Warws. RO, CR 2017/E42, f. 1; *VCH Leics.* II, 42–3.
121 NHLE, no. 1290220, 35–39 Church St (accessed 9 Aug. 2020); plaque on building extant 2020.
122 Warws. RO, CR 2017/E42, ff. 1, 5.
123 TNA, LR 2/255, f. 160; Goodacre, *Transformation*, 16.
124 Warws. RO, CR 2017/E42, f. 5.

an attempt by the Verduns to create a new suburb. In 1509 there were only three cottages and two crofts on the western side of Small Lane, suggesting that any attempt to extend the town had met with limited success.[125]

Visitors to Lutterworth from the south, after passing the hospital and crossing Spital bridge, would climb a steep road to a triangular area known as Wellgriffe and either turn left to Woodmarket or continue north to High Street. There were six shops between Wellgriffe and High Street in 1509.[126] The wide wood market, accessible from Watling Street without passing through the town, was where timber from the Arden and coal from the environs of Bedworth and Nuneaton (Warws.) were sold in their own specialist areas, preventing obstructions and the need to bring bulky goods past other market stalls. A stone cross stood at the west end of Woodmarket in 1509, marking the start of the market area where tolls applied, and there was a scaffold for the gallows on the south side of Woodmarket.[127] Pedlars' Cross stood at the bend on Coventry Road at Woodbridge Hill, and was where itinerant traders coming to sell their wares from baskets were probably encouraged to congregate and be supervised by market officials.[128] Lutterworth's role as a thoroughfare town is emphasised by the presence of five inns in 1509, and Woodmarket's importance is apparent from the three inns along this road: the Bull, the Pannier and the Saracen's Head, the latter two owned by Everard Feilding.[129] The Pannier or the Saracen's Head may have been occupied by the innkeeper William Parburne in 1515, when he was accused of negligence for allowing one of William Feilding's houses to burn down.[130] The two other inns in 1509 were the Crown, owned by Martin Feilding, and the Swan, owned by the hospital, both on High Street, with the latter facing the market place.[131]

The two oldest buildings in the town, other than the parish church, are believed to be the Shambles and the property immediately to its north, separated from the Shambles by a yard (Figure 5). Both are thought to date from the early to mid 16th century. The Shambles may be partly on the site of the 'Fleshamills' of 1509. Restored in 1984, it is of timber-framed box construction, in four bays of two storeys. The partitions between the bays extend to the apex of the roof, suggesting that each was once a separate unit.[132] The small timber-framed house to its north, with a cross wing, is also timber framed, with alterations made in the 19th and 20th centuries.[133]

125 Warws. RO, CR 2017/E42, f. 4; A. Watkins, 'The town of Lutterworth in the later Middle Ages', *Trans. LAHS* 92 (2018), 129–30.
126 TNA, E 179/133/121 m. 2; Warws. RO, CR 2017/E42, f. 4.
127 Warws. RO, CR 2017/E42, ff. 4, 16; Goodacre, *Transformation*, 27.
128 Warws. RO, CR 2017/E42, f. 10; ROLLR, Misc. 239.
129 Warws. RO, CR 2017/E42, f. 4; Goodacre, *Transformation*, 27.
130 Warws. RO, CR 2017/E42; TNA CP 40/1011, m. 272.
131 Warws. RO, CR 2017/E42, f. 3.
132 NHLE, no. 1218008, The Shambles Public House Bell St (accessed 9 Aug. 2020); Lutterworth Museum, Listed Buildings Records.
133 NHLE, no. 1211195, Valeska Restaurant Market St (accessed 9 Aug. 2020); Lutterworth Museum, Listed Buildings Records.

Figure 5 *The Shambles, on the north-eastern side of the market place, and the small property immediately to its north, just within this image, were probably both built in the early 16th century.*

Evolution of the Modern Town

When John Leland passed through Lutterworth *c.*1535 he recognised it as a town but 'scant half so bigge as Lughborow [Loughborough]', yet Lutterworth had the third-highest number of households in the county in 1563, behind only Leicester and Loughborough.[134] By 1607, the town had expanded to include a separate beast market (in addition to the neats market for young cattle), iron market, corn market, horse fair leys and more than 40 shops.[135] The Drapery contained 12 shops in 12 bays, had a tiled roof and measured 100 ft. by 20½ ft. The Shambles was thatched, measured 110 ft. by 12 ft., and contained seven shops, each of one bay.[136] Two shops had been 'lately built' adjacent to Westminster Hall, and there were two shops on Beast Market (later Market Street); eight on Ely Lane (later Station Road); seven shops on Woodmarket, including three in one building; two shops, including one within an inn, on High Street; one on Sheep Market; another on Iron Market; and a shop 'now being built' on the manorial waste.[137] By 1625, a 'decayed' shop on Neats Market had been rebuilt as two shops.[138] Some of these may have been workshops and others were perhaps open only on market days, but the overall impression is of a thriving small town.

134 L. Toulmin Smith (ed.), *The Itinerary of John Leland in or about the Years 1535–1543* (1907), I, 19; *VCH Leics.* III, 166–9.
135 TNA, LR 2/255, ff. 122, 124, 157, 131.
136 TNA, LR 2/255, f. 161.
137 TNA, LR 2/255, ff. 117, 124, 130, 140, 150, 151, 155, 162, 163, 166.
138 ROLLR, DE 1012/5.

Figure 6 *The market place in 2022, looking north.*

Only one inn was specifically identified in 1607, the Crown, occupied by Theophilus Greene, which had six bays and a malthouse of seven bays. John Halpeny's house, also on High Street (probably the Swan), had six bays and a separate brewhouse.[139] Two houses on Woodmarket were of five bays, occupied by John Garfield and Robert Greene. Garfield's house also had a malthouse of six bays. These were probably two of the three inns recorded on Woodmarket in 1509.[140]

A fire destroyed 80 bays of houses and barns in the town in 1653.[141] It may have been shortly after this that the southern part of the market place was filled with permanent buildings, perhaps a mixture of houses and shops, forming an island (Map 5). This central 'island' was swept away in 1960 to widen the main road through the town, returning the market place closer to its medieval size (Figure 6).[142] In addition to the church, the Shambles and its neighbour, there are perhaps six more buildings that predate the fire, some with their timber frames subsequently clad with brick.[143] About a dozen houses are recognised to survive from the later 17th century, and are also timber-framed beneath a brick shell.[144] The 'Old Bakehouse' on Bakehouse Lane is of cruck construction and may be a similar age.[145] Other houses were less substantial. In 1794 'by far the majority' of houses in the town were said to be built of 'semi-fluids (mud-walls) covered with thatch'.[146]

The built character of the modern town centre reflects a major period of rebuilding over the first four decades of the 19th century, largely in the Greek Revival style, when

---

139 TNA, LR 2/255, ff. 149, 155.
140 TNA, LR 2/255, ff. 150, 158; Warws. RO, CR 2017/E42, f. 4.
141 Ratcliff and Johnson, *Warwick County Records*, III, 215–16.
142 *Leic. Eve. Mail*, 1 Jan. 1960; see Figure 14.
143 NHLE, no. 1290220, 35–39 Church St; no. 1211221, The Springs Stoney Hollow; no. 1218060, Candlemas Cott. Chapel St; no. 1218074, 2 Church St; no. 1209173, The Cavalier Public House 31 Market St; no. 1292774, 58–62 Woodmarket (accessed 9 Aug. 2020).
144 NHLE, no. 1211248, 38 and 40 Woodmarket; no. 1209175, 25 Regent St; no. 1211157, 23 and 25 Market St; no. 1209166, 4–10 Church St (accessed 9 Aug. 2020).
145 J.S. Dodge, *A Look at Lutterworth 2000, or Thereabouts* (Lutterworth, 1999), 27.
146 *Universal Dir.* (1794), 603, parentheses original.

new commercial and mail-coach routes delivered economic confidence and prosperity. The two main inns, the Denbigh Arms and the Hind, both faced High Street with an entrance and exit for coaches on Bank Street. The Denbigh Arms (Figure 12) was largely rebuilt in the early 19th century, and the Hind's façade was updated in the same period, with a rusticated ground floor facing the street (Figure 2).[147] The so-called 'Manor House' on Market Street was also refronted and upgraded in this period (Figure 9).[148] The pair of three-storey shops immediately to the north of the Hind were possibly by William Flint, a Leicester architect, c.1828.[149] Lutterworth Hall (originally Lutterworth House) was built on Woodmarket for the attorney Francis Burges in 1820–1, to a design by William Firmadge, another Leicester architect. This property was enlarged in 1897, bought by Lutterworth RDC for offices in 1939 and restored in 1980–2 following its sale by the RDC.[150] Hythe House (Figure 7) has a single chimney stack, an off-centre door and a rusticated façade of c.1840, which may be hiding an earlier building. It takes its name from the birthplace of Herbert Fagge, a surgeon and general practitioner who lived there between 1867 and 1919.[151] A small property at 14 Bank Street was also modified in the late 1830s, possibly by Joseph Hansom, to present a Greek Revival façade, with rustication, gable pediment and pilastered porch.[152]

South of High Street, the six 'very ordinary terrace houses' comprising The Terrace (originally Wiclif Terrace) were built c.1840 with 'grand stuccoed façades with Grecian detail' including horizontal rustication to the ground floor. It is believed they may have been designed by Joseph Hansom.[153] The northwards expansion of the town in the early 19th century added three brick houses at the southern end of Bitteswell Road for the middling classes, who saw no need to disguise the building material.[154] Public buildings included the town hall, by Joseph Hansom (1836, Figure 2),[155] and the Union workhouse at the western end of Woodmarket, by George Gilbert Scott and William Bonython Moffatt (1840, demolished c.1970).[156]

There was little domestic building activity between 1840 and 1900, although this period did see the construction of the police station (1842, Figure 28) and

147 NHLE, no. 1209172, Denbigh Arms Hotel High St; no. 1292770, Hind Hotel 8 High St (accessed 9 Aug. 2020); Pevsner, *Leics. and Rutl.*, 301.

148 Below, Landownership (Manor Houses).

149 M. Mitchley, *William Flint: Leicester's Classical Architect* (Thurmaston, 2019), 218–19.

150 NHLE, no. 1292775, Lutterworth Hall Woodmarket (accessed 9 Aug. 2020); Pevsner, *Leics. and Rutl.*, 301; J.D. Bennett, *Leicestershire Architects 1700–1850* (Leicester, 2001), 27; below, Local Government (Local Government after 1894).

151 NHLE, no. 1209177, Hythe Ho. 68 Woodmarket (accessed 9 Aug. 2020); TNA, RG 10/3222/96/9; *Leic. Chron.*, 3 Aug. 1867; *Rugby Advertiser*, 20 June 1919.

152 NHLE, no. 1292200, 14 Bank St (accessed 9 Aug. 2020); Pevsner, *Leics. and Rutl.*, 301; P. Harris, 'Birmingham or Hinckley? Launching the career of Joseph Aloysius Hansom', *Trans. LAHS* 95 (2021), 154.

153 NHLE, no. 1209174, The Terrace 1–6 Rugby Road (accessed 9 Aug. 2020); Pevsner, *Leics. and Rutl.*, 301; Harris, 'Birmingham or Hinckley?', 154–5.

154 NHLE, no. 1209164, 2 and 4 Bitteswell Road; no. 1218025, 6 Bitteswell Road (accessed 9 Aug. 2020).

155 NHLE, no. 1211129, Town Hall High St (accessed 9 Aug. 2020); Pevsner, *Leics. and Rutl.*, 301; below, Local Government (Town Government).

156 http://www.workhouses.org.uk/Lutterworth (accessed 22 Aug. 2020).

Figure 7 *Hythe House, Woodmarket (south elevation).*

superintendent's house,[157] the restoration of the parish church[158] and the building of
Sherrier school (1874, Figure 17),[159] the mechanics' institute (1876, Figure 13)[160] and
the grammar school on Bitteswell Road (1881).[161] The opening of Lutterworth railway
station in 1899 ushered in a fresh period of building activity. A factory was built at the
end of New Street (east of Bitteswell Road) in 1902; foundries were built in 1906 and
1914 on the land between Leicester Road and the railway line; and a new factory was
built for George Spencer in 1912 to the east of Leicester Road. Air raids on Coventry in
1940 resulted in swift action by the Ministry of Supply, who provided a factory between
Leicester Road and the railway for Alfred Herbert Ltd, a major manufacturer of machine
tools from that city. This was soon followed by the relocation of Frank Whittle's
development work on his jet engine to Ladywood Works, in the same area, creating an
industrial 'zone' to the north east of the town.[162] Later factories and small industrial
units have also been built in this area.

157 Below, Local Government (Public Services); NHLE, no. 1228055, Magistrates' Court, Police Station,
     Superintendent's House Gilmorton Road (9 Aug. 2020); Pevsner, *Leics. and Rutl.*, 302.
158 Below, Religious Hist. (Architectural Development of St Mary's Church).
159 Below, Social Hist. (Education).
160 Below, Social Hist. (Communal Life).
161 Below, Social Hist. (Education).
162 Below, Economic Hist. (Manufacturing).

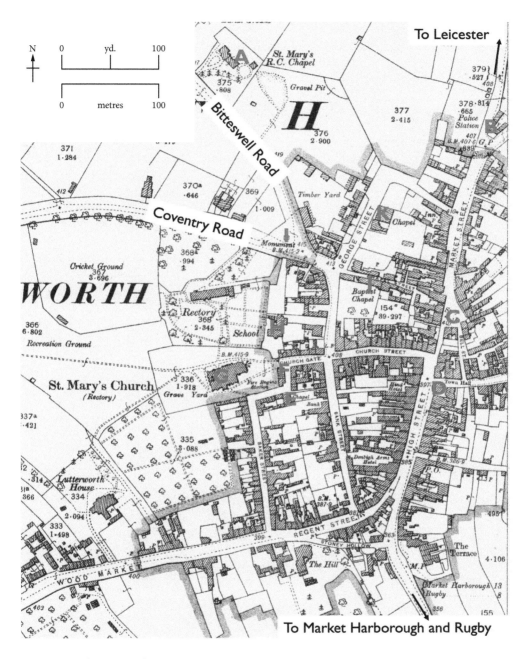

Map 5 *Central Lutterworth in 1904.*

A Catholic Church
B Police Station
C (Shrunken) Market Place
D Town Hall
E Wesleyan Methodist Church
F Mechanics' Institute

G St Mary's Church
H Sherrier School
I Wycliffe Memorial
J Particular Baptist Church
K Congregational Church

Houses had been built along New Street by 1904, including many owned by private individuals for rent in 1910.[163] On the recommendation of the parochial committee, Lutterworth RDC agreed in 1913 to provide 30 houses for the working classes between Leicester Road and the New Street factory. This became Crescent Road, and was one of the earliest council house developments in Leicestershire, although the impact of the First World War resulted in only 23 houses being completed by 1915.[164] The RDC purchased a further 38 a. to the west of Leicester Road in 1919 for another 200 houses, and appointed Walter Bedingfield as architect.[165] Plans for the first 54 were approved in 1920, and the tender of Lutterworth builder Peter Rourke was accepted.[166] The Ministry of Supply erected prefabricated semi-detached bungalows in 1941 on the unbuilt council land to the north of Crescent Road, creating Dunley Way, Denbigh Place, Swiftway and Sherrier Way, with these streets laid out in a grid pattern owing to the need for speedy and economic construction to house the Herbert employees. This plan became fossilised when the temporary dwellings were replaced by permanent council houses between 1955 and 1962. Following the Second World War, the RDC built further prefabricated bungalows off Coventry Road, the last of which were demolished between 1970 and 1972.[167]

An expanding middle class also needed new homes, and attractive individual pairs of semi-detached houses and detached houses were built on the north side of Coventry Road and along Bitteswell Road. The most notable addition to the housing stock in this period was Auburn Place on Bitteswell Road, completed in 1928 by Peter Rourke for George Spencer: a neo-Tudor house in large grounds, with stained glass windows designed at the William Morris factory featuring Queen Elizabeth I and Sir Francis Drake.[168]

By the early 21st century, Lutterworth had expanded further, especially following the opening of the M1 motorway in 1964, but it remained a small town. Houses were built to the south of Coventry Road between 1955 and 1968, and to its north between 1968 and 1985.[169] Although it was classed by the district council as a 'key settlement' in 1980, the 260 houses planned for that decade was a much lower number than for several Leicestershire villages: for example, 1,650 were planned at Enderby/Narborough, 1,160 at Broughton Astley and 980 at Groby.[170] Expansion in the closing years of the 20th century was to the north west of the town, and then to the south west in the early 21st century. The early 21st century also saw another business park added, near the motorway junction.

The limited bus service following the closure of the railway meant cars became an essential component of life, and Lutterworth became a dormitory town. The Harborough District Local Plan for 2011 to 2031 identified Lutterworth as 'an appropriate location for

163 OS Map 25", Leics. XLVIII.16 (1904 edn); TNA, IR 130/4/190; ROLLR, DE 2072/149.
164 *Leic. Daily Post*, 7 Feb. 1913; 4 Apr. 1913; 19 Sept. 1913; 4 Dec. 1913; ROLLR, DE 1379/457, pp. 2–3; Lutterworth Museum, Box 129, letter from Lutterworth RDC, 12 Feb. 1973, to Mrs I. Barker, daughter of one of the first residents.
165 ROLLR, DE 1379/450, pp. 4–5, 8, 37.
166 ROLLR, DE 1379/340, pp. 43, 46.
167 B. Wilkinson, 'Lutterworth's prefabs', *Lutterworth Local Hist. Group Jnl* (2002), 9–10.
168 Dodge, *A Look*, 90–3.
169 OS Map 1:2500, SP 5485 (1967, 1982 edns); SP 5484 (1967, 1972 and 1987 edns); SP 5384 (1964, 1971 and 1991 edns).
170 Leics. CC, *Leicestershire: Planning for the Eighties* (Glenfield, 1980), 14, 21.

significant housing and employment development to meet a large part of the District's requirement'. A controversial proposed development on farmland to the east of the motorway within Lutterworth civil parish is intended to provide 1,260 new houses by 2031, and a further 1,490 houses after 2031.[171] These would be linked to the town by a road bridge over the motorway,[172] but would effectively create a separate 'new town'.

Outlying Farms

Two separate farmhouses on Moorbarns, both (confusingly) known as Moor Barns in 1904, probably have their origins in the two houses built on that land in the 16th and 17th centuries.[173] Padge Hall, close to the junction of Watling Street and Coventry Road, may have been built in the 19th century, with the site absorbed within Magna Park at the close of the 20th century. Three farmhouses were built shortly after the enclosure award of 1792: Lutterworth Fields (later Glebe Farm) to the south of Coventry Road and, in the north of the parish, Edward's (later Riddlesden) Farm and Lord's (later Milord's) Farm, facing each other across Leicester Road. Leaders Farm, off Coventry Road, was recorded from 1928, and was purchased by the town council for a cemetery c.2013.[174] Woodbridge Farm, to its west, was first named on Ordnance Survey maps in 1964.[175]

---

171 Harborough District Local Plan 2011–31, adopted Apr. 2019, 20–1, 48, 51.
172 https://www.leicestershire.gov.uk/have-your-say/current-consultations/east-of-lutterworth-strategic-development-area/lutterworth-east-masterplan (accessed 22 Aug. 2020).
173 OS Map 6", Leics. LII.NE (1886 edn); Leics. XLVIII.SE (1886 edn); below, Landownership (Moorbarns).
174 *Kelly's Dir. of Leics. and Rutl.* (1928), 669; below, Local Government (Public Services).
175 OS Map 1:10000, SP58SW (1955 edn); 1:2500, SP 5284 (1964 edn).

The Pattern of Landownership

THE MANOR OF LUTTERWORTH WAS held by Earl Ralph before the Conquest. It had been granted to Mainou the Breton by 1086, and had been sub-infeudated to the Verdun family by the early 13th century. It passed by marriage, first to the Ferrers family in 1360 and then to the Greys of Groby in 1445. The manor and land were forfeited to the Crown in 1554 on the attainder of Henry Grey, duke of Suffolk.

The most important landowners in Lutterworth from the mid 16th century were the Feilding family, whose landholding reputedly dated back to the 13th century. Everard Feilding owned *c*.150 a. in 1509 and some of the key properties in the town. His descendants added to this landholding during the 16th century, and Everard's great-great-grandson Basil (d. 1633) purchased Lutterworth manor in 1629, in a transaction that also enabled 26 residents to purchase the freeholds of the land they occupied. The Feilding family continued to hold the manor, and remained the largest landowners in the parish into the 20th century. Pasture in the south of the parish known as Moorbarns had become an important enclosed estate by 1509, and was held by the Temple family in the 16th and 17th centuries.

A hospital was founded by Nicholas de Verdun and his mother Rose *c*.1216, and was endowed with seven yardlands in Lutterworth. This was divided into two equal portions in the 1590s, half of which was purchased by William Feilding in 1598, while the remainder, with the hospital site, was purchased in 1596 by Thomas Forren, a prominent Northamptonshire landowner. Forren's holding became part of the neighbouring Misterton estate in 1774.

A small number of properties were held 'for the use of the town', probably by the town guild, in 1509, and these became part of the Town Estate after the Reformation.[1] The Town Estate landholding in the parish in 1839 comprised *c*.16 a. of land, a workhouse, almshouses, two charity schools and 26 houses or tenements, mostly occupied by the poor and in bad repair.[2] It owned 29 properties in the town in 1910, mostly small cottages but including the town hall and the fire station, and held properties with a considerable total value in 2020.[3]

Lutterworth RDC became an important landowner (in terms of social benefit, not acreage) after purchasing land in the town in 1913 for council houses. It owned 594 houses in Lutterworth in 1972, including 431 built after 1939.[4] That number fell through 'right to buy' legislation, with all remaining houses sold in 2007 to Seven Locks Housing Ltd, a social housing provider operating across south Leicestershire.[5]

1   Below, Local Government (Town Government).
2   *Rpt of Charity Commissioners* (Parl. Papers 1839 [163], xv), p. 132.
3   ROLLR, DE 2072/149; Lutterworth Town Estates, Rpt and Financial Statements, 2020.
4   RDC of Lutterworth, *Handbook* (Lutterworth, 1971–2), unpaginated.
5   Ex inf. Sharon Iddison, Harborough District Council.

Lutterworth Manor before 1628

Lutterworth was held before the Norman Conquest by Earl Ralph, who also held one of the manors in neighbouring Misterton.[6] He was probably Earl Ralph of Hereford (d. 1057), the nephew of Edward the Confessor and grandson of Aethelred II.[7] Lutterworth, comprising 13 carucates of land, was held by Mainou the Breton in 1086, and formed part of Mainou's barony of Wolverton (Bucks.).[8] Mainou's descendants had sub-infeudated the manor by 1214 to the Verdun family, the descendants of Bertram de Verdun, the Domesday tenant of Farnham Royal (Bucks.).[9]

Nicholas de Verdun obtained Lutterworth's market charter in 1214.[10] His lands were forfeited when he joined the rebellious barons against King John in 1216, but were restored to him by Henry III in 1216–17.[11] After Nicholas died in 1231, the manor passed to his daughter Rose, who retained the Verdun name after her marriage.[12] She died in 1247, and was succeeded by her son John Verdun.[13] At John's death in 1274, he held the manors of Lutterworth, Cotesbach, 'Butlesby' (probably Bittesby, immediately west of Lutterworth) and Newbold (Verdon), with manors and lands in six other counties. He was succeeded by his son, Sir Theobald Verdun, who held the manor in 1279 for one knight's fee.[14] Theobald died in 1309. The agreed dower of his widow Eleanor included the manor of Lutterworth, 'excepting only £9 of villeinage land and cottages'.[15]

Theobald's heir was his son, also Theobald.[16] Theobald the younger had three daughters by his first wife, Maud, the daughter of Edmund, Lord Mortimer of Wigmore. After her death he married Elizabeth, the daughter of Gilbert de Clare, 7th earl of Gloucester and 6th earl of Hertford (d. 1295), and the widow of John de Burgh,[17] who appears in later records as Elizabeth de Burgh or Lady Clare.[18] Elizabeth was pregnant when Theobald died in 1316. She subsequently gave birth to their daughter, Isabel, who became a co-heiress with her three stepsisters.[19] Elizabeth received Lutterworth as part of her dower. She later married Sir Roger Damory (d. 1322), a member of King Edward II's court.[20]

6   *Domesday*, 645.

7   *ODNB*, s.v. Ralph [*called* Ralph the Timid], earl of Hereford, accessed 7 June 2020; https://opendomesday.org/name/earl-ralph-of-hereford; http://domesday.pase.ac.uk/ Domesday?op=5&personkey=38759 (accessed 14 May 2020).

8   *Domesday*, 645; *VCH Bucks.* IV, 506.

9   *Domesday*, 416; *VCH Bucks.* III, 227.

10   *Rot. Chart.*, 1199–1216, 201.

11   *VCH Bucks.* III, 227.

12   *Complete Peerage*, XIIB, 246–7; *Bk of Fees*, I, 521.

13   *VCH Leics.* II, 27; N. Tringham, 'Rose de Verdun (d. 1247) and Grace Dieu Priory: endowment charter and tomb', *Trans. LAHS* 93 (2019), 199–220; *Complete Peerage*, XIIB, 246–7; *Cal. Chart.* 1257–1300, 12.

14   *Cal. Inq. p.m.* II, 58–60; *Complete Peerage*, XIIB, 247–9; Nichols, *Hist.*, IV, 247.

15   *Cal. Inq. p.m.* V, 95; *Cal. Close* 1272–9, 322–3.

16   *Cal. Inq. p.m.* V, 95.

17   *Cal. Inq. p.m.* VI, 36; *Complete Peerage*, XIIB, 250–1.

18   TNA, E 179/133/1, m. 10d; E 179/133/2, m. 10d.

19   *Complete Peerage*, XIIB, 250–1; *VCH Bucks.* III, 227.

20   *Cal. Close* 1313–18, 381; *ODNB*, s.v. Clare, Elizabeth de [Elizabeth de Burgh; *known as* lady of Clare] (1294/5–1360), magnate and founder of Clare College, Cambridge, accessed 21 July 2020.

Elizabeth died in 1360. Her daughter Isabel had married Henry, Lord Ferrers of Groby, and Lutterworth manor became part of Isabel's inheritance, passing to Isabel and Henry's son William (I), Lord Ferrers of Groby.[21] After his death in 1371,[22] the manor passed first to William's son Henry (II),[23] then on Henry's death in 1388 to Henry's son William (II), Lord Ferrers, who died in 1445. William (II)'s son Henry (III) had died in his father's lifetime, so the manor passed to Henry (III)'s daughter Elizabeth, the wife of Sir Edward Grey, a younger son of Reynold Grey, Lord Grey of Ruthin, and Edward became known as Lord Ferrers of Groby.[24] The Ferrers and Greys of Groby were the second most influential family in Leicestershire (after Beaumont) in the reign of Henry VI.[25] Elizabeth (Lady Ferrers) outlived both her husband and their son Sir John Grey, who was killed in 1461 fighting on the Lancastrian side at the second battle of St Albans. Sir John's widow, Elizabeth (Woodville), the daughter of the 1st Earl Rivers, married the Yorkist King Edward IV in 1464. Sir John and Elizabeth's son Thomas was created 1st marquess of Dorset in 1475 and inherited the manor on the death of his grandmother Elizabeth (Ferrers) in 1483.[26] When Thomas died in 1501, the manor passed to his son, also Thomas, 2nd marquess.[27] Following the latter's death in 1530, it passed to his son Henry, created duke of Suffolk in 1551.[28] Suffolk was pardoned for his part in proclaiming his eldest daughter, Lady Jane Grey, queen in 1553, but was tried and executed in 1554 after conspiring to prevent the marriage of Queen Mary to Philip of Spain.[29] The manor became vested in the Crown, where it remained until 1628.

Principal Feilding Estate before 1628

The Feilding family, earls of Denbigh from 1622 and lords of Lutterworth from 1629, claimed to have been landowners in Lutterworth from the 13th century. Eager to prove an illustrious pedigree, Basil Feilding, 2nd earl of Denbigh (d. 1675), provided Nathaniel Wanley of Coventry with 'evidence' of his descent from the house of Habsburg, including 'charters' purporting to show the family's ancient landholding in Lutterworth.[30] The claim was comprehensively demolished in the early 20th century.[31] Feilding and Wanley stated that Nicholas de Verdun (d. 1231) gave five virgates of land to Nicholas's younger brother Bertram, who gave them to his daughter Cicely, the wife of John de Colville. The land passed to their daughter Maud, who was said to have married Geoffrey, son

21 *Cal. Inq. p.m.* VIII, 316–17; IX, 299; X, 509; M. Hagger, *The Fortunes of a Norman Family: the de Verduns in England, Ireland and Wales, 1066–1216* (Dublin, 2001), 119–23.
22 *Cal. Inq. p.m.* XIII, 68.
23 *Cal. Inq. p.m.* XVI, 211; XVII, 148.
24 *Complete Peerage*, V, 357–9.
25 *Hist. Parl. Commons*, 1422–61, II, 295.
26 *Complete Peerage*, V, 358–62; IV, 418; *ODNB*, s.v. Grey, Thomas, first marquess of Dorset (*c.*1455–1501), accessed 30 Aug. 2017.
27 *Complete Peerage*, IV, 418–20; *ODNB*, s.v. Grey, Thomas, second marquess of Dorset (1477–1530), accessed 30 Aug. 2017.
28 *Complete Peerage*, IV, 420–2.
29 *ODNB*, s.v. Grey, Henry, duke of Suffolk (1517–54), magnate, accessed 20 July 2019.
30 W. Dugdale, *The Antiquities of Warwickshire*, I (1730), 86–7; Nichols, *Hist.*, IV, 273–90.
31 J.H. Round, *Studies in Peerage and Family Hist.* (London, 1970 edn), 216–49.

of the earl of Habsburg, Lauffenberg and Rheinfelden, with Geoffrey taking the name Feilding. Geoffrey and Maud's heir was said to be their son, also named Geoffrey.[32] A Geoffrey Feilding was assessed for tax in Lutterworth in 1332.[33] The heralds identified a Geoffrey Feilding in Lutterworth in the 14th century and were satisfied that he was the ancestor of the earls of Denbigh, but they named this Geoffrey's father as William, and William's father as John.[34] The (genuine) 14th-century Geoffrey Feilding married Agnes, the daughter of Adam de Napton,[35] and this Geoffrey is said to have given his lands in Lutterworth to their son William (I) in 1329.[36]

William (I) married Joan Prudhome,[37] and is said to have transferred 'the manors of Misterton and Lutterworth' (although he possessed neither manor) to his son John (I) in 1361.[38] This John has been conflated with his grandson John in the published pedigrees.[39] John (I) died in 1403 (Figure 8), leaving a son William (II), of whom little is known beyond his attestation of a Warwickshire election in 1425.[40] William (II)'s son John (II) married Margaret Purefoy of Drayton,[41] and in 1433 purchased the manor of Newnham Paddox in the parish of Monks Kirby (Warws.), 5 miles west of Lutterworth, which became the main Feilding family home.[42] John (II)'s son and heir William (III) married Agnes Seyton. He was a merchant of the Staple at Calais, elected to Parliament for Leicestershire in 1449 and 1459,[43] and knighted on the battlefield shortly before his death in 1471, fighting for the Lancastrians at the battle of Tewkesbury.[44]

Sir Everard Feilding, William (III)'s son and heir, was also an active merchant of the Staple.[45] Everard held c.150 a. in Lutterworth in 1509, together with 'Westminster Hall', two inns, two shops and 27 houses.[46] He died in 1515, having bequeathed his land in Lutterworth to his son William (IV).[47] At his death in 1547, Sir William held 300 a. of arable land, 100 a. of pasture, 100 a. of meadow, eight messuages, 24 cottages and 20 shops in Lutterworth, worth £24 yearly.[48] His heir was his son Basil (I), who died in 1585.[49] Basil and his father, William (IV), have alabaster tombs with effigies in a chapel

32   Nichols, *Hist.*, IV, 277–9, 281.
33   TNA, E 179/133/2, m. 10d.
34   W. Camden (ed. J. Fetherston), *The Visitation of the County of Warwick in the Year 1619* (London, 1877), 11.
35   Nichols, *Hist.*, IV, 283; Camden, *Visitation*, 11.
36   Nichols, *Hist.*, IV, 251.
37   Nichols, *Hist.*, IV, 251; Camden, *Visitation*, 11; Dugdale, *Antiquities*, 86–7.
38   Nichols, *Hist.*, IV, 251.
39   Camden, *Visitation*, 10–12; Nichols, *Hist.*, IV, 294.
40   *Hist. Parl. Commons*, 1422–61, IV, 319.
41   Camden, *Visitation*, 11; Nichols, *Hist.*, IV, 294.
42   *VCH Warws.* VI, 175; Dugdale, *Antiquities*, 85–6; Nichols, *Hist.*, IV, 288.
43   Below, Economic Hist. (Trades and Services); Nichols, *Hist.*, IV, 265; *Cal. Pat.* 1446–52, 315, 590; *Hist. Parl. Commons*, 1422–61, IV, 319–22; E. Acheson, *A Gentry Community: Leicestershire in the Fifteenth Century, c.1422–c.1485* (Cambridge, 1992), 105, 125–6, 132, 230–1.
44   *Hist. Parl. Commons*, 1422–61, IV, 319–22; Nichols, *Hist.*, IV, 294.
45   Nichols, *Hist.*, IV, 251, 287; TNA, PROB 11/18/114.
46   Warws. RO, CR 2017/E42.
47   TNA, PROB 11/18/114.
48   ROLLR, 5D 33/189, citing TNA, E 150/1148.
49   Nichols, *Hist.*, IV, 288, 294; TNA, PROB 11/68/79.

Figure 8 *Brass memorial in St Mary's church, Lutterworth, to John Feilding (d. 1403) and his wife, Joan (d. 1418). The inscription is a faithful copy of the original, recorded in 1810 but subsequently lost.*

at the east end of the north aisle of St Edith's church, Monks Kirby.[50] Basil's son and heir, William (V), increased the family's landholdings in Lutterworth in 1598 through the purchase of 3½ yardlands from William Goodyeare of Market Harborough, once part of the landholding of the medieval hospital.[51] William (V)'s date of death is unknown; his son Basil (II) inherited the landholding at Lutterworth.[52] Basil (II) also held land in Martinthorpe (Rutl.) and became an MP for that county in 1614, but did not stand again in 1620.[53]

Lutterworth Manor from 1628

Lutterworth manor was granted by Charles I in 1628 to trustees for the mayor and commonalty of the city of London. They sold the manor in 1629, with the tolls of the market and fairs but excluding Lodge mill, to Basil (II) Feilding and George Varnham of

50   NHLE, no. 1034855, Church of St Edith Millers Lane (accessed 11 June 2020); monuments seen by author.
51   Nichols, *Hist.*, IV, 294; Camden, *Visitation*, 11; Warws. RO, CR 2017/D171.
52   Nichols, *Hist.*, IV, 288.
53   *Hist. Parl. Commons*, 1604–29, IV, 241–2.

London for £1,650.[54] Varnham was acting as trustee for 25 men and one woman who had each provided part of the consideration to obtain the freeholds of individual properties and land that they mostly occupied.[55] The conveyances of the freeholds to the individuals were completed between 1629 and 1631.[56]

Basil (II) died in 1633. His eldest son and heir, William (VI), had married Susan, the sister of George Villiers, 1st duke of Buckingham.[57] The marriage brought court offices and titles to the family, and William (VI) was created 1st earl of Denbigh in 1622. Following his death in 1643, the manor passed through the hands of each of the subsequent earls of Denbigh: William's son Basil (d. 1675);[58] Basil's nephew William, the 2nd earl of Desmond, who also became 3rd earl of Denbigh (d. 1685);[59] William's son Basil, 4th earl of Denbigh (d. 1717); Basil's son William, 5th earl (d. 1755); and William's son Basil, 6th earl (d. 1800). The 6th earl's eldest son William had died in 1799, leaving a son, William Basil Percy Feilding, who succeeded his grandfather as 7th earl of Denbigh and lord of Lutterworth.[60] He died in 1865 and was succeeded by his son Rudolph William, 8th earl (d. 1892),[61] and then by the 8th earl's son Rudolph Robert, who owned 378 a. in Lutterworth in 1910 and died in 1939.[62] No evidence has been found of subsequent family members claiming any manorial incidents.

Feilding Cadet Estate from 1509

The early history of the Feilding's second estate in the town is obscure. Martin Feilding, a younger brother of Everard (d. 1515), held *c*.24 a. in Lutterworth in 1509, with one inn, five shops, the horse-mill and six cottages.[63] Martin was probably the direct ancestor of George Feilding, who purchased the freehold of three messuages, three crofts, two cottages, two closes and 12 yardlands of land, occupied by five tenants, when Basil Feilding bought the manor in 1629.[64]

George's son and heir was also named George.[65] The latter's eldest son, Robert (widely known as Beau Feilding), lived a colourful life, which included a bigamous marriage.[66] He was later reconciled to his first wife, Mary (née Wadsworth), and in 1712 bequeathed

54 TNA, SP 16/229, f. 201; Warws. RO, CR 2017/D146; CR 2017/L11; Nichols, *Hist.*, IV, 252–3.
55 Warws. RO, CR 2017/D172.
56 Warws. RO, CR 2017/D173–94.
57 *Complete Peerage*, IV, 178.
58 *ODNB*, s.v. Feilding, Basil, second earl of Denbigh (*c*.1608–1675), parliamentarian army officer and politician, accessed 7 Dec. 2018.
59 *Complete Peerage*, IV, 178–80; subsequent earls held both peerages but are referred to in this text only as earls of Denbigh.
60 Warws. RO, CR 2017/D168/1.
61 *Complete Peerage*, IV, 182–3.
62 ROLLR, DE 2072/149; *The Times*, 27 Nov. 1939.
63 Warws. RO, CR 2017/D42.
64 Warws. RO, CR 2017/D181.
65 TNA, C 5/354/33.
66 TNA, PROB 11/339/216; *ODNB*, s.v. Feilding, Robert (1650/51–1712), rake and bigamist, accessed 1 Nov. 2020; Anon., *Cases of Divorce for Several Causes* (1715), I, i–xlvii, 1–48; II, 1–30.

to her and her heirs all his 'manors', messuages and lands in Lutterworth.[67] The will was challenged by Robert's younger brother William Feilding of Youghal (Co. Cork, Ireland), who claimed that the estate should have passed to him under an earlier settlement and that Robert had not been of sound mind when he made his will.[68] After winning his claim, William settled the lands in 1722 on his son, also William, a captain in the guards. Captain William's son, also William, inherited, and after his death the land and properties passed to his only child, Elizabeth, who never married. She was granted 253 a. in Lutterworth's enclosure award, and died in 1803.[69]

Following Elizabeth's death, the land passed to Charles Palmer of Coleshill (Warws.), a descendant of Andrew Palmer of Knowle (Warws.), who had married Elizabeth Feilding (the sister of Robert and William of Youghal) in 1674.[70] This land appears to have been settled by Charles Palmer on his eldest son, Albert, who owned 257 a. in Lutterworth in 1817.[71] Albert died in 1820 without issue, and his estate passed back to his father Charles, who died one month later.[72] Under Charles Palmer's will, his lands in Leicestershire and Warwickshire were divided between his surviving sons, Edward Feilding, Robert and Charles.[73] The Lutterworth land passed to Edward Feilding Palmer, who was a major landowner in Lutterworth in 1846 and who died in 1869.[74] His land in Lutterworth appears to have been settled on his son, the Revd Feilding Palmer, who died in 1897, having devised all his real estate to his widow, Frances.[75] In 1899 Frances gave land on Gilmorton Road for a cottage hospital to be built in her husband's memory.[76] She owned 49 a. in Lutterworth when she died in 1910, having devised this, together with £500, to the trustees of the Feilding Palmer cottage hospital.[77]

Manor Houses

A capital messuage was recorded in 1316.[78] This was worth 2s. annually in 1360, when there was also a dovecote worth 18d.[79] With no resident lords in the Middle Ages, the house probably fell into decay over time. It was said there was no manor house in 1445.[80]

A property on the west side of High Street owned by Everard Feilding was the only house in the town described as a 'chief messuage' in 1509.[81] By 1726, a 'kilne yard' at this

---

67 TNA, PROB 11/530/26.
68 TNA, C 5/354/33; Warws. RO, CR 2017/F108/1–9.
69 ROLLR, EN/AX/211/1; DE 2559/104; DE 2094/3; Warws. RO, CR 2017 F108/1–9; TNA, IR 27/17/037.
70 Warws. RO, CR 2017 F108/1–9; DR 0022/1.
71 ROLLR, DE 783/26.
72 ROLLR, Admons and wills 1821, A–S; Warws. RO, DRB 0081/23.
73 Lichfield RO, Lichfield, Original wills, admons and inventories 1820, P–R.
74 White, *Hist.* (Sheffield, 1846), 401; Warws. RO, DRB 0081/24; TNA, IR 27/370/3.
75 Principal Probate Registry, COW 425919g; COW 404513g.
76 *Leic. Chron.*, 15 Apr. 1899; 23 Dec. 1899; below, Social Hist. (Social Welfare).
77 *Cheltenham Chron.*, 30 July 1910; Principal Probate Registry, COW 404514g.
78 TNA, C 134/56/1.
79 TNA, C 135/152/5.
80 *Cal. Inq. p.m.* XXVI, 188, 195–6.
81 Warws. RO, CR 2017/E42, f. 3.

Figure 9 *The 'Manor House' on Market Street (west elevation).*

property had been converted into a bowling green.[82] This became known as the Denbigh Arms, one of Lutterworth's main coaching inns. Building work in the early 19th century largely disguised the timber framing of an earlier building behind a stone neo-Greek façade three storeys high, with pilasters at each end of the seven bays (Figure 12).[83] The property was divided into individual apartments in 2003 and renamed Denbigh Court.[84]

The 'Manor House' on the east side of Market Street (Figure 9) was probably Elizabeth Feilding's house recorded on Beast Market in 1790.[85] The property was given an updated façade and possibly extended in the early 19th century, also in neo-Greek style. The interior includes evidence of an earlier timber-framed building, a fireplace and mantelpiece of the 18th century (or earlier) and an 18th-century staircase.[86]

It has been suggested that 'Farmfield', on Station Road, includes part of the fabric of an old manor house and was possibly occupied by Maud, the wife of 'Geoffrey de

82   Warws. RO, CR 2017/D163/2.
83   Warws. RO, CR 2017/D235; NHLE, no. 1209172, Denbigh Arms Hotel High St (accessed 9 Aug. 2020); Pevsner, *Leics. and Rutl.*, 301; Dodge, *A Look at Lutterworth 2000, or Thereabouts* (Lutterworth, 1999), 30.
84   Date on building, extant 2019.
85   ROLLR, DE 2559/104; above (Feilding Cadet Estate from 1509).
86   NHLE, no. 1292772, The Manor Ho. Market St (accessed 9 Aug. 2020); Pevsner, *Leics. and Rutl.*, 302; Dodge, *A Look*, 27, 30–1.

Habsburg', in the 13th century.[87] There is no evidence of a manor house ever being in this road. Farmfield was probably built in the early 18th century as a farmhouse.[88]

Moorbarns

Moorbarns pasture, in the south of the parish, probably originated as demesne land and had been enclosed by 1509.[89] It was forfeited to the Crown with Lutterworth manor in 1554, but the duke of Suffolk's widow, Frances, was granted a life interest. Peter Temple of Burton Dassett (Warws.) obtained a reversionary lease of 348 a. at Moorbarns in 1557 for 40 years from the death of the duchess, for £37 annually and an entry fine of £84.[90] The duchess died in 1559, but Temple appears not to have taken possession until 1562, possibly after reaching an accommodation with the sitting tenant, Edward Ferrers, perhaps a relative of the Ferrers family, former lords of Lutterworth manor.[91] A new lease was granted in 1576 to Peter Temple and his eldest son, John, for 21 years from 1600, also at £37 annually.[92] An adjacent *c.*200 a. of land was enclosed and added to the pasture probably between 1562 and 1580.[93]

Peter Temple died in 1578.[94] The land passed to his son John (d. 1603), and then to John's son Thomas (1st baronet, d. 1637), under a series of Crown leases that extended to 1663 at an unchanged rent.[95] Sir Thomas ceased farming in 1624, and sublet the land for an annual rent of between £305 and £420.[96] He arranged for the head lease to pass to his second son, John, for 30 years, under terms that required John to pay a total of £1,000 to his four youngest siblings on Sir Thomas's death.[97] A bitter dispute followed between Sir Thomas and his eldest son, Peter, who had expected the land to pass to him.[98] The Crown sold the reversion in 1629, and this was purchased by John Temple in 1632. He died later that year.[99]

87 ROLLR, DE 1761/53/2; J. Thompson, 'The secular history of Lutterworth', *Trans. LAHS* 4 (1869–75), 165.

88 NHLE, no. 1211213, Farmfield 18 Station Road (accessed 9 Aug. 2020).

89 Warws. RO, CR 2017/E42, ff. 5, 6, 8.

90 *Cal. Pat.* 1557–8, 15; TNA, C 66/919, m. 1; Warws. RO, CR 2017/E42, m. 5.

91 *Complete Peerage*, IV, 422; N.W. Alcock, *Warws. Grazier and London Skinner, 1532–1555: The Account Book of Peter Temple and Thomas Heritage* (London, 1981), 233; E.F. Gay, 'The rise of an English country family: Peter and John Temple, to 1603', *Huntington Libr. Quarterly* 1.4 (1938), 377; *Cal. Pat.* 1557–8, 15.

92 *Cal. Pat.* 1575–8, 328; TNA, C 66/1158, mm. 26–7; Northants. RO, Temple (Stowe) 7/2/1; Alcock, *Warws. Grazier*, 233–5.

93 Below, Economic Hist. (Agriculture).

94 R. O'Day, *An Elite Family in Early Modern England: The Temples of Stowe and Burton Dassett, 1570–1656* (Woodbridge, 2018), 429.

95 *Cal. Pat.* 1580–2, 62; TNA, SP 16/229, f. 201; C 66/1204, mm. 20–1; TNA, PROB 11/101/373; *Cal. Pat.* 31 Eliz. I (L&I Soc. vol. 300), 22; TNA, E 315/151/5; Northants. RO, Temple (Stowe) 5/2; O'Day, *An Elite Family*, 431; Gay, 'The rise', 390; E.F. Gay, 'The Temples of Stowe and their debts: Sir Thomas Temple and Sir Peter Temple, 1603–1653', *Huntington Libr. Quarterly* 2 (1939), 422.

96 Gay, 'The Temples', 430; Gay, 'The rise', 377; TNA, E 134/12Chas1/East24, m. 9.

97 O'Day, *An Elite Family*, 263, 382, 390–1.

98 Ibid., 99–100, 263, 381–94; Gay, 'The Temples', 409, 412–16.

99 Nichols, *Hist.*, IV, 252, 258; TNA, PROB 11/162/453; TNA, E 134/12Chas1/East24, m. 3.

Moorbarns was sold in 1633 to Sir Thomas Puckering of Warwick for £8,000.[100] He died in 1637, leaving a daughter, Jane, who married Sir John Bale of Carlton Curlieu. They had no children.[101] Moorbarns was held by Sir Thomas's nephew Sir Henry Puckering (formerly Newton) of Warwick in 1663. Its extent was recorded as 551 a., 243 a. of which was let to William Vere until 1680, with the remaining 308 a. divided into nine smaller parcels ranging from 3 a. to 93 a., which were let individually, mostly to Lutterworth inhabitants.[102] Sir Henry Puckering sold the entire Moorbarns land in 1664 to Sir Edward Boughton of Little Lawford (Warws.),[103] who died in 1681.[104] His descendant Edward Boughton sold the western portion of the land (c.330 a.) to a Mr Evans in 1786, and the remainder in small parcels to Lutterworth inhabitants.[105] Moorbarns contained 564 a. in 1848, of which Mrs Dorothy Evans owned 325 a., with the residual 239 a. closest to the town owned by c.70 people.[106] Charles Marriott of Cotesbach Hall (owner of c.1,200 a. in Cotesbach) purchased Moorbarne Farm and 261 a. previously owned by Anne Evans, and two small adjoining pieces of land between 1879 and 1881.[107] He continued to own this land in 1910, when another 136 a. at Moorbarns was owned by R. Hill.[108] Hill's land and a further 16 a. in Moorbarns was owned by Ann Richardson in 1926, who bequeathed the reversion, after the death of her daughter, to Lutterworth church as additional glebe land.[109]

There was a keeper's house on Moorbarns by 1557.[110] This was probably a substantial property by 1614, when Robert Carr 'of Morebarne' died, leaving moveable goods worth £111 4s. 8d.[111] Sir John Temple lived on Moorbarns in the 1620s, presumably in this house.[112] It was known as Moorebarne House in 1636, when there was another house also on Moorbarns, built in 1632–3, probably by Sir Thomas Puckering, and known as High Field House.[113]

100 O'Day, *An Elite Family*, 385, 394–6; TNA, E 134/12Chas1/East24, m. 9.

101 TNA, PROB 11/175/379; C 5/452/67.

102 ROLLR, 35'29/381.

103 Warws. RO, CR 0026/1/9/39.

104 *Hist. Parl. Commons*, 1660–90, I, 692–3.

105 Nichols, *Hist.*, IV, 258; TNA, IR 18/4544.

106 TNA, IR 18/4544.

107 Cotesbach Educational Trust, CEA/1/1/182; CEA/1/1/166–7; CEA/1/1/185; CEA/1/1/720.

108 TNA, IR 130/4/191, 192, 225, 226; ROLLR, DE 2072/149.

109 CERC, CC/OF/19/141B; below, Religious Hist. (Church Origins and Parochial Organisation).

110 *Cal. Pat.* 1557–8, 15; TNA, C 66/919, m. 1.

111 ROLLR, PR/I/25/89; J. Goodacre, *The Transformation of a Peasant Economy: Townspeople and Villagers in the Lutterworth Area, 1500–1700* (Aldershot, 1994), 101.

112 O'Day, *An Elite Family*, 263.

113 TNA, E 134/12Chas1/East24, m. 4.

Hospital of St John the Baptist

St John's hospital was founded by Nicholas de Verdun and his mother, Rose, c.1216, and endowed with seven yardlands to maintain a priest and six poor men, and to provide hospitality for poor wayfarers. The hospital building had been erected by 1219.[114] The hospital survived the seizure of chantry lands, and the site was in the 'custody' of Henry Grey, marquess of Dorset (later duke of Suffolk) in 1547, and let to Richard Wingfield, his bailiff. It passed to the Crown with the manor in 1554.[115] The hospital's outlying possessions were sold by the Crown in 1569,[116] and the site was sold to Theophilus Adams and Thomas Butler, both of London, in 1585.[117] The Crown retained the advowson and made presentations of masters, purely a sinecure, in 1577, 1601, 1640 and 1672.[118]

The hospital site, with a mill that had been erected by at least 1546, was purchased by Thomas Forren in 1596, with ten messuages and 342 a. in Lutterworth and Misterton, including c.80 a. of enclosed pasture within Lutterworth parish.[119] Forren built a house at the hospital site, and successfully defended his title to the land in 1603 against Bernard Adams, who had been appointed master of the hospital in 1601.[120] In 1613 Forren devised the house, mill and land to his wife, Marie, for seven years, with the reversion to his son Anthony.[121] Anthony sold the site c.1622 to Sir William Faunt, another large-scale pastoral farmer. Faunt died in 1639, shortly after he had been fined £4,000 for enclosures in Foston, 9 miles north of Lutterworth, and his lands, including the hospital site, were seized by court order from his heir, his nephew George.[122] Spital mill and the land were subsequently released and were sold in 1661 to William Cole.[123] After Cole's death in 1698, these passed to his widow, Emma Cole, and after her death they passed to her son-in-law Richard Shuttleworth.[124] Richard's son James inherited these in 1728.[125] Robert Shuttleworth sold the mill and land to Aaron Franks in 1774,[126] and these were owned by Jacob Franks of Misterton Hall at his death in 1840.[127] He had devised Spital mill and land to his second son John (d. 1880). John Franks had no children and left his estate to be divided between two nieces.[128]

114 *VCH Leics.* II, 42–3.
115 TNA, E 134/6Chas1/Mich 39, mm. 7–7v.
116 *Cal. Pat. 1566–9*, 352.
117 *Cal. Pat. 27 Eliz. I* (L&I Soc. vol. 293), 42.
118 *Cal. Pat. 1575–8*, 229; *Cal. Pat. 43 Eliz. I* (L&I Soc. vol. 339), 43; *Cal. SP Dom. 1639–40*, 532; *Cal. SP Dom. 1671–2*, 138.
119 ROLLR, DE 1012/2–3; TNA, STAC 8/147/14; E 134/6Chas1/Mich39, mm. 7–7v.; A. Hamilton Thompson, 'The chantry certificates for Leicestershire', *Assoc. Archit. Soc. Rpts. & Papers* 30 (1909–10), 496; Goodacre, *Transformation*, 164.
120 TNA, STAC 8/147/14; *Cal. Pat. 43 Eliz. I* (L&I Soc. vol. 339), 43.
121 TNA, PROB 11/122/523.
122 Nichols, *Hist.*, IV, 170, 175.
123 ROLLR, DE 1012/12–16; *VCH Leics.* V, 216.
124 ROLLR, DE 1012/19, 27–30; DE 2094/1; Wills, 1698, f. 30.
125 ROLLR, Bishop's transcripts, Laughton; DE 1012/19, 31–2.
126 ROLLR, DE 1012/37–8.
127 *Leic. Chron.*, 18 Apr. 1840; TNA, PROB 11/1927/188.
128 *Leic. Chron.*, 20 Nov. 1880; 22 Jan. 1881; ROLLR, 18D 67/2520.

The 'Misterton Estate' of 2,520 a., including Spital House, the mill and 70 a. of meadow and pasture in Lutterworth, was offered for sale in 1883.[129] It was purchased in 1885 by Charles Bamford,[130] who had substantial business interests in Liverpool and North America, and an estate in Llanrhaeadr-yng-Nghinmeirch (Denbs.). They remained within the Misterton estate, passing after Bamford's death in 1891 to his son Arthur (d. 1894),[131] whose widow Anne (née Nash) married the Honourable Harold Brooke Hawke (son of the 6th Baron Hawke of Towton) in 1906.[132] The mill and 60 a. of land in Lutterworth were owned by A. Hawke in 1910.[133] By then the mill no longer functioned, the water supply having been cut when the Great Central Railway was built in 1899.[134]

129 *Leic. Jnl*, 12 Oct. 1883; ROLLR, 18D 67/2520, pp. 12–14, plan nos 308, 313–33.
130 *Northampton Merc.*, 6 June 1885.
131 *Nuneaton Advertiser*, 10 Jan. 1891; *Denbighshire Free Press*, 10 Jan. 1891; 14 Feb. 1891.
132 *Leic. Daily Post*, 10 Aug. 1906.
133 TNA, IR 130/4/205; ROLLR, DE 2072/149.
134 OS Map 6", Leics. XLIX.SW (1885 and 1904 edns).

ECONOMIC HISTORY

LUTTERWORTH'S LOCATION AND ITS RELATIVELY early market charter of 1214 were key to the success of the medieval town. By 1334, its tax assessment of £4 13s. 2d. was the seventh highest among Leicestershire's towns.[1] The town had several specialist market areas in the 16th and early 17th centuries and over 40 shops by 1607, including a large drapery and shambles. Although market trade declined in the 18th century, Lutterworth had the fifth highest assessment in the county for the shop tax in 1785, excluding Leicester.[2]

The medieval demesne was almost wholly arable in the 14th century, becoming enclosed pasture known as Moorbarns c.1500. By the 1560s, and probably earlier, a large flock of sheep was grazed on this land. Three residents of Lutterworth were merchants of the Staple at Calais in the 15th and early 16th centuries, and later there were wool dealers, probably selling to English cloth manufacturers. Following the enclosure of Lutterworth's open fields in 1792, arable land was swiftly laid down to pasture, and the main crop produced thereafter was hay. The town's economy in the 19th century was supported by 'neighbouring opulent farmers and graziers',[3] who attended the town's markets, frequented its shops and utilised the professional services available.

Some inhabitants manufactured cloth or leather goods in the late Middle Ages, and others were involved in victualling. Before the late 17th century, many of the town's craftsmen, innkeepers and shopkeepers also held some open-field land. One factory was opened in the late 18th century to spin cotton, but this enterprise was short-lived. In 1831, 42 per cent of adult male residents were employed in retail, 20 per cent in agriculture and just 11 per cent in manufacture.[4] The development of factories was held back by the absence of a railway and the lack of piped water. Both were provided in 1899.[5]

Two iron foundries and a hosiery factory opened in the first decade of the 20th century. Frank Whittle's company Power Jets, which developed a jet aero engine, moved from Rugby to Lutterworth in 1937, and engineering became a major industry in the town from 1940, when the machine-tool manufacturer Alfred Herbert Ltd relocated from Coventry. These businesses closed or moved away during the second half of the 20th century, to be replaced by many smaller service businesses, each with relatively few employees. Magna Park, a privately owned logistics and warehousing estate on the western parish boundary, was developed from 1988 and employed nearly 10,000 people

1   R.E. Glasscock (ed.), *The Lay Subsidy of 1334* (London, 1975), 159.
2   TNA, E 182/537, pt 2.
3   Pigot, *Dir. of Leics.* (1835), 63.
4   Census, 1831.
5   Above, Landscape and Settlement (Communication); below, Local Government (Public Services).

in 2020.[6] An extension, Magna Park South, was under development in 2021 on 220 a. of farmland within Lutterworth parish.[7]

Agriculture

The Agricultural Landscape

There is evidence of a three-field system by 1322, when one third of the agricultural land lay fallow (*ad warectum*).[8] Street Field (West Field in 1597) was adjacent to Watling Street. Cowhadens Field, sometimes recorded as Middle or North Field, largely lay under the modern built-up area and probably extended to the northern parish boundary. The third field was known as East Field from 1597 to 1606, as Thornborough Field between 1607 and 1679, and thereafter mostly either as Whitehill Field or (Gil)Morton Field.[9] Map 6 reconstructs the agricultural landscape as it would have been in 1607. The precise boundaries of the fields are not known.

Moorbarns pasture, in the south of the parish, was hedged by 1509, and contained 348 a. in 1557.[10] It was probably enclosed by Thomas Grey, 1st marquess of Dorset (d. 1501), who enclosed land at Bradgate (20 miles north of Lutterworth) and in four manors in south-west Leicestershire.[11] By 1607 this had become a butterfly-shaped enclosure (Map 6), largely bounded by the river and brooks, and was said to contain 507 a., including two large pastures of 200 a. and 250 a.[12] Six witnesses in 1636, whose memories of the land stretched back 50 years, had heard 'very old' men or deceased relatives say that some of the land in Moorbarns was formerly part of Street Field.[13] This extension probably took place between 1562 (when Peter Temple took possession) and 1580. The earliest enclosure is probably the part adjacent to Watling Street. Moorbarns contained 539 a. in 1786.[14] Another *c*.70 a. of pasture lay to the south and east of the river, and had been enclosed by 1603, when it was part of the land attached to the former hospital site.[15] It was farmed as part of Misterton estate in 1883.[16]

In 1607, excluding the glebe land, Street Field contained 198 a. of arable with 108 a. of meadow and leys (total 306 a.), Cowhadens Field contained 247 a. of arable and 96 a.

6   https://lutterworth.magnapark.co.uk (accessed 20 Dec. 2020); Univ. of Leicester, *Leicester Merc.* Archive, LMA, 2/3/3/2.

7   https://www.multimodal.org.uk/article/gazeley-has-bought-symmetry-park-db-symmetry-and-renamed-it-magna-park-south (accessed 1 Feb. 2022).

8   TNA, SC 6/1146/17.

9   BL, Add. Ch. 73016; Lincs. Arch., DIOC/TER/5, ff. 450–453v (1601); DIOC/TER /LEICS/ LUTTERWORTH (1606, 1674, 1721, 1724, 1745, 1762); DIOC/TER/23 (1709), pp. 592–8; TNA, LR 2/255 (1607); ROLLR, 1D 41/2/431 (1679); EN/MB/211/1 (1790).

10   Warws. RO, CR 2017/E42, ff. 5, 6, 8; *Cal. Pat.* 1557–8, 15; TNA, C 66/919, m. 1.

11   L.A. Parker, 'Enclosure in Leicestershire, 1485–1607' (Univ. of London PhD thesis, 1948), 11, 45–7, 51, 60, 86, 156–60, 202; I.S. Leadam, *The Domesday of Inclosures, 1517–1518* (London, 1897), I, 240–2.

12   TNA, LR 2/255, f. 160.

13   TNA, E 134/12Chas1/East24, mm. 7–10.

14   TNA, IR 18/4544.

15   Warws. RO, CR 2017/D171; TNA, STAC 8/147/14.

16   ROLLR, 18D 67/2520, plan nos 308, 313–33; above, Landownership (Hospital of St John the Baptist).

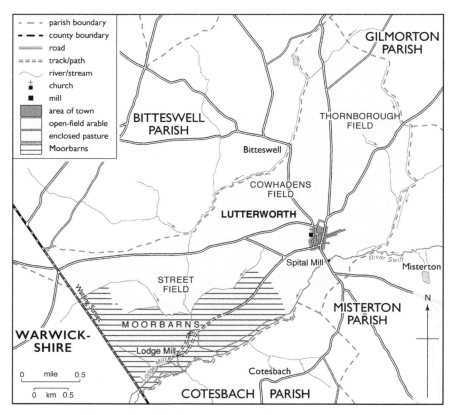

Map 6 *Reconstruction of the agricultural landscape in 1607.*

of meadow and leys (total 343 a.), and Thornborough Field contained 256 a. of arable with 109 a. of meadow and leys (total 365 a.). Leys of at least 153 a. were laid down as permanent pasture within the fields, but their precise location is unknown. The total area of meadow was at least 134 a. which may have been mostly adjacent to the many watercourses.[17] Heathland of 19 a. known as 'cow pasture' was probably close to a parish boundary and on once common land, but this was held by named landholders in individual unenclosed strips.[18]

The open fields were enclosed by an Act of Parliament of 1790 and an award of 1792. The Act specifically excluded Moorbarns, although only 118 a. of Moorbarns was included in the tithe apportionment of 1853, implying that the tithes on part of this pasture may have been extinguished within the enclosure award.[19] The original copy of the enclosure award does not survive, but an almost contemporary summary of the allotments shows that these totalled 1,737 a.[20] A damaged and partial enclosure map survives, which does not include the north or east of the parish, or Moorbarns.[21]

17   TNA, LR 2/255; H.L. Gray, *English Field Systems* (London, 1969), 35, 445.
18   TNA, LR 2/255.
19   ROLLR, EN/MB/211/1; Ti/211/1; TNA, IR 18/18/4544.
20   ROLLR, EN/AX/211/1.
21   ROLLR, Misc. 239.

Medieval Agriculture

There were nine ploughs in Lutterworth in 1066, and only seven in 1086, on 13 carucates of land (*c.*1560 a.), but such a low ratio of ploughs to carucates was not unusual for Leicestershire.[22] The reduction in ploughs suggests that land may have fallen out of cultivation by 1086, although the assessed value of the manor remained £7.[23] Three of the ploughs were on the demesne,[24] a high proportion, but in one sixth of Leicestershire manors the demesne ploughs exceeded one third of the total.[25]

Theobald de Verdun's demesne contained 3½ virgates (*c.*105 a.) in 1279, just 5 per cent of the total agricultural land. He also held another 6 virgates (*c.*180 a.) which were not considered to be part of his demesne. There were 40 virgates (*c.*1,200 a.) held by 36 villeins, 16 virgates (*c.*480 a.) held by six free tenants, and 7 virgates (*c.*210 a.) held by the prior of the hospital.[26] Few manorial accounts survive, but total income was stable in the 1320s and 1330s: £99 16*s.* 6*d.* in 1322,[27] £108 5*s.* in 1330 and £100 9*s.* 10½*d.* in 1339,[28] with the latter including £73 16*s.* 10¼*d.* from rents and leases, and £35 profit from cultivation (*de la Gainerie*).[29] Wage labourers on the demesne were paid to weed and hoe 129 a. in 1322,[30] and to winnow and thresh wheat in 1361.[31]

The demesne in 1316 comprised 103 a. of arable, with each acre worth 4*d.* annually, 100 a. of pasture, each worth 2*s.* 6*d.*, and 6½ a. of meadow, also worth 2*s.* 6*d.* per acre.[32] Sown crops in 1322 comprised wheat and dredge (140 a.) and barley and dredge (15 a.), with 77 a. out of cultivation (*frisc*) in addition to the fallow of 113 a.[33] A wider mix of cereal crops was grown in 1332–3, when 158 a. were sown with wheat (50 a.), oats (50 a.), barley (28 a.), maslin (18 a.) and dredge (12 a.).[34] Oats were an important food for horses, and the increase in this crop may reflect a change in the composition of plough teams, away from oxen (which fed on grass), although no oxen were recorded in 1322. Wheat (40 qr.), maslin (20 qr.), oats (20 qr.) and dredge (7 qr.) from the previous harvest were held in the barns.[35]

Lady Clare's livestock were concentrated on her Suffolk manors.[36] Demesne accounts for Lutterworth in 1322 record six affers (workhorses), three colts, a sow, two sheep, two swans and four geese.[37] In 1333 the livestock included a small dairy herd: there

22 *Domesday*, 645; *VCH Leics.* I, 305.
23 *Domesday*, 645.
24 Ibid.
25 *VCH Leics.* II, 152.
26 Nichols, *Hist.*, IV, 247–8; Bodleian Libr., Rawlinson MS B 350, f. 23.
27 TNA, SC 6/1146/17; *VCH Leics.* II, 162–3.
28 G.A. Holmes, *The Estates of the Higher Nobility in Fourteenth-century England* (Cambridge, 1957), 144, citing TNA, SC 11/799.
29 Holmes, *Estates*, 147, citing TNA, SC 11/801, where the individual components add up to more than the total recorded in SC 11/799.
30 TNA, SC 6/1146/17; *VCH Leics.* II, 162–3.
31 TNA, SC 6/908/33.
32 TNA, C 134/56/1.
33 TNA, SC 6/1146/17; *VCH Leics.* II, 162–3.
34 TNA, SC 6/1109/24; Holmes, *Estates*, 148.
35 TNA, SC 6/1109/24.
36 Holmes, *Estates*, 109–10.
37 TNA, SC 6/1146/17; *VCH Leics.* II, 162–3.

were 19 oxen, 11 workhorses, five colts, 13 bullocks, ten cows, six heifers, 11 calves and 30 pigs, with a total value of £28 10s.[38] The grazing land adjacent to Watling Street was used for short-term fattening for livestock on the hoof, including 52 oxen and eight cows that had been bought in 1339–40 as stock for Lady Clare's larder. Five grooms drove them from Caerleon (Monm.) to Lutterworth (c.120 miles), with two of the grooms accompanying the beasts for the final c.100 miles from Lutterworth to Clare (Suff.). These two grooms were each paid 2s. for '8 days in coming and 4 days in returning'. Some Lutterworth stock was for household consumption, including 60 pigs sold by Henry de Braundon, Lutterworth's reeve, to Lady Clare's household in 1340, for £7 10s.[39] Just 12 a. of meadow were noted in 1086, which seems very low given the extent of watercourses.[40] There were 40 a. of meadow in the demesne in 1322,[41] which had increased to 50 a. in 1333.[42] Herbage of 40 a. was sold in 1322, pasture produced a total income of 30s. that year, and a further 40s. was generated from the manorial waste.[43]

In her will dated 1355, Lady Clare bequeathed to her grandson, Sir William de Ferrers, seed corn for Lutterworth comprising oats (29 qr.), beans and peas (13 qr.), barley (13 qr.), wheat (12 qr.), rye (6 qr.), dredge (2 qr.) and maslin (2 qr.), with four carthorses, 18 oxen, six other draught animals, carts, ploughs and equipment, but no other livestock.[44] Over the five months to January 1360, 25 a. of wheat were sown and 23 a. of rye. Barley, wheat and oats were sold for £11 18s. 3½d. in one month in 1361, and rye, peas and barley were bought.[45] Lutterworth was one of just six manors on the extensive Ferrers estates that grew cereals and legumes in 1363, when wheat, rye, dredge, oats and peas were sown, with the same crops also held in the barns.[46]

Pastoral Farming

In addition to 25 oxen and six working horses, the demesne was stocked in 1359–60 with a bull, 43 cows, nine heifers, 17 steers and a flock of 649 sheep. Wages totalling 31s. 4d. over the five months to January 1360 were paid to three shepherds, a cow-man and a dairy worker in addition to a bailiff, a hayward and seven carters.[47] This is the earliest record of a significant number of sheep being grazed at Lutterworth, and indicates a substantial change in farming practice on the demesne following the Black Death.

There are no later manorial accounts, but by the end of the 15th century Lutterworth lay in the centre of an area of widespread enclosure, and wool production became an important part of the town's economy. By 1507, the Leicestershire villages of Bittesby, Cotes de Val, Knaptoft, Misterton, Poultney, Stormsworth, Westrill and Wigston Parva,

38   TNA, SC 6/1109/24.
39   J. Ward (ed.) *Elizabeth de Burgh, Lady of Clare (1295–1360): Household and Other Records* (Woodbridge, 2014), 18–19.
40   *Domesday*, 645.
41   TNA, SC 6/1146/17; *VCH Leics.* II, 162–3.
42   TNA, SC 6/1109/24; Holmes, *Estates*, 148.
43   TNA, SC 6/1146/17; *VCH Leics.* II, 162–3.
44   Ward (ed.), *Elizabeth de Burgh*, 146–7.
45   TNA, SC 6/908/33.
46   BL, Add. Roll 66077.
47   TNA, SC 6/908/33.

all within 7 miles of the town, had become wholly or substantially depopulated and their lands laid down to grass, Lutterworth's demesne land had become Moorbarns pasture and part of the hospital's land was probably enclosed.[48] Newnham Paddox, Copston Parva, Little Walton and Cestersover (all Warws.), and Downtown, Elkington and Sulby (Northants.) were also within 7 miles of Lutterworth and also depopulated.[49] These changes provided opportunities for some Lutterworth people to keep more livestock than would otherwise be possible. Sheep grazing on these fields may have provided the wool that was exported by three Lutterworth men who were merchants of the Staple at Calais between *c.*1450 and 1515, and traded by two wool merchants resident in the town in the 1520s.[50]

Lutterworth inhabitants known to have leased additional grazing outside the parish include Richard Pratt, a mercer, who was leasing land on the former village site of Cotes de Val (Gilmorton parish) and a close in Misterton by 1573;[51] Thomas Insley, who was grazing 280 ewes and nine beasts in Bittesby at his death in 1588 and 134 ewes, 39 lambs, 11 beasts and two bulls in 'Lutterworth Feeld';[52] John Halpeny, a cordwainer; widow Ellen Overend; Robert Billington, a baker; and an innkeeper, John Tarleton, who also leased land in Misterton in the late 16th and early 17th centuries.[53] Thomas Gore, a Lutterworth freeholder with 3½ virgates, leased a close in Gilmorton and a meadow in Kimcote (north east of Lutterworth). At his death in 1634, he owned 248 sheep, 22 cows, wool valued at £30 in his wool-house, and wheat, barley and oats that occupied over four bays of barn.[54] Nicholas Ratcliffe, a shoemaker, was fined in 1564 for keeping 480 sheep over his stint (the number and type of animals that the manorial court had agreed a person could graze on common land).[55] He may have been grazing them on a recent extension to Moorbarns and fined if the manor court still considered this to be open-field land. At his death in 1583, Ratcliffe had corn and hay worth £20 and a flock of 100 sheep worth £6.[56]

Most of Moorbarns was grazed by its leaseholders for their own profit, although the 'keeper' was permitted to keep some stock of his own.[57] A few residents in the late 16th and early 17th centuries grazed a few animals on Moorbarns for 8*d.* or 10*d.* weekly, and Lutterworth's rectors kept three or four cows there in lieu of tithes.[58] When Peter Temple took possession of Moorbarns in 1562, he allowed £217 for stocking the pasture, sufficient for 400 ewes and lambs.[59] In 1583, after the extension of Moorbarns, he granted 840 ewes with their grazing and 40 loads of hay annually for four years to his eldest

48 Parker, 'Enclosure', 16, 36–8, 58, 238, 242; J. Goodacre, *The Transformation of a Peasant Economy: Townspeople and Villagers in the Lutterworth Area, 1500–1700* (Aldershot, 1994), 32–3, 36, 94.

49 Goodacre, *Transformation*, 36; M.W. Beresford and J.G. Hurst, *Deserted Medieval Villages: Studies* (Woking, 1971), 192–3, 204–6, 197–8.

50 Below (Trades and Services).

51 TNA, WARD 2/39/146I/53; WARD 2/41/146M/9; WARD 2/41/146O/3.

52 ROLLR, PR/I/9/205.

53 TNA, WARD 2/56/199/67; WARD 2/56/199/58; WARD 2/56/199/65; E 44/425.

54 ROLLR, PR/I/37/119; TNA, LR 2/255, f. 126; WARD 2/56/199/18.

55 TNA, SC 2/183/84, m. 1; Goodacre, *Transformation*, 161.

56 ROLLR, W&I 1583/9B.

57 ROLLR, W&I 1541/47A.

58 TNA, E 134/12Chas1/East24, mm. 3v, 4v, 8v; ROLLR, PR/I/40/231.

59 N.W. Alcock, *Warws. Grazier and London Skinner, 1532–1555: The Account Book of Peter Temple and Thomas Heritage* (London, 1981), 206–7, 233.

son, John.[60] In 1607 John's son Thomas was grazing 1,200 sheep, 50 'runtes', 50 'coodes' (possibly 'cade', or motherless, lambs), 40 rams and 30 cows, and mowing 200 or 300 'loads' of hay each year.[61]

Corn was scarce in 1630, and Sir Thomas Temple agreed to plough 100 a. of Moorbarns.[62] The first crops on this land were flax and hemp, and probably woad, profitable crops that would have provided seasonal work and prepared the ground to receive the first planting of cereals.[63] In 1634 Francis Billington, a baker, had a crop of corn worth £20 'in Morebarne',[64] and in 1636 Robert Bradgate was growing 100 a. of corn on Moorbarns.[65]

Mixed Farming, c.1500–1790

Edward Hands, who died in 1575, had a sizeable mixed farm with wheat, rye, barley, peas, oats and hay worth £35 and seven cows, 53 sheep, 17 pigs and eight horses.[66] Most farms were much smaller, but even those with one virgate were far better off than the majority of the population. Eleven people held a single virgate in 1607, which was probably much reduced from its medieval size and contained a modest 12 a. of arable land with about 8 a. of meadow and pasture. Six people held 1½ or 2 virgates, nine people held 3 or 3½ virgates and three people held 4 virgates. Those with more than one virgate had a smaller proportion of meadow and pasture: John Wolman, for example, held two virgates containing 24 a. of arable land, 3 a. of meadow and 3 a. of leys, a total of 30 a.[67] The stint allowed three horses, three cows, beasts or plough horses and 35 sheep to be grazed for each virgate held. The occupiers of 44 cottages could each graze one horse and one cow.[68]

By the 17th century, the 'traditional' mixed farm hardly existed in Lutterworth. At his death in 1633, Thomas Witeman had wheat, maslin, barley, peas and hay valued at £21 on his one-virgate holding, with three horses, two cows, 12 sheep and a pig.[69] Although he was only using one third of his stint for sheep, this was one of the largest flocks held by a mixed farmer.[70] Some probably found it more profitable to sell their stints to a grazier and to grow additional corn for sale. John Newcombe, a husbandman who died in 1664, had corn, peas and hay worth £10, three horses and two cows, but no sheep.[71] In contrast, James Coltman, a grazier, died in 1658 owning 40 sheep and three cows, but no

60 Northants. RO, Temple (Stowe), 7/2/3.
61 TNA, LR 2/255, f. 160; E 134/12 Chas1/East24, mm. 3–3v.
62 TNA, E 134/12Chas1/East24; Goodacre, *Transformation*, 113; E.F. Gay, 'The Temples of Stowe and their debts: Sir Thomas Temple and Sir Peter Temple, 1603–1653', *Huntington Libr. Quarterly* 2 (1939), 412–16; R. O'Day, *An Elite Family in Early Modern England: The Temples of Stowe and Burton Dassett, 1570–1656* (Woodbridge, 2018), 381–94.
63 TNA, E 134/12Chas1/East24, mm. 3–3v., 4v., 9; Goodacre, *Transformation*, 116; J. Thirsk, 'Seventeenth-century agriculture and social change', in J. Thirsk (ed.), *Land, Church and People: Essays Presented to Professor H.P.R. Finberg* (Reading, 1970), 158–61, 171, 174.
64 ROLLR, PR/I/36/80.
65 TNA, E 134/12Chas1/East24, m. 9.
66 ROLLR, W&I 1574/32.
67 TNA, LR 2/255. Other examples are detailed in Gray, *English Field Systems*, 445.
68 TNA, LR 2/255, ff. 117–72.
69 ROLLR, PR/I/35/218.
70 Goodacre, *Transformation*, 149.
71 ROLLR, PR/I/62/95.

crops.[72] Lawrence Foster, a grazier who died in 1664, had ten cows, 65 sheep and a rick of hay, but no other farming assets.[73]

Agriculture from 1790

Lutterworth's open fields were enclosed under an Act of 1790, intended to cover 1,400 a. of open-field and common land, specifically excluding Moorbarns. The award of 1792 reallocated 1,737 a. between 48 people, with allotments ranging from nearly 397 a. (6th earl of Denbigh) to nine individual allotments of less than 1 a. each.[74] The smallest allotments were probably soon sold, and most of the former open-field land had been converted to pasture within a decade. Only 429 a. of arable crops were grown in 1801, with most of that for animal consumption: 120 a. of wheat, 105 a. of barley, 127 a. of oats, 52 a. of 'turnips or rape' and 25 a. of beans.[75] The arable acreage continued to decline steadily until the Second World War: 230 a. of cereal crops were grown in 1877, 133 a. in 1907, and 70 a. in 1927. By far the largest crop was hay: 1,424 a. in 1917, from a total of 2,061 a. of grassland.[76]

The cattle murrain of 1865–6 affected the Lutterworth district more than any other part of the county. Across Lutterworth petty sessional division, 312 cattle either died of disease or had to be slaughtered.[77] The high incidence may relate to the number of store cattle passing through the area to reach the fattening pastures less than 10 miles away in south-east Leicestershire. High numbers of store cattle are likely to explain the variation and lack of any trend in the number of cattle in the parish between 1867 and 1937. The numbers fluctuated between 700 and 1,100 head at the annual June return dates but probably understate the peak, as store cattle were generally sold in April and May. The number of sheep fell sharply, from 2,934 in 1867 to 1,001 in 1907, thereafter fluctuating between 1,000 and 1,600 until the Second World War.[78] The preponderance of small farms is striking. Only 15 of the 64 farmers returning statistics in 1917 occupied more than 50 a.,[79] with the largest farm containing 284 a.[80] Most farmers were tenants.[81]

The numbers of fowl were insignificant before the First World War, but F. and A.H. Sanders established a large poultry unit on Moorbarns in the 1920s, and won gold medals for egg production. They sold their poultry units in 1950.[82] Other farms of more than 50 a. were used for fattening bullocks,[83] or for dairy herds and/or sheep. Farms of less than 50 a. were mostly held by milk producer-retailers in 1943, although two had beef herds. Two of Lutterworth's largest farms converted 252 a. from pasture into arable

72 ROLLR, PR/I/53/33.
73 ROLLR, PR/I/63/23.
74 30 Geo. III, c. 41; ROLLR, EN/MB/211/1; EN/AX/211/1.
75 *Home Office Acreage Returns, 1801*, II (L&I Soc., vol. 190), 47.
76 TNA, MAF 68/533; 68/2243; 68/3356.
77 *Rpt of the Cattle Plague in G.B. during the years 1865, 1866 and 1867* (Parl. Papers 1867–8 [C 4060], xviii), pp. 395, 420.
78 TNA, MAF 68/134; 68/533; 68/1103; 68/1673; 68/2243; 68/2813; 68/3356; 68/3836.
79 TNA, MAF 68/2813.
80 ROLLR, DE 2072/149.
81 TNA, MAF 68/134; 68/533; 68/1103; 68/1673; 68/2243; 68/2813; 68/3356; 68/3836.
82 *Rugby Advertiser*, 19 Dec. 1930; 22 Sept. 1950.
83 TNA, MAF 32/389/181.

between 1939 and 1943. The number of pigs began to increase from the 1930s, from 124 in 1927 to 321 in 1967. Cereal crops, especially barley, increased alongside them, with 475 a. of the 566 a. of the total arable land (84 per cent) sown with barley in 1967.[84] Neither pigs nor poultry were kept in any numbers in the 1970s.[85] There were 11 farms in the parish in 1999,[86] excluding land farmed as part of the Bitteswell and Misterton estates.

Mills

Lodge Mill

Flowing towards the south west, the river Swift divides near the northern tip of Cotesbach parish. The eastern waters form the parish boundary between Cotesbach and Lutterworth, and this is probably the original course, which may have driven the watermill recorded at Cotesbach in 1086.[87] The western stream is straighter and may be an artificial leat created in the Middle Ages to improve the flow to Lutterworth's manorial mill, which stood 1½ miles from the town (Map 6). The earliest record of a watermill is from 1274, when Theobald de Verdun leased water and windmills to Ralph le Pedler for one year for 56 marks (£37 6s. 8d.), with the reservation of the fishing of pike of 12 inches or less, bream and tench of 9 inches, and perch of 6 inches.[88]

There was probably one functioning mill in Lutterworth in 1405–6, when William Mylner was the only miller amerced for taking excessive tolls.[89] Repairs to the manorial mill costing 106s. 9½d. were completed in the early 16th century. It was known as Lodge mill when it was set out to farm for 33s. 4d. in 1514, with the acquisition of a name suggesting that there was now a mill at the hospital.[90] Two millers were amerced in 1562 and 1564.[91] Lodge mill protected its trade by collecting corn from the town, accepting that the Spital miller would do likewise, provided he advertised his visits only through the jingling bells of his horses' collars. Those with private mills or querns were ordered by the manor court to 'pull them down' in 1547, with the exception of one quern, which was probably in the property that became the Denbigh Arms.[92]

Lodge mill came into the hands of the Crown with the manor in 1554, and was sold to Edward Ferrers and Francis Phillips of London in 1609.[93] A Crown lease of 41 years had been granted to John Sabine (probably acting for John Temple) in 1585, when the mill was 'greatlie in decaie'.[94] Sabine, William Nichols and Richard Fox let it in 1587 to Thomas Swancote for 21 years at an annual rent of £22 plus two pairs of capons and

84   TNA, MAF 68/3356; 68/3836; 68/4205; 68/4574; 8/5037.
85   TNA, MAF 68/4205; 68/4574; 8/5037; 68/5536.
86   OS Map 1:25000, sheet 222 (1999 edn).
87   *Domesday*, 635.
88   BL, MS catalogue of Lord Frederick Campbell's Charter, 20 vi, 983.
89   TNA, E 101/258/2.
90   TNA, SC 6/HENVIII/1824, m. 6.
91   TNA, SC 2/183/83, rott. 1, 7; SC 2/183/84, m. 1.
92   TNA, E 134/30Eliz/Hil5, mm. 3–4; E 134/40Eliz/East12, mm. 3–5; Goodacre, *Transformation*, 173.
93   Nichols, *Hist.*, IV, 252; *Cal. Pat.* 7 Jas. I (L&I Soc., vol. 121, 1976), 77; ROLLR, DE 1012/7.
94   TNA, E 134/30Eliz/Hil5, mm. 4–5; Nichols, *Hist.*, IV, 252.

the obligation to keep and preserve 'one Ayrie of swanns'.[95] Nichols and Fox were John Temple's 'servants'.[96] Swancote repaired the mill and added a second water wheel by 1588, when he threatened any competitor with legal action.[97]

John Temple (d. 1603) bequeathed the head lease of the mill to his son Thomas (1st baronet), who purchased the freehold with his own son Peter in 1631.[98] The mill was let to Thomas Insley c.1629, who spent £150 to convert the wheels from overshot to breastshot, yet they could still grind only half the requirement of the town.[99] The Temples and Insley lodged a suit in 1630 against Sir William Faunt, the owner of Spital mill, and his miller, Isaac Cook. A counter-suit followed, as both mills tried to establish the extent of their rights.[100] The court ruled that the carriers for Spital mill could no longer enter the town, and that tenants of the manor could use the Spital mill only if the Lodge mill could not grind their corn within 24 hours.[101]

Sir Richard Temple (4th baronet and great-grandson of Sir Thomas) sold Lodge mill in 1700 to a widow, Emma Cole, the owner of Spital mill, for £870.[102] Her grandson, James Shuttleworth, lost a legal case against the parishioners who were grinding their own corn in 1758, and may have closed Lodge mill shortly afterwards.[103] The site was sold to Aaron Franks, the owner of the Misterton estate, in 1774.[104] There may have been an attempt to replace the mill, as James Lea, the miller at the Spital mill, was also said to occupy Lodge mill in 1846, but there was no working mill there in 1863.[105] A small building on the site in 1886 had been demolished by 1903.[106]

The location of the manorial windmill that was let with the watermill in 1274 is unknown.[107] It was worth 5s. in 1360.[108] The lessee at Lodge mill, Thomas Chamberlain, built a windmill on the river islet adjacent to the watermill c.1610.[109] Chamberlain's son William inherited this in 1615, when the windmill was said to be worth £50.[110] No more is known about this mill.

95 Bucks. RO, D 104-51-2; Northants. RO, Temple (Stowe) 7/2/4; TNA, E 134/40Eliz/East12, mm. 5–5v.; Goodacre, *Transformation*, 165.
96 TNA, PROB 11/101/373.
97 TNA, E 134/30Eliz/Hil5, mm. 4–5; E 134/40Eliz/East12.
98 TNA, PROB 11/101/373; ROLLR, DE 1012/7.
99 TNA, E 134/7Chas1/East26; E 134/6Chas1/Mich39, m. 6v; Goodacre, *Transformation*, 165.
100 TNA, E 134/6Chas1/Mich39; E 134/7Chas1/East26.
101 ROLLR, DE 1012/7.
102 ROLLR, DE 1012/20–21, 24.
103 Nichols, *Hist.*, IV, 262.
104 ROLLR, DE 1012/37–8.
105 White, *Hist.* (Sheffield, 1846), 408; (Sheffield, 1863), 760.
106 OS Map 6", Leics. LII.NE (1886 and 1905 edns).
107 BL, MS catalogue of Lord Frederick Campbell's Charter, 20 vi, 983.
108 TNA, C 135/152/5.
109 TNA, E 134/7Chas1/East26, m. 3.
110 ROLLR, PR/I/26/53; PR/I/238/102.

Spital Mill

The hospital was letting a mill on its site by at least 1564.[111] Its proximity to the town gave it a natural advantage over Lodge mill, and the site had sufficient water to grind corn in all seasons, while Lodge mill sometimes ran dry.[112] Ownership passed with the hospital site.[113] Thomas Forren rebuilt the mill in the 1590s at a cost of £500.[114] The Lea family held the tenancy at the Spital in the 19th century: James Lea in 1846 and Richard Lea & Son in 1877.[115] Steam power was introduced by 1883, supplementing the overshot waterwheel.[116] The watermill continued until 1899 (Figure 10), when the construction of the Great Central Railway severed the water supply.[117]

Other Mills

There was a horse-mill by the churchyard in 1509, on the west side of Bakehouse Lane, held by Martin Feilding.[118] It was described as a malt mill in a very poor state of repair in 1512, when it was leased to Roger Topley for 2s. annually.[119] It came into the hands of the Crown with the manor in 1554, and was let to the Temple family by 1587, who sublet it with Lodge mill to Thomas Swancote.[120] Sir Thomas and Peter Temple probably purchased the freehold in 1631, when they bought Lodge mill.[121] The horse-mill was then said to be capable of grinding all the malt needed in Lutterworth 'if it may have reasonable time'.[122] James Shuttleworth, the son-in-law of Colonel and Emma Cole, owned the Bakehouse Lane malt mill in 1757 and brought a suit against four people for grinding their malt elsewhere.[123] Judgement was devolved to the local assizes, which decided in favour of the inhabitants. The Bakehouse Lane malt mill was taken down c.1760.[124]

Thomas Forren built a new windmill c.1595 on the Spital site to replace one that had burned down, and this was almost certainly used for malt.[125] Sir Richard Temple prepared a case against Colonel Cole at the Spital for grinding malt in 1698, but Cole died before this was heard.[126] Sir Richard Temple sold Lodge mill and the malt mill in 1700 to the colonel's widow, Emma.[127] She closed the malt mill at the Spital shortly afterwards.[128]

111 A. Hamilton Thompson, 'The chantry certificates for Leicestershire', *Assoc. Archit. Soc. Rpts. & Papers* 30 (1909–10), 496; *VCH Leics.* II, 42–3.
112 TNA, E 134/7Chas1/East26, m. 3; E 133/159/22.
113 Above, Landownership (Hospital of St John the Baptist).
114 TNA, STAC 8/147/14.
115 White, *Hist.* (Sheffield, 1846), 408; (Sheffield, 1877), 525.
116 ROLLR, 18D 67/2520, p. 12.
117 OS Map 6", Leics. XLIX.SW (1885 and 1904 edns).
118 Warws. RO, CR 2017/E42, f. 5.
119 TNA, SC 6/HENVIII/1824, m. 6.
120 TNA, E 134/30Eliz/Hil5, m. 4; Bucks. RO, D 104-51-2; ROLLR, DE 1012/4; Nichols, *Hist.*, IV, 252.
121 Nichols, *Hist.*, IV, 253–4; ROLLR, DE 1012/7.
122 TNA, E 134/6Chas1/Mich39, mm. 3, 6v.
123 TNA, E 134/30Geo2/Hil4; E 134/30Geo2/East6.
124 Nichols, *Hist.*, IV, 252–4; White, *Hist.* (Sheffield, 1846), 402.
125 TNA, E 134/6Chas 1/Mich39, mm. 7–7v.
126 TNA, E 134/30Geo2/Hil4; ROLLR, DE 2094/1.
127 ROLLR, DE 1012, 20, 21, 24.
128 TNA, E 134/30Geo2/East6, m. 8.

Figure 10 *Spital mill and the mill leat in 1892 (north-west elevation).*

A brick windmill had been built on Bitteswell Road by 1790.[129] It is believed to have been demolished in the 1870s.[130] A subscription windmill was built on Leicester Road in 1805 at a cost of *c.*£1,100. The Lutterworth subscribers included eight farmers, five members of the gentry, clergy or professions, 12 bakers, grocers and innkeepers, and 14 other tradesmen. The mill prospered until 1829 but then struggled financially.[131] It was badly damaged by fire in 1891 and never rebuilt.[132]

BOCM Silcock Ltd opened a mill for animal feeds on Leicester Road in 1969. The company merged with Pauls Agriculture to become BOCM Pauls Ltd in 1992.[133] The mill closed and was demolished in 1996.[134]

129 ROLLR, EN/AX/211/1; N. Moon, 'Bitteswell Road windmill', *Leics. Industrial Hist. Society Bulletin* 11 (1988), 43, citing property deeds in private hands; Pigot, *Dir. of Leics.* (1835), 149.
130 G. Smith (ed.), *Around Lutterworth* (Stroud, 2005), 63.
131 ROLLR, 18D 67/II/424; J. Goodacre, 'Observations on a mill: Lutterworth subscription windmill', *Leics. Historian* 2 (1980–1), 12–13.
132 Goodacre, 'Observations', 12–13; *Rugby Advertiser*, 16 Nov. 1895; 22 Feb. 1896; 23 May 1930.
133 *The Times*, 24 June 1992.
134 https://www.youtube.com/watch?v=sAOXe1teqXw (accessed 3 Jan. 2015).

Manufacturing

Maltsters, Brewers and Bottlers

After a poor harvest in 1630, John Price, a maltster, was accused of driving up prices by buying '22 quarters of barley a day'. Others protested his innocence, and an investigation found that 12 qr. of barley in his home had been brought to him by others for malting.[1] Francis Porter was also a maltster, and owned 40 qr. of malt on his death in 1653.[2] John Foster had 15 qr. of malt and barley in his kiln when he died in 1678,[3] and John Langham had 40 qr. in his malthouse on his death in 1696.[4] There were three maltsters in the town in 1846 but no maltsters or brewers in 1863.[5]

Arthur Bannister opened a steam brewery in 1879, on a site between Market Street and George Street.[6] Poor water quality caused the business to close. The premises were purchased in 1901 by Thomas Buck, the owner of a small brewery in Walton, who agreed a supply of water with Lutterworth Land Society, which had built a waterworks in 1899.[7] The business ceased brewing in the 1920s but continued to bottle drinks until the 1970s, when it changed its focus to sales. It closed in 1982.[8]

William Mawson began manufacturing mineral water in Lutterworth in 1869, and incorporated the business in 1893.[9] By 1907 the company was also manufacturing lemonade, ginger ale and cordials. It ceased trading in 1917.[10]

Textile Industries

Spinning and Weaving

William Plompton, a weaver in Wyken (Warws.) in 1443, had been apprenticed to William Audeley in Lutterworth, perhaps also a weaver.[11] Only one probate inventory survives for a weaver, William Iliffe (d. 1676), who held four yards of woollen cloth at his death within an inventory value of £91 6s. 2d.[12] By 1782 there were 60 worsted looms in the town, and silk ribbons were produced here in the 18th and 19th centuries.[13] At least

1   TNA, SP 16/188, f. 114; SP 16/191, ff. 5, 36; PC 2/40, f. 505; W.G. Hoskins, 'Harvest fluctuations and English economic history, 1620–1759', *Agricultural Hist. Review* 16 (1968), 20.
2   ROLLR, PR/I/53/37.
3   ROLLR, PR/I/80/131.
4   ROLLR, PR/I/101/44.
5   White, *Hist.* (Sheffield, 1846), 410.
6   *Nuneaton Advertiser*, 2 Apr. 1887; *Northampton Merc.*, 22 Sept. 1883; *Kelly's Dir. of Leics. and Rutl.* (1891), 747.
7   *Rugby Advertiser*, 4 May 1901; *Kelly's Dir. of Leics. and Rutl.* (1908), 513; below, Local Government (Public Services).
8   *Lutterworth Independent*, Sept. 1985, 8.
9   Lutterworth Museum, Box 92, typescript of note by F.P. Mawson; J.G. Harrod & Co., *Dir. of Leics.* (London, 1870), 546.
10   Lutterworth Museum, Box 92, letter dated 28 Oct. 1907; *Rugby Advertiser*, 26 May 1917.
11   *Cal. Pat.* 1441–6, 120.
12   ROLLR, PR/I/78/163.
13   Nichols, *Hist.*, IV, 257; White, *Hist.* (Sheffield, 1863), 753.

nine Lutterworth children were apprenticed to weavers within the town between 1691 and 1767, including two to silk weavers.[14] An area on the west side of Bitteswell Road, close to the town, was labelled 'Tenters' on the enclosure map of 1792 and may have been where newly woven woollen cloth was stretched.[15] There were 12 weavers living in Lutterworth in 1861.[16]

A factory was built 'on the border of the town towards Hinckley' (probably on Bitteswell Road) in the late 18th or early 19th century by William Buszard, the brother of the Lutterworth banker Marston Buszard (d. 1824). William owned a factory in Manchester that produced fustian and dimity (heavy and sheer cotton fabrics).[17] Cotton arrived at his Lutterworth factory 'nearly in its raw state', and there it was spun and sent on to Manchester.[18] William Buszard died in 1812, and the factory may have closed shortly afterwards. It was no longer trading in 1822.[19] Benson Turner Ltd, worsted spinners of Bradford (Yorks. W.R.), moved some operations to Lutterworth in 1947 because of difficulties in recruiting labour in Yorkshire, and leased part of the Vedonis (Spencer's) factory. They closed c.1958.[20]

Hosiery and Knitted Fabrics

The earliest record of a framework knitter in the town was in 1757.[21] One child was apprenticed by the parish to a stocking-maker in 1776 and three more to framework knitters between 1798 and 1809.[22] In 1844 there were 90 frames in the town, mostly working for Leicester manufacturers, and 18 framework knitters in 1861.[23] A framesmith, R. Holmes, was recorded in 1822, and William and Thomas Holmes were framesmiths in 1846.[24]

George Spencer, with the brothers Herbert and Frank Barrowcliff, opened a factory in New Street in 1902 to produce hosiery.[25] Following the dissolution of the partnership in 1908, George Spencer and Co. was established by Spencer with the backing of the Nottingham lace manufacturer and hosiery machine builder William Revis.[26] In 1911 the company became one of three UK businesses licensed to produce a newly developed woollen 'interlock' fabric for underwear, 'Vedonis', which became a well-known

14   ROLLR, DE 2559/89/28, 30, 41, 55, 67, 78, 112, 139, 211.

15   ROLLR, Misc. 239.

16   1861 census statistics, from http://icem.data-archive.ac.uk (accessed 25 Nov. 2020).

17   *Scholes Manchester and Salford Dir.* (Manchester, 1794), 25; (Manchester, 1798), 24.

18   Nichols, *Hist.*, IV, 257.

19   Cheshire wills, 1812, on https://www.findmypast.co.uk; Pigot, *Dir. of Leics.* (1822), 226.

20   *Bradford Observer*, 8 Jan. 1954; *Rugby Advertiser*, 9 Sept. 1947; 'Obituary: Wilfred Turner', *Jnl Textile Institute Proceedings* 48 (1957), 199; *PO Telephone Dir.* (1960).

21   TNA, E 134/30Geo2/East6 (Henry Hastings).

22   ROLLR, DE 2559/89/120, 225, 238, 248.

23   *VCH Leics.* III, 21; White, *Hist.* (Sheffield, 1846), 402; 1861 census statistics, from http://icem.data-archive.ac.uk (accessed 25 Nov. 2020).

24   Pigot, *Dir. of Leics.* (1822), 227; (1835), 149; White, *Hist.* (Sheffield, 1846), 407.

25   *London Gaz.*, 13 Nov. 1903, 6968; *Rugby Advertiser*, 1 Feb. 1946.

26   *London Gaz.*, 15 Sept. 1908, 6724; *Manchester Courier and Lancashire General Advertiser*, 25 Sept. 1908; J.S. Dodge, *Notes for a Brief Life of George Spencer* (Lutterworth, 2001) 3–4; *Kelly's Dir. of Leics. and Rutl.* (1912), 555.

brand-name protected by patent until 1928.[27] The business had moved to new premises by 1912 (Vedonis Works), which stretched between Gilmorton Road and Leicester Road.[28] Further factories opened in Hucknall and Basford (both Notts.) in the 1920s.[29]

The Lutterworth factory was requisitioned for war work in 1941, with the employees retained for that purpose. Part of it was taken over by the Raleigh Cycle Co., and part by the Rover Cycle Co., to produce munitions. Underwear manufacture recommenced in Lutterworth in 1946, shortly after the death of George Spencer.[30] The business was the largest independent producer of hosiery and knitwear in the United Kingdom in 1969, with 2,094 employees in five factories in Lutterworth and Nottinghamshire.[31] The Lutterworth factory made knitted fabrics, babies' and children's clothes and (through a subsidiary, J.R. Fulton) ladies' jersey clothes.[32] Business declined from the late 1970s, as fashions changed. The children's clothes business was sold to Vee Children's Wear c.1984, who also took on part of the Vedonis factory, but that business failed c.1989.[33] The Spencer fabrics business closed in the late 1980s, and, although a second factory for Fulton opened in Leicester c.1987, that business ceased to trade in the early 1990s.[34]

Other hosiery businesses included Johnson & Barnes, which opened in 1906 but closed in 1918, and K. Leigh (Stockings) Ltd, which moved from Countesthorpe (8 miles north of Lutterworth) to a factory on Crescent Road in 1972 and closed c.1990.[35]

Elastic Web Manufacture

George and John Pettit established George Pettit & Son Ltd in part of the former Barrowcliff and Spencer factory on New Street in 1914,[36] making elastics and trimmings for haberdashery and the hosiery and corsetry trades.[37] They described themselves as successors to France and Bradsworth, elastic web manufacturers of Leicester who patented a method of weaving India-rubber threads into elastic webs in 1875.[38] Part of the premises was requisitioned by the Ministry of Aircraft Production in 1943.[39] The business was taken over by Tubbs, Lewis & Co. of Wotton-under-Edge (Glos.) in 1948, one of Britain's largest elastic manufacturers, but the Lutterworth factory had closed by 1950.[40]

---

27 S. Chapman, *Hosiery and Knitwear: Four Centuries of Small-scale Industry in Britain* (Oxford, 2002), 170; Dodge, *Notes*, 3–4.
28 *Kelly's Dir. of Leics. and Rutl.* (1912), 555.
29 *Nottingham Jnl*, 24 Aug. 1925.
30 *Rugby Advertiser*, 1 Feb. 1946; 23 Aug. 1946.
31 Chapman, *Hosiery*, 284.
32 *Leic. and Leics. Industrial Directory* (1982), 199, 331.
33 Memories of P. Wetton in T. Hirons and J. Woodford (eds), *Lutterworth Memories, 1950–1980* (Lutterworth, 2021), 14; *Phone Book, Leic. Dist.* (1989), 652.
34 *Phone Book, Leic. Dist.* (1987), 225, 591; (1992), 252.
35 Kibworth Hist. Society, 'Johnson & Barnes Ltd'; ROLLR, DE 4234/12; *Leic. Chron.*, 3 Nov. 1972; *Phone Book, Leic. Dist.* (1989), 381; (1992).
36 ROLLR, DE 3799/3, pp. 1–10; *Rugby Advertiser*, 1 Feb. 1946.
37 *Rugby Advertiser*, 20 Mar. 1931.
38 ROLLR, DE 3799/13; *Leic. Chron.*, 11 Sept. 1875; 15 Jan. 1876; A. Barlow, *The Hist. and Principles of Weaving by Hand and by Power* (London, 1878), 297–8.
39 ROLLR, DE 3799/2, pp. 41–2, 47, 51.
40 ROLLR, DE 3799/2; DE 3799/13; *Classified Telephone Dir. East Midlands* (1950).

Standring Burgess & Co. had opened an elastic web factory on Bitteswell Road by 1932.[41] The premises were gutted by fire in 1936,[42] and the company ceased trading in 1938.[43] Hills (Lutterworth) Ltd, elastic and ribbon manufacturers, commenced business on Bitteswell Road in 1939, possibly on the same site, and closed in 1985.[44] John Swann & Sons (later Swann Elastics) manufactured elastic web in a factory in Crescent Road in 1928, which closed in the 1940s.[45]

Leather and Footwear

In 1512–13 the market tolls brought in 18s. 4d. from shoemakers (33 per cent) and 12s. 8d. from tanners (23 per cent).[46] Thomas Parkins had leather 'in the Tann yard' valued at £75 at his death in 1678, and £650 owing to him against bonds 'and other writings'.[47] No other tanners have been identified.

Nicholas Ratcliffe, a shoemaker, was sufficiently wealthy to be assessed for tax in 1571.[48] By the 17th century, shoemaking had become one of the main trades in the town. On his death in 1600, Richard Palmer had lasts and 18 pairs of shoes in his shop worth £4.[49] William (d. 1609) and John (d. 1632) Newcombe were both shoemakers,[50] as were two John Youngs, who died in 1613 and 1638. The latter had leather and tools of his trade worth £7 10s. 2d. on his death, and a lease on a headland, valued at £10.[51] John Clarke, another shoemaker, held half a yardland with corn, hay, peas, five cows and 12 sheep on his death in 1676, in addition to leather, shoes and book debts.[52] Ten Lutterworth children were apprenticed to shoemakers in the town between 1700 and 1801.[53] There were 31 shoemakers in the town in 1782, and 15 in 1861.[54]

Clock and Watchmaking

Thomas and William Bates, who were making clocks between 1698 and 1740, generally signed them 'Market Harborough', but at least one was signed 'Lutterworth', suggesting that they visited the town to take orders on market days.[55] Similarly, an early

41 *Kelly's Dir. of Leics. and Rutl.* (1932), 708.
42 *Rugby Advertiser*, 7 Feb. 1936.
43 *London Gaz.*, 27 May 1938, 3442.
44 *Birmingham Daily Post*, 3 Jan. 1939; *Kelly's Dir. of Leics. and Rutl.* (1941), 1023; Moon, 'Bitteswell Road windmill', 42.
45 *Rugby Advertiser*, 16 Mar. 1928; *Leic. Eve. Mail*, 30 Apr. 1929; *Kelly's Dir. of Leics. and Rutl.* (1941), 1023; *Classified Telephone Dir. East Midlands* (1950).
46 TNA, SC 6/HENVIII/1824; CP 40/998, m. 188; *List of Early Chancery Proceedings, Preserved in the Public Record Office* (London, 1926), VII, 335.
47 TNA, PROB 4/9507.
48 TNA, E 179/134/205, rot. 1; Goodacre, *Transformation*, 161.
49 ROLLR, PR/I/18/29.
50 ROLLR, Wills, 1609/3; PR/I/35/30.
51 ROLLR, Wills, 1613/120; PR/I/40/157.
52 ROLLR, PR/I/78/87; Goodacre, *Transformation*, 191–2.
53 ROLLR, DE 2559/89 nos 40, 44, 58, 60, 83, 101, 109, 117, 156, 235.
54 Nichols, *Hist.*, IV, 257; 1861 census statistics, from http://icem.data-archive.ac.uk (accessed 25 Nov. 2020).
55 Ex inf. Brian Loomes.

18th-century clock signed 'William Jackson, Lutterworth' was almost certainly made by William Jackson of Loughborough.[56] Joseph Pickering (d. 1715) was a Lutterworth silversmith and clockmaker, with one yardland in the open fields.[57] The Corrall family included several Lutterworth clockmakers: Francis (d. 1770) from c.1720,[58] Thomas between 1750 and 1795, Powell between 1777 and 1795, and William in the mid 18th century.[59] Another Francis (d. 1850) and a later William were listed as clock- and watchmakers in 1846, and Francis's widow, Mary Ann Corrall, continued the business in 1855.[60] Timothy Hallam was a watchmaker in 1822, and Thomas Hallam was listed as a clock- and watchmaker in 1846, as was Thomas Harris.[61] Thomas Hallam and Thomas Harris were still trading in 1881.[62] A member of the Haswell family was making clocks c.1840; Edward John Haswell was a watchmaker on High Street in 1895; and his widow continued the business in 1912 under her husband's name.[63]

Brickmakers

Robert Saunders of Lutterworth and John Taylor of North Kilworth, bricklayers, were granted a 60-year lease in 1758 to dig clay on ground owned by the 6th earl of Denbigh adjoining Leicester Lane. Their annual rent was £9 plus 1,000 good bricks from every 20,000 they made, with the condition that they pull down seven cottages on High Street, replacing them with six or more new houses of three storeys, which were to be kept in good repair for the term of the lease.[64] A Mr Bickley was making bricks and tiles in 1784.[65] In 1821, during the town's building boom, William Neale was granted a 21-year lease of c.3 a. between Coventry Road and Bitteswell Road to dig for clay, build two kilns and make bricks and tiles, for an annual rent of seven guineas plus 1s. 6d. for every 1,000 bricks and tiles made, and 1d. for every dozen crests, gutters, kiln bricks and quarries.[66] Victoria Brickworks occupied 8 a. near the north-western parish boundary and probably opened before Queen Victoria's death in 1901. A tramline of 750 yd. had been built by 1904 to link this site to Coventry Road.[67] Another brickworks and kiln, closed by 1886, occupied a site to the west of Bitteswell Road.[68]

56   B. Loomes, 'William Jackson, mysterious maker of Loughborough and Leicester', *Clocks Magazine* (Mar. 2019); image in Goodacre, *Transformation*, 205.
57   ROLLR, 1D/41/4/L091, ff. 13–15; Wills, 1715 Pe–Z; example in Lutterworth museum.
58   Example in Lutterworth Museum; J.A. Daniell, 'The making of clocks and watches in Leicestershire and Rutland', *Trans. LAHS* 27 (1951), 35, 46, 60.
59   Daniell, 'The making of clocks', 46, 47, 61.
60   White, *Hist.* (Sheffield, 1846), 410; *PO Dir.* (1855), 90.
61   Pigot, *Dir. of Leics.* (1822), 227; White, *Hist.* (Sheffield, 1846), 410.
62   *Kelly's Dir. of Leics. and Rutl.* (1881), 672.
63   Daniell, 'The making of clocks', 48; *Kelly's Dir. of Leics. and Rutl.* (1895), 281; (1912), 554.
64   Warws. RO, CR 2017/D238/1.
65   Warws. RO, CR 2017/E17, f. 1v.
66   Warws. RO, CR 2017/D258/1–2.
67   OS Map 25", Leics. XLVIII.SE (1904 edn).
68   OS Map 25", Leics. XLVIII.SE (1886 edn).

Figure 11 *Wycliffe foundry employees, c.1908.*

Iron Foundries

Land adjacent to the railway was let in 1906 to Wycliffe Foundry Co. Ltd, which initially made locomotive axle boxes.[69] A siding for 11 wagons was constructed and let to the company.[70] The company purchased the land and had extended the premises twice by 1914.[71] They employed a significant number of women before the First World War (Figure 11), especially in the core shop, where they made the sand cores that would create the hollow areas within each casting. The company invested in a new type of furnace in 1929, to produce a high-quality low-carbon iron.[72] The company was licensed by Follsain Syndicate Ltd in 1932 to carry out a new process to treat steel to protect it against sea-water corrosion and oxidation at high temperatures.[73] The two companies set up a joint venture in 1934, Follsain Metals Ltd, to market the process. A public share issue in 1936 aimed to raise £100,000 to 'quadruple' production facilities at Lutterworth, to produce a new metal alloy that could withstand extreme heat, for use in brake blocks for locomotives and trams.[74] Follsain Metals Ltd and Wycliffe Foundry & Engineering Ltd merged to create Follsain–Wycliffe Foundries Ltd in 1948. The business expanded in

69 Lutterworth Museum, *Follsain–Wycliffe Newsletter*, 15 (1956), 2–3.
70 Lutterworth Museum, T. West, 'Lutterworth: iron foundries and sidings' (draft MS).
71 Lutterworth Museum, *Follsain–Wycliffe Newsletter*, 15 (1956), 3; Lutterworth Museum, West, 'Lutterworth: iron foundries'.
72 H. Morton, 'Progress in iron foundry practice with reference to locomotive castings', *Jnl of the Institute of Locomotive Engineers* (1940), 480–2.
73 Lutterworth Museum, *Follsain–Wycliffe Newsletter*, 15 (1956), 4; Follsain–Wycliffe Foundries Ltd, *Penetral Process: The Impregnation Treatment of Mild Steel* (Lutterworth, *c.*1939), 1–4.
74 *The Times*, 2 Jan. 1934; 6 Dec. 1935; 27 Apr. 1936; Lutterworth Museum, *Follsain–Wycliffe Newsletter*, 15 (1956), 5.

1951, and acquired part of the Spencer's factory.[75] The company was acquired by Clayton Dewandre, a foundry and engineering group based in Lincoln, in 1961.[76] Plans were announced in 1975 to extend the site and increase the number of employees from 290 to 370 over two years.[77] These were confounded when American Standard Inc. acquired the parent company in 1977.[78] The new owners divested themselves of this business, which then struggled financially, and a winding-up order was made in 1982.[79] The business was purchased from the liquidators but ceased trading in 1996.[80]

General Foundry and Engineering Co. Ltd (GFE) was incorporated in 1914 by Robert Duffus, manager of the pattern shop at British Thomson-Houston Co. Ltd (BTH), a manufacturer of electric motors and generators based in Rugby (Warws.), his colleague P.H. Wardlow and two farmers from Rugby.[81] They built foundry premises (Ladywood Works) to the north of the Wycliffe foundry, and railway sidings were agreed in 1921, but the GFE business was transferred to Arlesey (Beds.) that year, and the premises were sold.[82] They were purchased by BTH, probably at that time, and the siding was constructed in 1926. BTH vacated the building c.1933.[83]

Engineering

Power Jets Ltd was formed in 1936 by the RAF officer Frank Whittle, his agents (Dudley Williams and James Tinling), a firm of investment bankers (Falk & Partners) and the Air Ministry to exploit Whittle's design ideas for a jet engine, which was to be developed in prototype by BTH at Rugby. The first combustion tests did not run smoothly. In 1937 BTH offered Power Jets the use of their disused foundry building in Lutterworth (Ladywood Works) for their continuing experiments. Development and ground testing of Whittle's engine continued in Lutterworth. A newly designed aircraft, the E.28/39, was manufactured concurrently by the Gloster Aircraft Co. at Brockworth (Glos.) to Air Ministry specifications to take the engine. Taxiing trials were completed satisfactorily, and the maiden flight took place in May 1941 at RAF Cranwell (Lincs.).[84] Subsequent adjustments to the engine and testing continued in Lutterworth until 1942, when development work moved to a larger factory in Whetstone. The engine went into production with Rolls Royce, and entered service as part of the Gloster Meteor, Britain's

75   *Rugby Advertiser*, 9 Nov. 1948; 3 Aug. 1951.
76   *The Times*, 8 Nov. 1961; https://www.gracesguide.co.uk/Clayton_Dewandre_Co (accessed 23 Aug. 2020).
77   *Coventry Eve. Telegraph*, 1 Nov. 1975.
78   *The Times*, 3 Oct. 1977.
79   *London Gaz.*, 24 Dec. 1982, 16936.
80   Ex inf. Mick Gamble, Lutterworth resident; *London Gaz.*, 2 Aug. 1996, 10428.
81   *Birmingham Daily Gaz.*, 6 May 1914; *Rugby Advertiser*, 15 Aug. 1930.
82   Lutterworth Museum, West, 'Lutterworth: iron foundries'; *Rugby Advertiser*, 3 Dec. 1920; 24 Nov. 1925; 15 Aug. 1930.
83   Lutterworth Museum, West, 'Lutterworth: iron foundries'; R. Stead, *Lutterworth as I Remember It* (Leicester, 1983), 31.
84   J. Golley, *Jet: Frank Whittle and the Invention of the Jet Engine* (Fulham, 2010), 64–70, 78–91, 96, 164–9; NHLE, no. 1392641, Ladywood Works (the Offices and that part known as B3 Unit B adjacent to the north, once occupied by Sir Frank Whittle and Power Jets Ltd.) (accessed 9 Aug. 2020).

first production jet aircraft, in 1944.[85] The Ladywood Works continued to be used until 1945 as a training school for Power Jets' engineers.[86]

Alfred Herbert Ltd began as a partnership founded in Coventry in 1887. By 1914, the business had become the largest machine toolmaker in Europe.[87] Following the bombing of Coventry in 1940, the production of lathes (vital to the war effort) was transferred to a new factory in Lutterworth built by the Ministry of Supply on Leicester Road.[88] Manufacture continued in these premises after 1945, and by 1967 the factory building had been extended to cover 5 a., stretching east from Leicester Road to the railway.[89] The factory produced a die-sinking machine in 1960, weighing 22 tons, in a joint venture with the US aerospace company Pratt & Whitney.[90] Following a company reorganisation in 1968, Lutterworth became the centre of the boring and drilling division.[91] The industry was badly hit by foreign competition in the early 1970s, and the government took a controlling interest in Alfred Herbert Ltd in 1975, in exchange for up to £25 million of state aid.[92] Further government cash injections followed, but ceased after the general election of 1979.[93] The company was broken up in 1980.[94] The DeVlieg Machine Co. of Detroit took over the drilling, milling and boring business at Lutterworth, which had been building DeVlieg jigmills since 1956.[95] DeVlieg sold the company to the US conglomerate Stanwich in 1987.[96] Production continued until 1991, when the company went into liquidation.[97]

The electrical appliance manufacturer Hotpoint transferred its service centre from Coventry to Lutterworth in 1965.[98] It had a large warehouse and employed 310 people in the town in 1976, when the warehouse was consumed by fire and the business relocated to Peterborough.[99]

Other Manufacturing

Midland Electric Wire Co. Ltd was established in Leicester in 1882 and made insulated wire for use on dynamos, motors and telephones.[100] The company moved to Lutterworth in 1914, taking part of the former Spencer and Barrowcliff factory on New Street, where

---

85 Golley, *Jet*, 220; *ODNB*, s.v. Whittle, Sir Frank (1907–96), aeronautical engineer and inventor of the jet engine, accessed 3 Dec. 2013.

86 G. Smith, *Around Lutterworth: Second Selection* (Stroud, 2002), 40.

87 R. Lloyd-Jones and M.J. Lewis, *Alfred Herbert Ltd and the British Machine Tool Industry, 1887–1983* (2017), 1.

88 Ibid., 149; *The Times*, 30 Oct. 1945.

89 OS Map 1:2500, SP 5485 (1967); M. Gamble, *Alfred Herbert, Lutterworth and Beyond* (Anstey, 2014), 35.

90 *The Times*, 11 Apr. 1960.

91 Lloyd-Jones and Lewis, *Alfred Herbert*, 322, 329–30.

92 *The Times*, 31 Oct. 1974; 10 July 1975; 28 Oct. 1975; Lloyd-Jones and Lewis, *Alfred Herbert*, 294–5, 315–16.

93 *The Times*, 1 July 1980.

94 Lloyd-Jones and Lewis, *Alfred Herbert*, 317.

95 *The Times*, 17 June 1980; Gamble, *Alfred Herbert*, 26; Lloyd-Jones and Lewis, *Alfred Herbert*, 317.

96 Gamble, *Alfred Herbert*, 56.

97 Ibid., 57; http://vintagemachinery.org/mfgindex/detail.aspx?id=10762 (accessed 22 Sept. 2020).

98 *Coventry Eve. Telegraph*, 31 May 1965.

99 *Coventry Eve. Telegraph*, 2 Oct. 1976; 5 Oct. 1976; 8 Dec. 1976.

100 *Whitaker's Red Book of Commerce* (1914).

they employed *c.*50 people, more than half of whom were women.[101] The business had moved to Station Yard by 1925.[102] The company closed in 1939.[103]

Lady Clare Table Mats was founded by Lady Clare Pigott (daughter of the 9th earl of Denbigh) and her nephew, the Hon. Basil Feilding (brother of the 10th earl), in 1946. The business manufactured handcrafted place mats featuring a central printed panel. It occupied part of the Vedonis factory from 1947, moving to newly built premises on Leicester Road in 1960.[104] The Hon. Basil Feilding died in 1970.[105] His widow resigned as a director in 1999, and the business relocated to Stonehouse (Glos.), where it continued to trade in 2021.[106]

Trades and Services

Markets and Fairs

Rights and Tolls

A charter of 1214 granted a market to Nicholas de Verdun and his heirs at his manor of Lutterworth every Thursday.[107] The nearest markets were then at Naseby (Northants.) and probably Hinckley, both almost 10 miles away. The major market towns of Leicester and Coventry were, respectively, 13 and 14 miles distant. Another 14 places within 10 miles of Lutterworth were granted a market by 1300, but Lutterworth's earlier foundation gave it time to become established before these rivals.[108] A fair was recorded in 1316, probably without a charter.[109] In 1414 William de Ferrers obtained a charter that confirmed the weekly market and granted an annual fair on the vigil and day of Ascension, 'as he and his ancestors have had time out of mind'.[110] A grant for two additional fairs, on 22 March and 5 September, was obtained by the 4th earl of Denbigh in 1694, for the sale of cattle, beasts and all kinds of goods, together with a grant for all kinds of horses to be sold at the weekly markets.[111] After the calendar was changed in 1752, these fairs were moved to 2 April and 16 September.[112]

---

101 *Leic. Chron.*, 21 Nov. 1914; *Rugby Advertiser*, 19 Dec. 1914; *Directory of Manufacturers in Engineering and Allied Trades* (London, 1918), 463.
102 *Kelly's Dir. of Leics. and Rutl.* (1925), 617.
103 *London Gaz.*, 13 Oct. 1939, 6683.
104 *Rugby Advertiser*, 8 Aug. 1947; *Coventry Eve. Telegraph*, 15 Apr. 1971.
105 *Coventry Eve. Telegraph*, 9 Mar. 1971.
106 ROLLR, NRA 31906; Companies House, company information service, company 00408870; *Phone Book, Leic. Dist.* (June 1996), 157; (2005–6); http://lady-clare.com (accessed 26 Nov. 2020).
107 *Rot. Chart.*, I, 201.
108 These were, in Leics., Narborough (1219), Kibworth Beauchamp (1223), Arnesby (1292); in Warws., Brinklow (1218), Bretford (1227), Rugby (1255), Churchover (1257), Hillmorton (1266), Monks Kirby (1266), Wolvey (1326); and in Northants., Lilbourne (1219) Welford (1222), West Haddon (1292), Sibbertoft (1300): S. Letters, 'Gazetteer of Markets and Fairs in England and Wales to 1516', http://www.history.ac.uk/cmh/gaz/gazweb2.html (accessed 15 Feb. 2014).
109 *Cal. Inq. p.m.* VI, 36; TNA, C 134/56/1.
110 *Cal. Pat.* 1413–16, 181.
111 TNA, SP 44/343. f. 503.
112 White, *Hist.* (Sheffield, 1846), 401.

The annual value of market tolls in 1316 was assessed at 46*s.* 8*d.*[113] They were worth 30*s.* annually in 1322, when the market was leased out for £20.[114] The value fluctuated widely, between 25*s.* and 47*s.* just between 1359 and 1362.[115] Timber was subject to a toll of 1*d.* in the 1450s.[116] This had been reduced to ½*d.* in 1512–13, when the toll was paid on 233 cartloads, generating 9*s.* 8½*d.* (17 per cent of the 55*s.* 1*d.* collected at that year's markets), with the Ascension fair generating another 16*s.* 7*d.*[117] These figures understate the level of trade, as some sales would have been exempt from tolls.

The tolls were let out in the 17th century, to Thomas Forren in 1613, to John Fletcher in 1670, and from 1676 to 1682, with the leases from 1676 including an obligation to maintain the drapery building. Tolls on grain were reintroduced in 1670, having not been taken 'of late tyme'.[118] Disputes in 1847 and 1854 suggest that tolls had been reintroduced after perhaps a lengthy period when none had been charged. In 1857 visitors paid 2*d.* for every horse or beast purchased, 1*d.* for a pig and 4*d.* for every score of sheep, with the toll doubled for sheep purchased at a fair. Lutterworth inhabitants paid half these rates.[119] Lord Denbigh (the 9th earl) was approached in 1922 by an individual offering to buy his market rights, but he indicated that he would prefer to sell to the town. They were purchased by the Town Estate in 1923 for £150.[120]

Market Trade

There are few records of goods sold in the Middle Ages. Seed corn and bread corn were recorded in 1279, and John Pulteney of Misterton took Henry Smith of Lutterworth to court in 1459 over 6 qr. of corn worth 40*s.*[121] There was a dispute in 1436 between John Feilding and William Vynton of Stormsworth over 20 sheep,[122] and in 1493 Robert Meyell of Ullesthorpe sought redress over 50 sheep purchased in Lutterworth from William Cave.[123] Presentments were made in 1406–7 against three butchers, three bakers, three brewers and an ostler, with the latter fined 2*s.* for selling victuals at excessive prices.[124] Six fishmongers were recorded in 1564, five of them from Leicester, Burbage, Harborough Parva (Warws.) Harborough (probably Harborough Magna) and Rugby. The 25 butchers who were amerced that year included men from Burbage, Hinckley, Laughton, Shawell and Swinford (all Leics.), Kilsby, Lilbourne and Welford (Northants.), and Clifton-on-Dunsmore (Warws.).[125]

113 *Cal. Inq. p.m.* VI, 36.

114 TNA, SC 6/1146/17.

115 TNA, SC 6/908/33; C 135/152/5.

116 TNA, SC 6/947/3.

117 TNA, SC 6/HENVIII/1824.

118 TNA, PROB 11/122/523; Warws. RO, CR 2017/E115; Goodacre, *Transformation*, 185.

119 Warws. RO, CR 2017/M37/3–4, 10–13.

120 ROLLR, DE 1379/457, p. 119; J. Sumpter, *A Brief Historical Review of the Charity known as the Lutterworth Town Estate Trust* (Lutterworth, c.1926), 11.

121 *Rot. Hund.*, 239; TNA, CP 40/793, m. 241.

122 TNA, CP 40/703, m. 270.

123 TNA, CP 40/934, m. 322; A. Watkins, 'The town of Lutterworth in the later Middle Ages', *Trans. LAHS* 92 (2018), 133.

124 TNA, E 101/258/2, m. 1.

125 TNA, SC 2/183/84.

The timber used to build many houses in south Leicestershire and north-west Northamptonshire in the late medieval period was purchased at Lutterworth.[126] In 1432–3 the bailiff of Murcott (Northants.) paid 10s. for 60 'sparr' (rafters), 4s. 4d. for 1,400 laths, and 3s. for 'lathnayle' in Lutterworth.[127] Merton College, Oxford, bought timber from Lutterworth in 1448 for a house in Kibworth,[128] and during the 1450s the prioress of Catesby abbey (Northants.) bought four pieces of timber, 54 beams, two 'sydpese', 650 lathes and a 'joyste tre' in the 1450s from John Sharpe of Lutterworth to repair her barn at Theddingworth.[129]

Livestock trade benefited from Lutterworth's proximity to Watling Street. Henry Russell, a Lutterworth grazier, sold cattle to Robert Fox, a London butcher, in 1538.[130] Peter Temple sold two little bullocks at Lutterworth in 1561.[131] In 1554, 58 wethers were purchased at Lutterworth for Misterton estate, including 40 from Thomas Lloyd, probably a Welsh drover, with other Misterton records mentioning an unnamed 'Welsh drover' who supplied the estate with beasts.[132]

Successful Lutterworth traders established business links elsewhere. In 1203 Robert de Lutterworth was received by Reynold the tailor in Northampton,[133] and men from Lutterworth appear in a dispute in Coventry in 1221.[134] In 1349 Roger Lucas of Lutterworth held a tenement in Coventry.[135] Several Lutterworth men were members of Leicester's guild merchant.[136] William Norreys was trading with Robert Collier of Atherstone in 1387.[137] John Tryp owed money to a London merchant in 1426,[138] traders from Lutterworth were active in Nuneaton[139] and Henry Karman of Lutterworth owed money to a tanner from Burbage in the 1530s.[140]

The market was renowned for the quality of its corn and the diversity of other goods in 1622 and 1673,[141] but the introduction of additional 'fairs' and specialised markets may indicate that regular trade was declining. One-day 'horse fairs' were held by 1607 on the

126 C. Dyer, 'Medieval peasant buildings 1250–1550: documents and historical significance', in N. Alcock and D. Miles, *The Medieval Peasant House in Midland England* (Oxford, 2013), 106.

127 C. Dyer, 'Building in earth in late medieval England', *Vernacular Architecture* 39 (2008), 68–9.

128 Merton College Muniments 6324; C. Howell, *Land, Family and Inheritance in Transition* (Cambridge, 1983), 143–4; N. Finn, 'Mud and frame construction in south Leicestershire', *Vernacular Architecture* 40 (2009), 70.

129 TNA, SC 6/947/3.

130 TNA, C 1/986/32.

131 Alcock, *Warws. Grazier*, 78.

132 Goodacre, *Transformation*, 159, 161.

133 D.M. Stenton (ed.), *The Earliest Northamptonshire Assize Rolls AD 1202 and 1203* (Northamptonshire Rec. Soc. 5, 1930), no. 692.

134 D.M. Stenton (ed.), *Rolls of the Justices in Eyre for Gloucestershire, Warwickshire and Staffordshire 1221, 1222* (Selden Society, 59, 1940), nos 517, 726, 826, 906.

135 CARC, BA/B/16/361/1.

136 M. Bateson (ed.), *Records of the Borough of Leicester*, I, *1103–1327* (London, 1899), 150, 64, 356, 259; H. Hartopp, *Register of the Freemen of Leicester, 1196–1170* (Leicester, 1927), 61, 64.

137 Warws. RO, MR 13/3, 13/5, 13/6, 13/8, 13/14, 13/16.

138 *Cal. Pat.* 1422–9, 314.

139 A. Watkins, *Small Towns in the Forest of Arden in the Fifteenth Century* (Dugdale Society, Occasional Paper 38, 1998), 13, 25.

140 *Early Chancery Proceedings*, VII, 335.

141 Burton, *Description*, 170; R. Blome, *Britannia, or, A Geographical Description of the Kingdoms of England, Scotland, and Ireland* (1673), 139; Watkins, 'The town of Lutterworth', 140–2.

first three Thursdays after Epiphany (6 January) on a meadow beyond the core of the town known as Horse Fair Leys.[142] The weekly horse sales from 1694 may have been an attempt to capture trade from horse dealers from the Warwickshire parishes adjoining Watling Street, who were attending Market Bosworth market.[143] In the 1790s Lutterworth formed part of a network of markets where stallions of good pedigree attended for the day to cover local mares.[144] A large sheep market was held on the Thursday after 'Old Michaelmas' (10 October) in 1846, suggesting that this annual custom had been introduced before the calendar change in 1752.[145] The market was said to be 'of no great note' in 1790.[146] By 1809, the September fair was including cheese, and, in an apparent attempt to concentrate livestock sales on a monthly basis, the markets held in the 1830s on the first Thursdays after 19 February, 10 March, 15 April, 23 July, 3 October and 10 November were being described as 'fairs'.[147] Butter, eggs, poultry and meat were sold from the market hall on the ground floor of Lutterworth town hall, built in 1836.[148] The sides were fully enclosed in 1907,[149] and it may have ceased to be a market hall at that time.

The lack of a railway station at Lutterworth before 1899 resulted in a loss of some market trade. A sale of over 700 sheep and five tons of cheese was held in the small village of Ullesthorpe in 1840, near the railway station.[150] Livestock markets were suspended during the cattle murrain of 1865–6, but a monthly stock sale was introduced in Ullesthorpe in 1871.[151] Some Welsh beasts were still driven along Watling Street, with the Jonathan family of Dihewyd, near Lampeter (Cards.) selling beasts in Lutterworth between 1856 and 1869.[152] By 1872 Lutterworth's livestock markets had become monthly occasions.[153] The Leicestershire Farmers' Co-operative Society reinstated weekly sales in the 'New Smithfield' in Ridley's Yard, Bitteswell Road, from 1920, but livestock markets ceased in 1926, when the yard, its sheds and weighbridge were sold.[154]

By the 1970s, the street market comprised between 12 and 15 stalls, but the Town Estate trustees believed that any expansion could result in a loss of business for the shops. There was also local opposition to plans for a Saturday market.[155] A small weekly market continued on Thursdays in 2021, with items sold including fruit and vegetables, clothes, baked goods and plants.

---

142 TNA, LR 2/255, ff. 131, 161.
143 TNA, SP 44/343, f. 503; P.R. Edwards, 'The horse trade of the Midlands in the seventeenth century', *Agricultural Hist. Review* 27 (1979), 96–8.
144 For example, *Northampton Merc.*, 27 Mar. 1790; 30 Apr. 1791; 11 Feb. 1792.
145 White, *Hist.* (Sheffield, 1846), 401.
146 J. Throsby, *The Supplementary Volume to the Leics Views: Containing a Series of Excursions in the Year 1790* (London, 1790), 212.
147 W. Pitt, *General View of the Agriculture of the County of Leic.* (London, 1809), 318; J. Curtis, *Topographical Hist. of the County of Leic.* (Ashby-de-la-Zouch, 1831), 122.
148 White, *Hist.* (Sheffield, 1846), 401.
149 P. Harris, *The Architectural Achievement of Joseph Aloysius Hansom (1803–1882), Designer of the Hansom Cab, Birmingham Town Hall, and Churches of the Catholic Revival* (Lampeter, 2010), 96.
150 *Leic. Jnl*, 15 Sept. 1848.
151 *Leic. Chron.*, 21 Jan. 1871; 28 Jan. 1871.
152 R.J. Colyer, *The Welsh Cattle Drovers* (Cardiff, 1976), 105, 109, 137, 110–11.
153 *Leic. Chron.*, 28 Sept. 1872.
154 *Rugby Advertiser*, 2 July 1920; 2 July 1926.
155 *Leic. Merc.*, 18 Aug. 1972; 21 Mar. 1977.

Wool Merchants

In 1260 Lutterworth was one of seven places in the county where foreign merchants could buy wool, which suggests that sheep farming was important in south Leicestershire even in the 13th century.[156] John Reynolds (d. 1473) was a merchant of the Staple at Calais, and had a memorial brass in Lutterworth church.[157] He was probably a member of the Reynold family of Leicester, which provided five mayors of the town over five generations, including Nicholas Reynold (d. c.1553), also a merchant of the Staple.[158] Staplers bought the clip (shorn wool) from farmers, monastic houses and middlemen. The wool was then sorted, graded and packed, and sent by the Stapler to a port for shipment to Calais, where it was inspected, warehoused and sold to foreign dealers and cloth manufacturers.[159] William Feilding (d. 1471), head of the Feilding family in Lutterworth, was also a member of the Company of the Staple, and was involved in the export of wool in the 1450s and 1460s.[160] He had trading links with Coventry and London, and in 1465, with his kinsmen Thomas and Richard Feilding, brought an action against a London merchant relating to a substantial transaction, with an attached penal sum of £10,000.[161] His son Everard (d. 1515) was also a merchant Stapler, and bequeathed £100 from his stock at Calais to his daughter Jane.[162] Everard had been in dispute with the abbot of Combe (Warws.) in 1512 over £200, which may relate to the abbey's wool clip.[163] No later merchant Staplers have been identified in the town, but membership of the Company of the Staple declined steeply in the early 16th century, when higher wool prices had made the trade less profitable and English wool exports faced increasing competition from Spanish wool.[164]

Robert Paver, described as an ironmonger in 1509 and a mercer in 1536, was a freeman of Leicester, as was his brother Ralph, who was described as a mercer when he was admitted to Leicester's Chapman's Guild in 1517.[165] Although not merchant Staplers, they were almost certainly wool dealers. Robert Paver's tax assessment of £143 6s. 8d. on goods in 1524 was among the highest in Leicestershire.[166] Margaret Paver, probably the widow of one of these men, had a wool chamber in her house containing wool worth £10 on her death in 1550, and a warehouse and shop with linen cloth and 'other wares'

156 Bateson (ed.), *Records*, I. The others were Leicester, Breedon on the Hill, Hinckley, Loughborough, Market Bosworth and Melton Mowbray.
157 *Cal. Pat.* 1467–77, 212; Nichols, *Hist.*, IV, 265.
158 Goodacre, *Transformation*, 154; H. Hartopp (ed.), *Roll of the Mayors of the Borough of Leic. and Lord Mayors of the City of Leic., 1209 to 1935* (Leicester, 1935), 272, 58–9.
159 E.E. Power, 'The wool trade in the fifteenth century', in E.E. Power and M.M. Postan (eds), *Studies in English Trade of the Fifteenth Century* (London, 1966), 49–61.
160 *Cal. Pat.* 1446–52, 315; *Hist. Parl. Commons*, 1422–61, IV, 320.
161 TNA, CP 40/392, m. 7; *Cal. Pat.* 1367–70, 26, 229; TNA, CP 40/546, m. 123; C 241/275/37; CP 40/753, m. 185; TNA, CP 40/1005B, m. 556; TNA, C 241/249/27; C 241/254/161; A. Watkins, 'The town of Lutterworth', 140–2.
162 TNA, PROB 11/18/114.
163 TNA, CP 40/1001, m. 7; Watkins, 'The town of Lutterworth', 141.
164 S. Rose, *The Wealth of England: The Medieval Wool Trade and its Political Importance, 1100–1600* (Oxford, 2018), 123–4, 158–62, 175.
165 Hartopp (ed.), *Register of the Freemen*, 61, 64; TNA, WARD 2/61/241/122, f. 4.
166 TNA, E179/133/122, rot. 9d; E179/133/121, rot. 2; Goodacre, *Transformation*, 155.

valued at £30.[167] John Kirby, assessed for tax of £22 in 1552, was also a wool merchant.[168] William Paddy was described as a wool-comber in 1794 and a wool-stapler in 1822, and Thomas Paddy was a wool-stapler in 1846.[169] Their business would have involved buying wool from farmers and selling it to spinners and weavers.

Agricultural Merchants

Staffordshire Farmers Ltd was a farmers' co-operative founded in Staffordshire in 1919.[170] By 1961 it had 19 branches across the Midlands, including one on Leicester Road, Lutterworth.[171] Many farmers in Lutterworth and the surrounding villages were members. The company bought fertilisers, seeds and other essential products cheaply in bulk, sold these to members, and also helped members to find markets for their crops.[172] The company went into liquidation in 1990.[173]

Shops

The drapery offered a covered venue for merchants to sell their wares, including cloth, wool and other commodities. It contained two 'selds' in 1322, which might have been single stalls, or arcades accommodating several traders.[174] In 1509 the 'fleshamills' probably contained a number of traders selling meat, and there were at least 16 other separate shops.[175] Some of these may have been workshops, and many others may have been open only on market days. Robert Sowter, a draper, owned cloth and 'other stuff' in his shop, valued at £40 on his death in 1551. He had employed a chapman to sell his wares in surrounding villages.[176] Thomas Clerk had 'mersery wares' worth 26s. 8d. in his shop at his death in 1576.[177] Two other residents in the 16th century were described as mercers, Robert Mowre in 1559[178] and Richard Pratt in 1571,[179] but no information survives about their stock.

There were 12 shops in the Drapery in 1607, seven in the Shambles, seven on Woodmarket and at least ten others, including one within John Halpeny's inn on High Street and one under construction on the manorial waste.[180] A 'decayed' shop near the

167 ROLLR, W&I 1550/40.
168 TNA, E 179/134/176, m. 2; Goodacre, *Transformation*, 151, 156.
169 *Universal British Dir.* (1794), 605; Pigot, *Dir. of Leics.* (1822), 227; White, *Hist.* (Sheffield, 1846), 407.
170 *Staffs. Advertiser*, 17 May 1919.
171 *Commercial Motor*, 15 Dec. 1961.
172 Ex inf. John Goodacre.
173 *London Gaz.*, 2 Jan. 1991, 100.
174 TNA, SC 6/1146/17; D. Keene, 'Sites of desire: shops, selds and wardrobes in London and other English cities, 1100–1550', in B. Blondé, P. Stabel, J. Stobart and I. Van Damme (eds), *Buyers and Sellers: Retail Circuits and Practices in Medieval and Early Modern Europe* (Turnhout, 2006), 127–36.
175 Warws. RO, CR 2017/E42 ff. 1–4; Goodacre, *Transformation*, 12.
176 ROLLR, W&I 1551/78.
177 ROLLR, Administrations 1573–85/41B.
178 TNA, E 41/119.
179 TNA, WARD 2/41/1460/3.
180 TNA, LR 2/255.

Neats Market owned by Sir William Faunt was rebuilt as two shops *c.*1625.[181] Francis Pope, a mercer, died in 1626 holding over 700 yd. of cloth in 41 different combinations of type and colour. He also had a sizeable farm, and probably leased land outside Lutterworth, as he owned 260 sheep and 25 cows, which suggests that there was insufficient trade within Lutterworth for his shop to occupy all his energies or capital. His total inventory value was £341 4*s.* 2*d.*[182] John Almey's shop carried stock worth £112 12*s.* 4*d.* when he died in 1666, of which 26 per cent was cloth, 42 per cent haberdashery, 25 per cent household goods and 7 per cent grocery. Described as a mercer and chandler, he also had 4 cwt. of tallow, and a farm with 20 sheep and four beasts.[183] Daniel Ogden's shop had stock of a similar value to Almey's in 1695, but it had a much wider range of groceries, with rice, liquorice, many more types of spices and 2½ cwt. of sugar. He also had a small shop in Dunton Bassett, but no farm.[184] Another Francis Pope (d. 1680) was a woollen draper, with stock including 'Devonshire', 'Burton', 'Tamworth' and 'Yorkshire' cloth.[185] At least seven Lutterworth traders issued their own tokens when low-value coins were in short supply.[186] None are known to have been issued by Daniel Ogden, but his probate inventory included a parcel of 'farthings', which were probably tokens.[187] Other shops were occupied by producer-retailers or concentrated on particular goods. Henry Mason, a hatter, had a stock of 251 hats and caps on his death in 1707, and 63 lb. of wool.[188] Edward Carr, a barber who died in 1694, had a stock of hair and wigs.[189] Richard Tant was described as a tobacconist in 1695. On his death in 1724 his entire stock consisted of tobacco and alcoholic drinks, together worth £43 7*s.* 0*d.*[190]

The total assessed shop tax for Lutterworth of £3 19*s.* 10½*d.* in 1785 was the fifth highest in the county (excluding Leicester).[191] There were 65 shopkeepers noted in 1835, with a wide range of wares. The main shopping area was High Street, with 29 shops. There were 11 in Church Street, six on Bakehouse Lane, six in Ely Lane, six in Beast Market, five in Woodmarket, one in Back Lane (later Bank Street) and one on Dixon's Square (near the modern Shambles Court).[192] There were 55 shops in 1910, concentrated in Church Street (22 shops) and High Street (18 shops).[193] In the 1950s the shops stocked almost everything one could want.[194] The majority of shops in 2021 were in High Street, Church Street, Market Street and George Street, almost all occupied by independent local businesses or by charities. There were four supermarkets, on Bitteswell Road, Leicester Road, Linden Drive (off Coventry Road) and by the motorway junction.

181 ROLLR, DE 1012/5; Goodacre, *Transformation*, 211.
182 ROLLR, PR/I/32A/121.
183 ROLLR, PR/I/65/14.
184 ROLLR, PR/I/100/97A.
185 ROLLR, PR/I/82/68.
186 Goodacre, *Transformation*, 212.
187 ROLLR, PR/I/100/97A.
188 ROLLR, PR/I/114/41.
189 ROLLR, PR/I/99/102.
190 ROLLR, DE 2559/89/82; Wills, 1724.
191 TNA, E 182/537, pt 2.
192 Pigot, *Dir. of Leics.* (1835), 64–5.
193 ROLLR, DE 2072/149.
194 Memories of P. Fretter in Hirons and Woodford (eds), *Lutterworth Memories*, 2–4.

Warehousing and Distribution

Freudenberg, a German-based group of companies manufacturing non-woven textiles for many different industries, including construction, automotive and aerospace, moved part of its distribution business from Northampton to Lutterworth in 1971. In 2014 it consolidated its customer service and logistics support for the aerospace industry at Lutterworth.[195] Warehousing and distribution became the most important industry in the vicinity of the town in the late 20th century. The first phase of the Magna Park warehousing and logistics estate (550 a.) was mostly developed in Bitteswell parish. The neighbouring Magna Park South, under development from 2021, will occupy 220 a. in Lutterworth, largely on the former Moorbarns pasture, with outline planning permission also agreed for Magna Park North (590 a.) in Bitteswell, adjoining the original development.[196] Magna Park employed 9,300 people in 2021, before the completion of Magna Park South, with occupiers including Asda, BT, DHL, Renault and Toyota.[197]

Inns and Hotels

There were five inns in 1509: the Crown and the Swan on High Street, owned respectively by Martin Feilding and the hospital; the Saracen's Head and the Pannier on Woodmarket, both owned by Everard Feilding; and the Bull, also on Woodmarket, owned by Agnes Cotts.[198] Three women and 27 men were charged for breaking the assize of bread in 1564, with 22 of those men sharing a surname with 22 of the 28 women who broke the assize of ale, although some of these couples may only have provided food and drink on market days from stalls.

In 1686 the town was able to provide 94 beds and stabling for 302 horses, a much higher ratio of stables to beds than other Leicestershire towns.[199] With Lutterworth yet to benefit from the long-distance coaching trade, the number of stables probably reflects the success of the market, and perhaps especially the horse fairs from 1607. Lutterworth's inns could offer a range of accommodation and services to suit people with different needs and means. Isaac Billington (d. 1676) and John Lakin (d. 1678) each served a fixed-price midday meal. George Tilley (d. 1695) could offer some of the most comfortable guest rooms in the town, with the 'Chamber over the House' containing furniture and furnishings valued at £11 11s. 8d., while Billington's 'Blew' chamber had furniture valued at £7 10s. 0d.[200]

Thirty-four licences were issued to victuallers in 1754.[201] Trade was sufficiently profitable for a new inn to be built in Beast Market in 1772–3, with stabling for 15 horses. This was probably the Greyhound, so named by 1778, although the present

195 *Coventry Eve. Telegraph*, 26 Feb. 1971; https://www.fst.com/-/media/files/pr/2014-07/ash/2014-07-09_ash_eu_en.pdf (accessed 6 Sept. 2021).
196 https://lutterworth.magnapark.co.uk (accessed 15 Aug. 2021).
197 Harborough District Council, *Lutterworth Town Centre Masterplan* (draft, 2021); https://lutterworth.magnapark.co.uk (accessed 9 Oct. 2020); https://www.multimodal.org.uk/article/gazeley-has-bought-symmetry-park-db-symmetry-and-renamed-it-magna-park-south (accessed 1 Feb. 2022).
198 Warws. RO, CR 2017/E42, ff. 3, 4.
199 TNA, WO 30/48.
200 ROLLR, PR/I/78/121 (Billington); PR/I/80/44 (Lakin); PR/I/100/163 (Tilley).
201 ROLLR, QS 36/2/1.

Figure 12 *Denbigh Court, formerly the Denbigh Arms, on the west side of High Street. The property on this plot was described as a capital messuage in 1509, when it was owned by Everard Feilding.*

building is said to date from the early 19th century.[202] The number of inns gradually declined, and only 19 licences were issued in 1800.[203] The Denbigh Arms, Hind, Greyhound and Crown were extending and improving their premises, and appear to have driven the smaller inns out of business. As the coaching trade ended, the largest inns adapted their facilities to accommodate the growing interest in hunting. In 1883 the Hind had 13 bedrooms, stables for 14 horses and hunters for hire, while the Denbigh Arms (Figure 12) had boxes for 60 horses.[204] The number of inns and public houses had fallen to nine in 1941[205] and to seven in 2019, including two outside the town centre.

202 *Northampton Merc.*, 2 Aug. 1773; 18 May 1778; NHLE, no. 1211135, The Greyhound Coaching Inn 9 Market St (accessed 9 Aug. 2020).
203 ROLLR, QS 36/2/8.
204 ROLLR, 18D 67/2520, p. 17; *Sporting Gaz.*, 10 Mar. 1883.
205 *Kelly's Dir. of Leics. and Rutl.* (1941), 1022–3.

Printing and Publishing

Bottrill's printing business is said to have been established in Lutterworth in 1802.[206] John Bottrill was the proprietor and also a stationer and bookseller on High Street in 1822.[207] He was followed in the business by E. Bottrill, who was publishing hymns and sermons in 1838,[208] with the business becoming known as Elizabeth Bottrill & Son by 1846.[209] Frederick William Bottrill, a grandson of the founder, produced four editions of an *Illustrated Handbook of Lutterworth* between 1882 and 1900.[210] F.W. Bottrill died in 1914. The business was taken over by Edwin Woodford, Bottrill's foreman, who retained the business name, publishing *Bottrill's Lutterworth and District Household Almanack* in 1938.[211] Edwin Woodford died in 1942 while his son John, who had also worked in the business, was away on active service. The business had closed by 1945 through insolvency.[212]

F.W. Bottrill described part of his business in 1877 as a 'depot' of the Religious Tract Society,[213] which had been founded in the 18th century. The business later became the Lutterworth Press, which by the 20th century had become a medium-sized publishing house. It has no other known connection to the town.[214]

There were several attempts to establish a newspaper in Lutterworth. The *Lutterworth Mercury and General Advertiser* ran from 1869 to 1870. The *Lutterworth News and General Advertiser* took its place in 1870 but ran only to 1871. The *Lutterworth Guardian* was published between 1923 and 1928.[215]

Gideons International is an evangelical Christian organisation founded in the USA in the early 20th century which spreads the word of God through the printing and distribution of Bibles and New Testaments to businesses and organisations, including hotels, hospitals, schools, colleges and prisons.[216] The UK administrative headquarters moved from Reading to Lutterworth in 1975 for ease of supplying material to their 142 UK branches.[217] The UK arm of the organisation was renamed Good News for Everyone! in 2019, following a decision to amend its constitution to accept women as members, which was not welcomed by the organisation in some other countries.[218]

Banking

Lutterworth's first bank, Goodacre & Co., had been established by 1803. The partners in 1812 were John Goodacre the younger and Marston Buszard (d. 1824).[219] It was taken

206 *Rugby Advertiser*, 3 June 1949.
207 Pigot, *Dir. of Leics.* (1822), 227.
208 BL catalogue.
209 White, *Hist.* (Sheffield, 1846), 408.
210 Leics. Libraries catalogue; *Rugby Advertiser*, 7 Mar. 1914.
211 *Leic. Eve. Mail*, 28 May 1914; *Rugby Advertiser*, 3 June 1949; ROLLR, DE 1379/567.
212 Ex inf. John Woodford (grandson of Edwin).
213 White, *Hist.* (Sheffield, 1877), 524.
214 https://lutterworthpress.wordpress.com/about (accessed 29 Nov. 2020).
215 Lutterworth Museum.
216 https://gideonsinternational.org.uk (accessed 11 Aug. 2021).
217 *Lutterworth Independent*, Aug. 1975, 8.
218 https://goodnewsuk.com; 'Gideons UK lose trademark battle', *Premier Christian News*, 3 Dec. 2019.
219 M. Dawes and C.N. Ward-Perkins, *Country Banks of England and Wales: Private Provincial Banks and Bankers, 1688–1953* (Canterbury, 2000), II, 352–3.

over in 1831 by Clarke & Philips, a Leicester bank, but failed in 1843. Creditors included 156 Lutterworth inhabitants with deposits totalling over £34,000.[220] Pares's Leicestershire Banking Co. had opened an office in Lutterworth by 1846.[221] Through a series of mergers, it became the National Westminster Bank in 1970.[222] The branch closed in 2017.[223] The Midland Counties District Bank had opened by 1899.[224] Following mergers, this became Barclays Bank in 1916.[225] The branch closed in 2018.[226]

The Rugby Building Society opened a branch office in Lutterworth in 1946.[227] After a series of mergers with other building societies from 1967, it became the Cheltenham and Gloucester Building Society in 1993, which was acquired by Lloyds Bank in 1995.[228] Lloyds Bank continued to have a branch in Bell Street in 2020.

A savings bank opened in 1822.[229] Situated within Bottrill's stationery business on High Street, it opened for one hour weekly on Thursdays. In 1848 it held 918 accounts, with an average balance of £27.[230] It closed in 1866, when it had 1,016 depositors, 876 of whom transferred their accounts to the Post Office Savings Bank, which had opened a branch in Lutterworth in 1861.[231]

Other Services

Small service businesses dominated Lutterworth's economy in 2020, and most occupied units on the town's business and industrial estates off Leicester Road, and on St John's Business Park near the motorway junction. Services offered included kitchen and bathroom design and installation, vehicle servicing, advertising, energy services, security, warehousing, accounting and counselling, and fairground rides could be hired from a firm located off Coventry Road. Individually, these businesses were not major employers, but collectively they provided a wide range of employments and self-employment options for many people.

220 Ibid., 325, 352–3; Pigot, *Dir. of Leics.* (1835), 64; J. Orbell and A. Turton, *British Banking: A Guide to Historical Records* (Abingdon, 2017), 152; *Leic. Chron.*, 17 June 1843.
221 White, *Hist.* (Sheffield, 1846), 408.
222 R. Reed, *National Westminster Bank: A Short Hist.* (1983), 38–40, 43.
223 *Sun*, 5 Dec. 2017, https://www.thesun.co.uk/money/5041069/natwest-banks-which-closing-full-list-branch-closures (accessed 2 Sept. 2020).
224 *Kelly's Dir. of Leics. and Rutl.* (1899), 288.
225 https://www.archive.barclays.com/items/show/5254; https://www.archive.barclays.com/items/show/5249 (accessed 2 Sept. 2020).
226 https://home.barclays/content/dam/home-barclays/documents/citizenship/Reports-Publications/Branch%20Closure%20Feedback/Lutterworth%20Branch%20Closure%20Feedback%20booklet.pdf (accessed 2 Sept. 2020).
227 *Rugby Advertiser*, 20 Dec. 1946.
228 https://www.bsa.org.uk/information/consumer-factsheets/general/mergers-and-conversions (accessed 5 Apr. 2021).
229 H.O. Horne, *A Hist. of Savings Banks* (London, 1947), 382; *Return of Savings Banks* (Parl. Papers 1893–4 (274)), p. 79.
230 *Return of Savings Banks* (Parl. Papers 1849 (344), xxx), p. 412; *Return of Savings Banks* (Parl. Papers 1852 (521), xxviii), p. 784.
231 *Return of Savings Banks* (Parl. Papers 1893–4 (274)), p. 79; *Return of Post Office Savings Banks* (Parl. Papers 1865 (489), xxxi), p. 417.

SOCIAL HISTORY

Social Character

LUTTERWORTH IN 1086 CONTAINED A broad mix of free and unfree tenants, with 12 sokemen, six *villani*, seven bordars and, in the demesne, three slaves.[1] Labour services had been commuted for cash by 1316.[2] In 1279 there were 25 burgesses (37 per cent of the recorded population), six free tenants (9 per cent) and 36 villeins (54 per cent).[3] The burgesses lived in their own area along High Street, while mention of a 'Bonde end' in 1403 suggests that the unfree peasants (bound to their lord) had once occupied a street or distinctive area of their own.[4] No plots were described as burgages in 1509, when the main social distinction was between the sole chief messuage (owned by Everard Feilding), 19 other messuages and *c.*79 cottages.[5]

Before 1629, Lutterworth's lords probably rarely visited. Mainou the Breton, the lord in 1086, held 24 manors in chief (15 forming his demesne), mostly in Buckinghamshire.[6] The Verduns held extensive estates in England, the Welsh Marches and Ireland.[7] Theobald de Verdun I (d. 1309) served Edward I in the Welsh and Scottish wars, and also spent substantial time in Ireland.[8] His son and heir, Theobald II (d. 1316), was appointed justiciar of Ireland in 1313.[9] The estates of the Ferrers and Grey families, successors to the Verduns from 1360, were based around Groby, 17 miles north of Lutterworth.

Two people stood well above the remainder of the population in the early 14th century, in terms of their wealth: the master of the hospital, assessed for 12*s.* tax in 1327 and 10*s.* in 1332, and Theobald de Verdun's widow, Lady Clare, assessed for 10*s.* in 1327 and 20*s.* in 1332. Beneath them was a band of moderately wealthy people, with 20 residents assessed for between 1*s.* and 5*s.* tax in 1327, and 16 people assessed for between 2*s.* and 6*s.* 8*d.* in 1332, when the tax rate was higher. Geoffrey Feilding appears in the 1332 list, assessed at 3*s.* 4*d.*, which was also the median value of all the assessments.[10]

---

1   *Domesday*, 645.
2   TNA, C 134/56/1; *VCH Leics.* II, 173–4.
3   Bodleian, Rawlinson MS B 350, p. 23; Nichols, *Hist.*, IV, 247.
4   Lincs. Arch., Bishop's Register 13, f. 58.
5   Warws. RO, CR 2017/E42; J. Goodacre, *The Transformation of a Peasant Economy: Townspeople and Villagers in the Lutterworth Area, 1500–1700* (Aldershot, 1994), 46, 59–60.
6   https://domesday.pase.ac.uk/Domesday?op=5&personkey=40863 (accessed 14 Sept. 2021).
7   M. Hagger, *The Fortunes of a Norman Family: the de Verduns in England, Ireland and Wales, 1066–1216* (Dublin, 2001), 130, 135–7.
8   Ibid. 98–115, 138, 235.
9   Ibid. 117, 234.
10   TNA, E 179/133/1, m. 10d; E 179/133/2, m. 10d; W.G.D. Fletcher and F. Hopper, 'The earliest Leicestershire lay subsidy roll, 1327', *Assoc Arch. and Hist. Soc. Rpts. & Papers* 19 (1887–8), 307.

A small mercantile class began to appear from the 1450s. At its heart were the town's three merchant Staplers, John Reynolds (d. 1473), William Feilding (d. 1471) and Everard Feilding (d. 1515), and the wealthy wool merchants and mercers Robert and Ralph Paver.[11] In 1552, 13 people were assessed for tax of £10 or more, with the list headed by Edward Ferrers, the tenant at Moorbarns and possibly Lodge mill (£33); Margaret Paver, a widow (£30); John Kirby, a wool buyer (£22); and William Peak (£22).[12] By the end of the 16th century, the owner of the hospital site (Thomas Forren) and the occupier of Moorbarns (John Temple) were both resident in Lutterworth. Forren was a large-scale pastoral farmer in Northamptonshire and became the main beneficiary of the contentious enclosure of Cotesbach in 1607. Temple had substantial landholdings in Buckinghamshire and Warwickshire.[13] In addition to the Spital mill and land, Forren also held the common bakehouse, the drapery, the shambles and a lease over the 'bailiwick' (which appears to have stretched no further than Lutterworth itself), including the tolls of the markets and fairs, giving him substantial influence within the town.[14]

The Feildings were the most prominent and influential of these people, through the land and properties they owned; their contacts beyond the town; and their positions as feoffees, first to the town guild, then in due course to the Town Estate. From 1629 they were also lords of the manor.[15] Everard Feilding was one of the 12 feoffees appointed by Edmund Muryell, who established the guild in 1478 through its first gift of property. The 12 feoffees of the guild in 1517 included Basil Feilding and Everard Feilding, possibly the son and brother of the then head of the family, Sir William Feilding (d. 1547).[16] The feoffees of the Town Estate in 1571 included Everard Feilding and Basil Feilding (the latter almost certainly William's son, d. 1585).[17] There are suggestions of tensions in the town in 1520. John Paybody left money for the highways and pavements of the town, if this could be paid 'w[i]t[h]owt stryff'.[18] The friction may have related to the degree of control exercised by the Feildings. Sir William Feilding's will set out in 1540 that there should be two keys to the box containing the town's money, and if his heirs had any concerns the box was to be kept at 'Monks Kirby' (the Feilding family home at Newnham Paddox, in Monks Kirby parish, Warws.).[19] The Feildings may have been instrumental in ensuring that some assets moved seamlessly from the town guild to the Town Estate, a move that provided ongoing benefits to residents over subsequent centuries.[20]

A few individual residents purchased Crown leases of their houses and open-field lands during Elizabeth's reign, and others became freeholders as part of the purchase of the manor by Basil Feilding in 1629.[21] They may have served in local office and acquired the confidence to defend the value of their investment. In 1627 the townspeople

11   Above, Economic Hist. (Trades and Services).
12   TNA, E 179/134/176, m. 2; Goodacre, *Transformation*, 151.
13   Goodacre, *Transformation*, 105; L.A. Parker, 'The agrarian revolution at Cotesbach, 1501–1612' *Trans. LAHS* 24 (1948), 41, 50, 57–76; E.F. Gay, 'The Temples of Stowe and their debts: Sir Thomas Temple and Sir Peter Temple, 1603–1653', *Huntington Libr. Quarterly* 2 (1939), 422–3.
14   TNA, PROB 11/122/523; LR 2/255, f. 161.
15   Above, Landownership (Lutterworth Manor from 1628).
16   Warws. RO, CR 2017/D199.
17   *Rpt of Charity Commissioners* (Parl. Papers 1839 [163], xv), p. 129.
18   ROLLR, Will register 1515–26, f. 374–374v.
19   TNA, PROB 11/31/690.
20   Below, Local Government (Town Government).
21   TNA, LR 2/255; above, Landownership (Lutterworth Manor from 1628).

successfully petitioned for a full examination by the Lord Chief Justice of why Sir Thomas Temple paid no rates for Moorbarns.[22] An agreement was reached that the Temples, or their tenants, should pay one quarter of the total amount paid by the resident ratepayers in the parish.[23] When corn was in short supply in 1630, it appears to have been the pressure of local opinion that resulted in Sir Thomas Temple ploughing part of Moorbarns.[24] By 1673, the town had also obtained annual payments towards poor relief from the owners of land in neighbouring depopulated parishes: £2 14s. from Misterton and Poultney, £2 10s. from Cotesbach, £2 from Westrill and Starmore, £1 10s. from Bittesby and £1 from Cotes de Val.[25]

There would have been tensions in the town during the Civil War. William Feilding, 1st earl of Denbigh, was a Royalist who died in April 1643 from injuries sustained supporting Prince Rupert's assault on Birmingham.[26] His son and heir, Basil, fought for Parliament, and was nominated commander-in-chief of the associated counties of Warwickshire, Staffordshire, Shropshire and Worcestershire in June 1643.[27] Lutterworth's churchwardens gave £2 to 'Prince Rupert's trumpeters' in 1643, perhaps when the king's army moved from Daventry to Ashby in July, probably passing along Watling Street.[28] In 1658 the constables paid 8s. for 'Ribben which was given to those w[hi]ch proclaimed the Lord Richard protector'.[29]

The growth of Lutterworth's population between c.1570 and 1670, partly following migration from neighbouring parishes that were being enclosed, would have had a major impact on the town. It is difficult to assess the degree of poverty in Lutterworth, but the occupiers of 33 of the 117 homes identified in 1607 (28 per cent) had no rights in the open fields. A further seven households could graze only one beast, and 44 households could graze one cow and one horse (total 44 per cent of households). Some of these households may have been headed by skilled craftsmen with no need for land, but potentially almost three-quarters of the population may have lived at no more than a bare subsistence level.[30] In 1670 the occupiers of 83 of Lutterworth's 225 houses (37 per cent) were too poor to pay the hearth tax.[31] The median number of hearths in 1664 was just two, but 29 people had four or more hearths (including the inns).[32] The main beneficiaries of population growth were the bakers and innkeepers, as the needs of the

22 E.F. Gay, 'The rise of an English country family: Peter and John Temple, to 1603', *Huntington Libr. Quarterly* 1.4 (1938), 377; Gay, 'The Temples', 430.

23 ROLLR, DE 2559/18, f. 46v; QS 6/1/2/1, f. 157r; Goodacre, *Transformation*, 70.

24 W.G. Hoskins, 'Harvest fluctuations and English economic history, 1620–1759', *Agricultural Hist. Review* 16 (1968), 20; TNA, E 134/12Chas1/East24; Goodacre, *Transformation*, 113; Gay, 'The Temples', 412–16; R. O'Day, *An Elite Family in Early Modern England: The Temples of Stowe and Burton Dassett, 1570–1656* (Woodbridge, 2018), 381–94.

25 ROLLR, DE 2559/35; DE 2559/99; Goodacre, *Transformation*, 70.

26 *ODNB*, s.v. Feilding, William, first earl of Denbigh (c.1587–1643), naval officer and courtier, accessed 7 Dec. 2018.

27 *ODNB*, s.v. Feilding, Basil, second earl of Denbigh (c.1608–1675), parliamentarian army officer and politician, accessed 7 Dec. 2018.

28 ROLLR, DE 2559/18.

29 ROLLR, DE 2559/24.

30 TNA, LR 2/255.

31 TNA, E 179/240/279; *VCH Leics.* III, 172.

32 TNA, E 179/251/4, pt 7, f. 180.

larger population exceeded the manor's capacity to mill corn and bake bread, and it is notable that a baker held the first lease that followed the pioneer crops on Moorbarns in 1634, after the land was ploughed.[33]

By the end of the 17th century, a wide range of goods was available in Lutterworth's shops, including many originating in continental Europe and beyond. The arrival of regular coach services from the 1780s increased the attractiveness of Lutterworth. The town's social life included horse races, balls, assemblies and musical entertainment. Private schools provided lessons in both commercial and cultural subjects, including accounting, music and languages. Lutterworth's charity schools ensured that potential servants or apprentices received a basic education, and the lack of alternative factory work would have kept their wages low. By 1846, the town contained three lawyers, five medical practitioners (including two with an MD qualification), and one commercial and one savings bank.[34] By the late 19th and early 20th centuries, town meetings that had once been chaired by the earls of Denbigh or the rectors were led by resident professional men such as Lupton Topham Topham and Marston Buszard, both barristers.[35] Topham lived at Lutterworth House between 1902 and 1920, and also owned Middleham House, Middleham (Yorks. N.R.).[36] Buszard (d. 1921), a QC/KC and MP for Stamford (Lincs.) from 1880 to 1885, was the grandson of the Lutterworth banker Marston Buszard (d. 1824) and the son of the physician Marston Buszard (d. 1879).[37] Yet the town centre remained small, with Woodmarket, for example, containing both spacious homes in large plots and small cottages occupied, in 1851 for example, by agricultural labourers and framework knitters.[38]

From the mid 19th century, Lutterworth had a strong 'middle-class' character, through the strength of its retail and service businesses, and residents fought in the 1870s for a separate grammar school. The factories of the early 20th century brought large-scale employment but did not change the character of the town, as the factory owners and managers were generally residents, while the working classes were mostly housed at a distance from the historic core. A greater change was seen from the 1970s, as Lutterworth became a dormitory town to other centres, including Coventry and Rugby, following the closure of local manufacturing businesses and the loss of the district council offices to Market Harborough, and it lost some of its distinctiveness.

33   Above, Economic Hist. (Mills; Agriculture).
34   White, *Hist.* (Sheffield, 1846), 404, 408, 410.
35   *Leic. Jnl*, 25 Jan. 1861 (earl, railway); Lutterworth Museum, Resolutions of Meeting held in 1835 (rector, town hall); *Northampton Merc.*, 8 Jan. 1881 (Buszard, opening of grammar school); *Leic. Chron.*, 13 Sept. 1890 (Buszard, railway); *Leic. Daily Post*, 18 Sept. 1920 (Topham, war memorial).
36   *Rugby Advertiser*, 10 Feb. 1928; *Melton Mowbray Merc.*, 28 Feb. 1907; *VCH Yorks. N.R.*, I, 251.
37   *Northampton Merc.*, 16 Sept. 1921; *Derbyshire Advertiser*, 2 Apr. 1909; TNA, PROB 11/1692/408; ROLLR, DE 2094/3, 2094/4, 2094/12.
38   TNA, HO 107/2078/329/6.

Communal Life

Friendly Societies

The Lutterworth Tradesmen's Original Benefits Society was founded in 1747, and provided medical care and sickness benefits to members.[39] It was dissolved in 1872.[40] A female friendly society was registered in 1836.[41] By 1873, there were at least six friendly societies, including the Earl of Denbigh Lodge (Manchester Unity), with 207 members and funds of £3,285; a branch of the Nottingham Ancient Odd Fellows, with 24 members; a 'Wickliffe' lodge of the Nottingham Albion Odd Fellows, with 52 members; an unaffiliated friendly society with 56 members; and an enrolled club.[42] There were 12 friendly societies or sick and benefit clubs in the town in 1937.[43]

Social Activities of the Churches

In addition to the football teams mentioned below, the Congregational church had a cycling club in 1910. A social club open to 'all young men of the town connected to the Free Churches' was established by the Congregational church in 1921, and met in the schoolroom of the Wesleyan church. It outgrew the premises and an adjacent 'semi-ecclesiastical structure' was built in 1925 comprising a large room for billiards and a smaller room for quiet games or reading.[44] The parish church formed a young men's club in 1929; it had a youth club by 1955, and the Methodist church had its own youth club in the 1960s and 1970s.[45] The former mechanics' institute was purchased by St Mary's church in 2007. Renamed the Churchgate Centre, it was used by church and wider community groups.[46] A food bank was run from there by the parish church in 2019.[47]

Libraries and Museum

A subscription library provided by stationer and bookseller John Bottrill contained over 3,000 volumes in 1808.[48] It continued until the death of John's grandson Frederick Bottrill in 1914.[49] Henry Ryder, Lutterworth's rector, provided books for a parish library in 1809,

39   ROLLR, DE 66, Box 2217.
40   *Rpt of Registrar of Friendly Societies, 1872* (Parl. Papers 1873 (323), lxi), p. 62.
41   *Rpt of Chief Registrar of Friendly Societies, 1875* (Parl. Papers 1876 (424), lxix), p. 512.
42   *Rpt of Registrar of Friendly Societies, 1873* (Parl. Papers 1874 (355), lxii), pp. 196–8.
43   *Bottrill's Lutterworth and Dist. Household Almanack and Dir. for 1938* (Lutterworth, 1937), unpaginated.
44   *Rugby Advertiser*, 11 June 1910; 27 Mar. 1925; P. Bruce, R. Gates and B. Gates, *A Brief Hist. of Lutterworth United Reformed Church* (Lutterworth, 1997), 29.
45   *Rugby Advertiser*, 1 Nov. 1929; 16 Sept. 1955; *Coventry Eve. Telegraph*, 28 Dec. 1973.
46   Ex inf. Phillip Jones, member of St Mary's congregation, 2012.
47   https://lutterworthchurch.org/wp-content/uploads/2018/02/Lutterworth-Cotesbach-Bitteswell-Curacy-Profile-2018.pdf (accessed 8 Dec. 2020).
48   *Coventry Herald*, 15 July 1808.
49   *Rugby Advertiser*, 7 Mar. 1914.

Figure 13 *Mechanics' institute and reading room, built in 1876.*

with a small endowment for repairs and purchases.[50] It contained 290 volumes in 1846.[51] The Independent chapel had its own library in the late 19th century.[52] The mechanics' institute, founded in 1841, also established a library with 600 volumes in 1846.[53] It was open each evening and on Thursday afternoons.[54] It moved into a new building erected by the Town Estate in 1876, adjacent to the churchyard gates (Figure 13).[55] The county council opened a library on High Street in 1950.[56] It moved to larger premises on Coventry Road in 1968[57] and to George Street *c.*2009, and continued to be run by the county council in 2021.

Members of Lutterworth Historical Society started collecting items for a museum in the early 1950s.[58] A steering committee was formed in 1989, with support from the town council and the Town Estate, and Lutterworth Museum opened in the mechanics' institute on Church Gate in 1991.[59] It moved to Wycliffe House on Gilmorton Road in 2003,[60] and to new premises in the town centre in 2021.

50   *Rpt of Charity Commissioners*, p. 139.
51   White, *Hist.* (Sheffield, 1846), 405.
52   Bruce, Gates and Gates, *Brief Hist.*, 13.
53   White, *Hist.* (Sheffield, 1846), 405.
54   White, *Hist.* (Sheffield, 1863), 757.
55   A.H. Dyson, *Lutterworth: The Story of John Wycliffe's Town* (London, 1913), 177; *Leic. Chron.*, 29 Jan. 1876; J. Sumpter, *A Brief Historical Review of the Charity known as the Lutterworth Town Estate Trust* (Lutterworth, *c.* 1926), 4.
56   *Rugby Advertiser*, 21 Jan. 1955.
57   *Coventry Eve. Telegraph*, 12 Feb. 1968.
58   *Coventry Eve. Telegraph*, 6 July 1966; 10 Dec. 1969; *Lutterworth Independent*, May 1984.
59   Lutterworth Museum, typescript history of the museum.
60   *Rugby Observer*, 13 Feb. 2003.

Other Social Activities

The Lutterworth Gooseberry Show Society ran its first show for gooseberry growers in 1811. This remained an annual event until 1939.[61] The Lutterworth Horticultural Society held an annual show from 1861,[62] which continued until at least 1970.[63] Lutterworth Agricultural Society was established in 1890,[64] and held annual shows until at least 1939.[65]

The Wycliff (later Wiclif) Lodge of freemasons was consecrated in 1905.[66] Edward Sherrier Lodge was formed in 1948.[67] The Lutterworth Masonic Association was established in 1962. It purchased the former Ritz cinema, which was converted into a freemasons' hall (for both lodges) and dedicated in 1963.[68] The building was refurbished in 1998, and renamed the Wiclif (later Wycliffe) Rooms.[69] Lutterworth Rotary Club was formed in 1952, and Lutterworth Inner Wheel in 1954.[70] An additional evening group, the Rotary Club of Lutterworth Wycliffe, was formed in 1987, and a connected Inner Wheel group was established in 1988.[71] A Round Table for Lutterworth and district received its charter in 1958.[72] All of these groups continued to meet in 2020. A branch of the British Legion was formed in 1922, and acquired a clubhouse on Leicester Road in 1936.[73] Lutterworth had a branch of the Women's Institute in 1930, and a morning group also started in 1983, which subsequently amalgamated with the Ullesthorpe branch.[74] The closest branch of the Women's Institute in 2021 was at Bitteswell.

There was a Scout troop by 1916; Cubs had formed by 1924, and Rovers by 1927 for older boys.[75] A Beavers group (for six- to eight-year-olds) was started in 1981.[76] Beavers, Cubs and Scouts continued to meet in the town in 2021.[77] Girl Guides and Brownies were meeting by 1927, and Rangers for older girls by 1930.[78] A Rainbows group for girls aged five to seven was formed in the late 1980s.[79]

61 *Northampton Merc.*, 3 Aug. 1811; *Rugby Advertiser*, 1 Aug. 1939; Dyson, *Lutterworth*, 179–81.
62 *Leic. Merc.*, 28 Sept. 1861; *Nuneaton Advertiser*, 27 Aug. 1870.
63 *Coventry Eve. Telegraph*, 1 Aug. 1970.
64 *Wright's Dir.* (1900), 151; *Leic. Chron.*, 12 Sep. 1891.
65 *Market Harborough Advertiser*, 4 Aug. 1939.
66 A. Newman, *A Hist. of the Masonic Province of Leics. and Rutl.* (Leicester, 2010), 30, 72.
67 Newman, *Hist.*, 37, 61, 80.
68 Ibid. 59, 72; *Coventry Eve. Telegraph*, 3 May 1962.
69 Newman, *Hist.*, 59.
70 *Rugby Advertiser*, 10 July 1953; https://www.innerwheel.co.uk/our-districts/district-7.html (accessed 2 May 2019).
71 T. Bailey (ed.), *Rotary in an English Market Town* (Lutterworth, 2012), 2–3, 6–7; https://www.innerwheel.co.uk/our-districts/district-7.html (accessed 2 May 2019).
72 *Coventry Eve. Telegraph*, 21 Sept. 1979.
73 *Rugby Advertiser*, 23 June 1922; 1 Dec. 1922; 25 Dec. 1936.
74 Ex inf. Frances Smith, president, 2011.
75 *Rugby Advertiser*, 26 Aug. 1916; 14 Nov. 1924; *Lutterworth Guardian*, 8 July 1927.
76 Ex inf. Jean Truman, leader of Beavers, 2011.
77 https://www.scouts.org.uk/groups/?loc=lutterworth (accessed 9 July 2021).
78 *Lutterworth Guardian*, 8 July 1927; *Rugby Advertiser*, 6 June 1930.
79 Ex inf. Gemma Hill, member of the first Rainbow group.

Social Venues

Seven innkeepers were each fined 12*d.* for allowing unlawful games to be played in 1562, and a further four men were fined 4*d.* for 'playing at the shovelboard', a forerunner of the board game 'shove ha'penny'. Four innkeepers were amerced for the same offence in 1564, and ten people were fined for playing 'Shovegroat'.[80] Isaac Billington's inn had a room known as the 'Shoveboard chamber' in 1676.[81] Occasional balls were held at the Denbigh Arms and at the Hind in 1770, and monthly assemblies were held at the Denbigh Arms later in that decade.[82] In 1872 the Hind was the chosen venue for the first hunt ball to be held in Lutterworth. It was attended by '120 of the elite of the neighbourhood'. Hunt balls were held in the town hall (which opened in 1836) between 1873 and 1890.[83]

The 8th earl of Denbigh encouraged the opening of the People's Club on Coventry Road in 1885, where working men could read newspapers and books, play games, enjoy public entertainments or (from 1889) take a hot or cold bath. It had closed by 1897.[84] The Ex-Service and Working Men's Club and Institute opened on Leicester Road in 1923, with a bowling green, tennis courts, a skittle alley and quoits pitches from 1924.[85] A building on Swiftway, owned by Lutterworth Rural District Council, was let as a sports and social centre in 1952. A boys' club opened in Regent Street in the 1950s and moved to the Swiftway premises *c.*1964, offering snooker, table tennis, darts and a gym.[86] Membership was opened to girls from 1979, and discos were held there.[87] The premises were rebuilt in 1982 to provide a sports hall, meeting rooms and kitchen for the whole community, and became known as Swiftway Community Centre.[88] The site was marketed in 2019 with outline planning for the demolition of the centre and the construction of ten flats.[89]

Entertainment

Horse-racing meetings took place on many occasions in the early 18th century with substantial cash prizes, including a plate of £10 value 'the day after the great Plate' in 1704, and a gold tumbler worth 40 guineas in 1722.[90] Races for £50 were held on two days in 1770, with a ball at the end of each day, held at the Denbigh Arms and the Hind.[91] A Lutterworth steeplechase of four races around the Coventry Road cricket and recreation ground took place in 1867, and there were pony and Galloway races at the same location in 1899.[92]

80   TNA, SC 2/183/83; SC 2/183/84; B. Waddell, 'Governing England through the manor courts, 1550–1850', *Historical Jnl* 55 (2012), 287.
81   ROLLR, PR/I/78/121.
82   *Northampton Merc.*, 17 Sept. 1770; 13 July 1772; 19 July 1773; 25 July 1774.
83   *Nuneaton Advertiser*, 17 Feb. 1872; 31 Jan. 1874; *Morning Post*, 8 Feb. 1873; *Leic. Chron.*, 23 Feb. 1889.
84   *Leic. Chron.*, 17 Oct. 1885; 2 Mar. 1889; *Rugby Advertiser*, 22 Jan. 1910.
85   *Lutterworth Guardian*, 12 Oct. 1923; 13 June 1924.
86   *Rugby Advertiser*, 25 Jan. 1952; *Coventry Eve. Telegraph*, 19 July 1975; Memories of P. Wetton in T. Hirons and J. Woodford (eds), *Lutterworth Memories 1950–1980* (Lutterworth, 2021), 75–7.
87   *Coventry Eve. Telegraph*, 29 Nov. 1975; 24 Oct. 1977; 4 July 1979; 26 Oct. 1979.
88   *Leics. Merc.*, 19 May 1981; *Lutterworth Independent*, Dec. 1982.
89   Agent's details, Wells McFarlane.
90   *London Gaz.*, 31 Aug. 1704; *Stamford Merc.*, 9 Aug. 1722.
91   *Northampton Merc.*, 17 Sept. 1770.
92   *Leic. Chron.*, 2 Mar. 1867; 26 Aug. 1899.

The earliest reference to an annual feast week is from 1839, when those attending this August event were joined by 800 men employed by Midland Counties Railway, who were laying the track between Ullesthorpe and Rugby.[93] The week included a funfair, cricket matches, visiting attractions such as Wombwell's menagerie and (from 1861) the Horticultural Society show.[94] The September hiring fair was largely a pleasure fair by 1869, with swings, roundabouts and shooting galleries alongside its traditional function. Hirings had 'almost died out' by 1899, and this fair merged into the August fair in the early 20th century.[95] Tractor-drawn floats appeared in the 1950s,[96] but interest dwindled. In an attempt to revive the event in the 1970s, it was moved to June and renamed 'Carnival Week'. An estimated 4,000 people attended in 1976. The event reverted to August in 1986.[97]

Vocal and instrumental performers from Worcestershire, Staffordshire, Oxfordshire and Leicester presented a programme of music in St Mary's church in 1778, followed by a ball at the Greyhound.[98] Lutterworth Choral Society was established in 1876, and was re-established as the Orchestral and Choral Society in 1897.[99] This had become Lutterworth Musical Society by 1925, and reformed after the Second World War as Lutterworth Choral Society. Renamed Lutterworth and District Choral Society, it had 70 members in 2018.[100] Lutterworth Opera Group was formed in 1968 to perform classical operas and Gilbert and Sullivan operettas.[101] Lutterworth had a brass band in 1860.[102] A drum and fife band was formed in 1893.[103] Lutterworth town band was formed c.1890 (Figure 14).[104] It had frequent engagements until the 1930s, and reformed after the Second World War.[105] The band later folded, but was reformed in 1982, and played at events across Leicestershire in 2019.[106]

An inn on Beast Market in 1773 (probably the Greyhound) had a room that had 'often been used for a Play-House and Dressing-Room', suggesting occasional theatrical performances.[107] Payne's Theatre Royal visited in 1866 and 1868, with their travelling premises erected in a field adjoining Leicester Road.[108] They returned in 1915, erecting their portable theatre adjacent to Rugby Road, where they held a special performance for the wounded soldiers in the Voluntary Aid Detachment hospital at Ullesthorpe.[109]

93 *Northampton Merc.*, 17 Aug. 1839; 14 Aug. 1839.
94 *Northampton Merc.*, 27 Aug. 1864.
95 *Leic. Chron.*, 18 Sept. 1869; 14 Oct. 1899; *Rugby Advertiser*, 26 Aug. 1938.
96 *Rugby Advertiser*, 27 Aug. 1954.
97 *Leic. Merc.*, 27 Oct. 1975; 18 Nov. 1975; 13 Feb. 1976; 2 July 1976; 4 June 1986.
98 *Northampton Merc.*, 18 May 1778.
99 *Leic. Chron.* 19 Feb. 1876; 1 Feb. 1913.
100 *Rugby Advertiser*, 24 Apr. 1925; 11 Jan. 1946; 25 Dec. 1959; *Coventry Eve. Telegraph*, 15 Apr. 1971; http://www.lutterworthchoral.co.uk/page11.html (accessed 6 May 2019).
101 http://www.lutterworthchoral.co.uk/page4.html (accessed 6 May 2019); Memories of T. Hirons in Hirons and Woodford (eds), *Lutterworth Memories*, 83–4.
102 *Rugby Advertiser*, 19 May 1860.
103 *Nuneaton Advertiser*, 8 Apr. 1893; 29 Dec. 1894.
104 *Rugby Advertiser*, 1 June 1901; *Leic. Daily Post*, 22 Aug. 1906.
105 *Rugby Advertiser*, 10 June 1932; 19 Aug. 1949; 14 Apr. 1950.
106 Ex inf. Simon Maher, band member, 2011; http://www.lutterworthtownband.com (accessed 6 May 2019).
107 *Northampton Merc.*, 2 Aug. 1773.
108 *Rugby Advertiser*, 26 May 1866; *Leic. Chron.*, 30 May 1868.
109 *Rugby Advertiser*, 2 Oct. 1915.

Figure 14 *Lutterworth town band outside the Hind Hotel on High Street, c.1890. The shop facing the camera, near the junction with Church Street, was demolished in 1960 to widen the road.*

There was an amateur dramatic society in 1893.[110] Lutterworth and District Drama Group was formed in 1949, changing its name the following year to Wycliffe Drama Group. It staged several performances in 2019 and planned a pantomime for 2021.[111] A Saturday stage school called 'Future Faces' opened in the grammar school in 2000. It became Lutterworth Youth Theatre Academy in 2008, providing classes in acting and musical theatre and running schools' programmes.[112] A school of dance was formed in 1977, and there continued to be a dance school in the town in 2020.[113]

William and Annie Sanger opened a cinema in 1916.[114] Shortly afterwards, Thomas Green converted a former factory on Market Street for use as a theatre and cinema and offered films, music-hall acts, comedy and boxing. It was known as the Empire Picture Cinematograph Hall in 1925.[115] The proprietor was J.F. Horrocks in 1930, when the premises burned down. Horrocks opened another cinema in 1932 in the Old Bank House in Bank Street.[116] Clarence Spencer took over the business in 1934.[117] He built a new cinema in George Street, the Ritz, which opened in 1938 and seated 364 people on two levels, replacing the premises in Bank Street.[118] It closed in 1961 because of falling attendances.[119]

110   *Leic. Chron.*, 6 May 1893.
111   Wycliffe Drama Group Archive, Minutes of Inaugural Meeting of Lutterworth and District Drama Group, 24 Nov. 1949; https://www.wycliffedramagroup.co.uk (accessed 14 Sept. 2021).
112   Interview with Bradley Woodward, principal of Lutterworth Youth Theatre Academy, 17 Nov. 2011.
113   www.warrington-schoolofdance.co.uk (accessed 6 Sept. 2011); http://www.lmsdlutterworth.com (accessed 4 Aug. 2020).
114   *Rugby Advertiser*, 14 Oct. 1916.
115   P. Morgan, *Lutterworth Independent*, Feb. 1978, 6–7; *Rugby Advertiser*, 23 May 1930; 11 Oct. 1935; *Kelly's Dir. of Leics. and Rutl.* (1925), 617.
116   *Rugby Advertiser*, 23 May 1930; 17 July 1931; *Kelly's Dir. of Leics. and Rutl.* (1932), 708.
117   *Era*, 25 July 1934; *Kelly's Dir. of Leics. and Rutl.* (1936), 879.
118   *Rugby Advertiser*, 4 Dec. 1936; 7 Oct. 1938; Lutterworth Museum, Box 77, souvenir programme.
119   *Coventry Eve. Telegraph*, 3 May 1962.

Allotments and Open Spaces

Over 40 a. of land was let as allotments for poor families in 1846.[120] In 1896 the 9th earl of Denbigh offered the field adjoining the grammar school to the parish council for allotments at a fixed rent on a seven-year lease.[121] The offer does not appear to have been accepted, but allotments had been created to the west of Leicester Road (13 a.) and on the north side of Coventry Road (13 a.) by 1901.[122] The Leicester Road allotment land was later developed for housing (Central Avenue), but land was purchased by the RDC in 1946 for further allotments west of Crescent Road (5 a.) and south of Council Street (4.7 a.). The council allotments on the north of Coventry Road had become a recreation ground by 1955, and the allotment land near Council Street was developed for housing in the 1980s.[123] The Crescent Road allotments remained in 2019, and new allotments opened that year to the south east of Wood bridge (Coventry Road).[124]

Glebe land on the south side of Coventry Road was partly being used as a cricket field and recreational ground by at least the mid 19th century.[125] The memorial gardens and war memorial at the corner of Church Street and George Street were laid out and opened in 1921.[126] Lutterworth Country Park opened in 2003 on the western edge of the parish.[127]

Sports

A succession of statues from 1363 had required men to practise archery on Sundays,[128] and in 1569 Thomas Saunter accidentally shot and killed 13-year-old John Saunter, possibly his son, with an arrow.[129] Concentric circles are marked on the enclosure map in the south-west corner of an unnamed field on the western side of Bitteswell Road, near the parish boundary, and this would have been an appropriate site for archery butts.[130]

The Denbigh Arms had a bowling green by at least 1726.[131] Lutterworth Bowling Club was formed in 1936, and played on a green at the Coventry Road recreation ground.[132] The green was extended in 1971.[133] Women were originally not able to join, and formed their own club in 1972. The two clubs had merged by the end of the 20th century, and continued to play at Coventry Road in 2021.[134] The Follsain Wycliffe Sports and Social

120 White, *Hist.* (Sheffield 1846), 406.

121 *Leic. Chron.*, 7 Mar. 1896.

122 *Leic. Chron.*, 27 Apr. 1895; OS Map 25", Leics. XLVIII.12 (1904 edn); XLVIII.16 (1904 edn).

123 Lutterworth Museum, Lutterworth RDC, min. 4 July 1946; OS Map 1:2500, SP 5484 (1955, 1972 and 1987 edns).

124 https://www.lutterworth.org.uk/allotments1.html (accessed 19 Oct. 2020).

125 OS Map 25", Leics. XLVIII.16 (1904).

126 *Leic. Chron.*, 28 May 1921.

127 Harborough District Council, Community Forum Lutterworth, min. 7 June 2005.

128 S. Gunn, 'Archery practice in early Tudor England', *Past & Present* 209 (2010), 53.

129 *Cal. Pat.* 1566–9, 415–16.

130 ROLLR, Misc. 239.

131 Warws. RO, CR 2017/D163/1; D170, f. 8; D235.

132 L. Williams, *Hist. of the Wycliffe Bowling Club* (Lutterworth, undated), 10.

133 *Coventry Eve. Telegraph*, 15 Sept. 1971.

134 Ex inf. Peter Jackson, groundsman and member for 40 years, 2011; https://www.facebook.com/LutterworthBowlsClub (accessed 9 July 2021).

Figure 15 *Lutterworth cricket team, 1932. The Lutterworth factory owner George Spencer, the club's president, is in the centre of the front row.*

Club had a team and a green in 1956. The club continued as Wycliffe Bowls Club when the company ceased to trade in 1982, but lost its green. A new green was seeded at Dunley Way in 1986. A ladies' section was formed in 1992. The club moved to Bitteswell in 1993 and continued to play there in 2021.[135]

A Lutterworth team played a team from Ullesthorpe at cricket in 1789.[136] A club began to play regularly on glebe land at Coventry Road from about 1850.[137] The ground was enlarged in 1874, when Lutterworth Cricket Club was one of the strongest clubs in the county.[138] Other cricket clubs in the town in the 1860s and 1870s included Lutterworth Aurora, Lutterworth Morning Star and Lutterworth Tradesmen.[139] The Wycliffe Cricket Club was formed in 1884 'for those who are engaged in business during the day'. The Wycliffe and Lutterworth clubs amalgamated in 1887.[140] In 1937 George Spencer (Figure 15), bought nearly 10 a. of glebe land between the churchyard and Coventry Road, including a field rented to the cricket club, and conveyed the cricket ground to the Town Estate.[141] The following year, two of Spencer's sons, Herbert and

135 Williams, *Hist.*, 34; https://www.hugofox.com/community/wycliffe-bowls-club-15034/home (accessed 9 July 2021).
136 E.E. Snow, *A Hist. of Leicestershire Cricket* (Leicester, 1949), 15.
137 Dyson, *Lutterworth*, 164.
138 *Leic. Chron.*, 16 May 1874; Snow, *Hist.*, 80.
139 *Leic. Chron.*, 22 June 1867; 3 June 1871; *Leic. Jnl*, 9 Apr. 1869.
140 *Leic. Chron.*, 14 June 1884; 8 Jan. 1887.
141 CERC, ECE/7/1/77948; *Leicester Advertiser*, 24 July 1937.

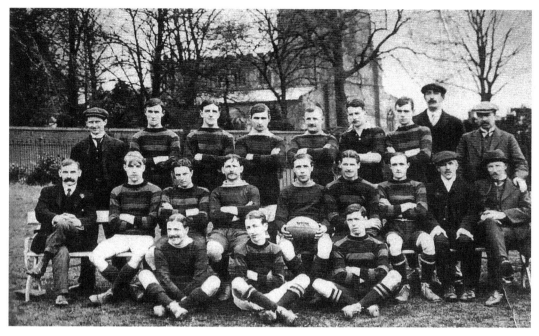

Figure 16 *Lutterworth Rugby Football Team, c.1905, on the old Coventry Road recreation ground, behind (south of) the cricket ground.*

George, provided a thatched pavilion.[142] This burned down *c.*1995, and a new pavilion was built.[143] Lutterworth Cricket Club played in the Leicestershire and Rutland Premier League in 2021.[144]

Lutterworth Football Club was formed in 1870 to play rugby football, and is believed to be the first rugby club established in the county outside Leicester (Figure 16).[145] In 1888 it agreed to play all matches under Rugby Union rules.[146] It had a squad of 60 players in 1926, probably assisted by the grammar school switching winter games from association to rugby football in 1923.[147] In 1927 it was said that 'Lutterworth prides itself in being a thorough Rugger town', but the club struggled to find players in the 1930s.[148] The club was revived after the Second World War, and moved to a new ground in Bitteswell *c.*1972, where it continued to play in 2021, with sections for men, women, boys and girls (from the age of five).[149]

142 *Rugby Advertiser*, 15 Feb. 1938; photograph in Lutterworth Museum.
143 G. Smith, *Around Lutterworth* (Stroud, 2005), 88; G. Smith, *Around Lutterworth, Second Selection* (Stroud, 2002), 78.
144 https://lutterworth.play-cricket.com (accessed 14 Sept. 2021).
145 *Leic. Jnl*, 23 Dec. 1870; 26 Jan. 1872; *VCH Leics*. III, 286.
146 *Leic. Chron.*, 15 Sept. 1888.
147 G. Irving, *Lutterworth Grammar School, Anniversary Book 1956, Centenary Revision* (Lutterworth, 1980), 49–50.
148 *Rugby Advertiser*, 16 Sept. 1927; 1 Sept. 1931.
149 Ex inf. Colin Hudson, secretary, Lutterworth Rugby Football Club, 2011; https://www.facebook.com/LuttsRFC; https://www.pitchero.com/clubs/lutterworthrfc/teams#m (accessed 9 July 2021).

Wycliffe Association Football Club was formed *c.*1895, apparently by the rector and curate of the parish church.[150] Lutterworth Town Football Club was formed in the 1920s, but was 'defunct, or moribund at best' in 1927. The churches rallied round in 1930, when the Lutterworth and district league included teams from St Mary's, the Congregational and Wesleyan churches. Lutterworth United, largely comprising the former St Mary's players, formed in 1931.[151] Lutterworth Town joined the Leicestershire Senior League in 1955.[152] It played on the Coventry Road recreation ground until 1970, when it relocated to a purpose-built ground on Dunley Way, which opened with a match against a Leicester City side before 2,000 spectators. Lutterworth Town moved to a ground in Bitteswell in 1991, returning to Coventry Road in 2011.[153] Lutterworth Juniors and Youth Football Club was formed in 1983, and became Lutterworth Athletic in 1993. Its home ground was at Bitteswell.[154]

Lutterworth Old Girls' Hockey Club was formed in 1922 from former grammar school pupils.[155] The club played at Coventry Road in 1925, when it affiliated to the Leicestershire Women's Hockey Association, and membership was widened in 1932 to include those who had been educated elsewhere. The club was renamed Lutterworth Ladies Hockey Club in 1973. In 1991 Leicestershire league rule changes meant that the game had to be played on a synthetic surface, so training and home matches were moved to a pitch at Guthlaxton College, South Wigston. The club returned to Lutterworth in 2001, to a synthetic pitch at the grammar school.[156]

The golf club dates from 1904, when *c.*40 a. were leased in the south of the parish. A new nine-hole course was constructed in 1916. The club owned 74 a. in 1969, when the membership stood at 475. The course was increased to 15 holes in 1979 and to 18 holes in 1987. It was redesigned in 1994, when the town's southern bypass was built.[157] The clubhouse burned down in 2021, but is to be rebuilt.[158] Lutterworth had a tennis club by 1910, which played at Coventry Road.[159] The club reformed in 1944, with a junior section from 1954.[160] It moved to Bitteswell in 1997.[161]

The 8th earl of Denbigh gave a piece of ground next to the river for a bathing place, which opened in 1874, replacing a smaller facility. A subscription raised £64 to cover the cost of the work and to provide sheds for changing.[162] In the 1960s, the public raised £12,000 towards the cost of a swimming pool. Leicestershire Education Authority

150 *Rugby Advertiser*, 22 Sept. 1894; *Nuneaton Advertiser*, 19 Oct. 1895.
151 *Rugby Advertiser*, 16 Sept. 1927; 7 Oct. 1927; 25 Sept. 1931.
152 Football Club Hist. Database, http://www.fchd.info/LUTTERWT.HTM (accessed 9 May 2019).
153 *Coventry Eve. Telegraph*, 29 Apr. 1970; 6 Aug. 1971; Ex inf. Peter Knight, committee member, Lutterworth Town AFC, 2011.
154 https://www.lutterworthathleticfc.com; https://www.lutterworthathleticfc.com/lutterworth-athletic-fc-about-us/lutterworth-athletic-history (accessed 4 May 2020).
155 Irving, *Lutterworth Grammar*, 49.
156 Ex inf. Jeanne Lewis, president, Lutterworth Ladies Hockey Club, 2011.
157 G. Reeve, *Lutterworth Golf Club Centenary Book, 1904–2004* (Lutterworth, undated).
158 *Harborough Mail*, 24 June 2021.
159 *Leic. Daily Post*, 27 May 1910.
160 H. Mainwaring and others, *Lutterworth Tennis Club: in Celebration of the Golden Jubilee 1993* (Lutterworth, 1993), not paginated.
161 Ex inf. Elvin Haigh, secretary, Lutterworth Tennis Club, 2011.
162 *Leic. Chron.*, 16 May 1874; *Rugby Advertiser*, 24 Apr. 1875.

offered a site at the grammar school, and agreed to contribute £15,000 towards the construction if the RDC agreed to cover running costs when it was open to the public. The pool opened in 1966.[163] A swimming club had been formed by 1968, and a sub-aqua club was founded in 1979.[164] A sports centre opened on the north side of Coventry Road in 2004, with a swimming pool, gym and sports hall, and the pool at the grammar school was demolished.[165]

Education

Sunday Schools

Anglican Sunday schools for boys and girls were opened in 1789.[166] They were attended by 90 boys and 120 girls in 1818.[167] The Congregational church had a Sunday school from 1807,[168] which had an average attendance of 111 in 1851.[169] There was also a Wesleyan Sunday school in 1851, attended by 25 people.[170]

Day Schools before 1870

The 'Church-gates' School

A 'scolehouse' stood in the corner of Bakehouse Lane in 1509, near the churchyard gate.[171] It may have been associated with the chantry established by Edmund Muryell in 1478.[172] Some of the schoolmasters in the 17th century were graduates, including John Newbolt (licensed 1674) and William Vincent (licensed 1685).[173]

Robert Poole gave the rent from two cottages to this school in 1630 for the education of eight fatherless or poor children born and living in Lutterworth.[174] His son, also Robert, left half a yardland and a small close in Lutterworth in 1699 for an apprenticeship for one boy each year educated through his father's gift.[175] The trustees of Margaret Bent's charity of 1693 provided £4 annually to this school in 1838, to educate another four poor boys.[176] John Durrad bequeathed £20 in 1724 to teach poor children to read, 'as well the children of dissenters as others'.[177] This was paying for another two boys

163 Irving, *Lutterworth Grammar*, 93–4; RDC of Lutterworth, *Handbook*, not paginated.

164 *Coventry Eve. Telegraph*, 25 Mar. 1968; http://www.lsac.co.uk/history.php (accessed 13 Aug. 2011).

165 https://sports-facilities.co.uk/sites/view/1002948 (accessed 21 Jan. 2021); Memories of J. Grey in T. Hirons and J. Woodford (eds), *Lutterworth Memories, 1950–1980* (Lutterworth, 2021), 22.

166 *Northampton Merc.*, 25 July 1789.

167 *Digest of Parochial Returns to Select Committee on Educ. of the Poor* (Parl. Papers 1819 (224), ix), p. 462.

168 Bruce, Gates and Gates, *Brief Hist.*, 10.

169 TNA, HO 129/408/28.

170 TNA, HO 129/408/27.

171 Warws. RO, CR 2017/E42, f. 1.

172 Warws. RO, CR 2017/D199.

173 ROLLR, 1D 41/34/2/206 (Newbolt); 1D 41/34/3/8 (Vincent).

174 *Rpt of Charity Commissioners*, pp. 133–5.

175 ROLLR, Wills, 1699, f. 70; *Rpt of Charity Commissioners*, p. 135.

176 *Rpt of Charity Commissioners*, pp. 135, 139–40.

177 TNA, PROB 11/613/144; *Rpt of Charity Commissioners*, p. 135.

in 1838, when there were also *c.*26 paying pupils. All the charity boys were learning to read, and nine of them were also learning writing and 'accounts'.[178]

The schoolhouse was taken down in 1781 and a new building, with schoolroom and master's residence, was erected on the same site by the townmasters. The cost, almost £58, was more than covered by donations and the sale of materials from the old school.[179] The contributions suggest a desire among some for the school to continue, probably to provide an alternative to the Anglican ethos of the Sherrier school, which had opened in 1733. There were only ten pupils at the 'church-gates' school in 1833, and it closed in 1834.[180] It had reopened by 1839, when 40 boys attended, including those educated through the Poole, Bent and Durrad charities.[181]

The Sherrier School

In his will of 1731, the Revd Edward Sherrier of Shawell (3 miles south of Lutterworth) bequeathed the interest on £200 to pay for the education of five boys at Lutterworth until the deaths of his widow and daughter. After their deaths, his land and property were to be conveyed to trustees, with £200 and the interest and profits on the remainder used to buy land in Lutterworth to build a new school, schoolmaster's house and almshouse, and to provide a salary for a schoolmaster. The trustees were always to include the rector of Lutterworth, the vicar of Shawell and five other Anglican clergy.[182] Sherrier's widow and daughter had both died by 1732. A house on George Street with a garden and yard was purchased for a schoolmaster, and the Town Estate agreed that a building could be erected on their adjacent land, with an almshouse for two people on the ground floor, and a schoolroom above for up to 90 children.[183] The school opened in 1733, and Charles Powel, 'late Master of the publick School of Daventry', was appointed master.[184] Only 20 boys attended in 1818.[185] The school became affiliated to the National Society in 1820 at the request of the rector, the Revd Robert Johnson, and the school's governors and trustees. The boys were taught the Anglican catechism and attended worship in the parish church on Sundays.[186] In 1834 the school was attended by 80 or 90 boys, 'a great part of them of the lowest class'.[187]

The Newton Bequest

Alderman Gabriel Newton of Leicester conveyed land to the corporation of Leicester in 1760, with the income to be used for the religious education of the children of the poor, and schools were established in nine towns in six counties. Newton made a further bequest in his will, but this was challenged after his death in 1762 by his heir-at-law.

178 *Rpt of Charity Commissioners*, p. 135.
179 ROLLR, DE 914/1; *Rpt of Charity Commissioners*, p. 133.
180 *Abstract of Education Returns* (Parl. Papers 1835 (62), xlii), p. 20; G.A. Chinnery (ed.), *Records of the Borough of Leicester*, V (Leicester, 1965), 509–11.
181 *Rpt of Charity Commissioners*, p. 135.
182 ROLLR, DE 126/1/3/2.
183 *Rpt of Charity Commissioners*, pp. 135–8; ROLLR, DE 126/1/39.
184 *St James's Eve. Post*, 1 Mar. 1733.
185 *Digest of Parochial Returns*, p. 462.
186 CERC, NS/7/1/8135.
187 Chinnery (ed.), *Records*, V, 371, 378.

The heir's claim became time barred in 1808, when the corporation reviewed the funds available and offered payment to further towns, subject to the conditions specified by Newton.[188] The rector and churchwardens of Lutterworth were offered £26 to teach and clothe 25 poor boys, and the conditions were accepted in 1813.[189]

The rector and churchwardens directed the payments to the 'church-gates' school until that school closed in 1834, when the funding was redirected to the Sherrier school. Representatives from Leicester Corporation visited Lutterworth in 1834 and found that the 25 Alderman Newton boys had been chosen from the boys already attending the school, and were said to have been given the green coat, waistcoat and hat that the Newton charity provided, although no more than 12 boys were wearing these. The corporation cancelled the annual payment in 1835, because the conditions for the payment, including the provision of additional places, were not being met.[190]

Bishop Ryder's School

The Revd Henry Ryder, Lutterworth's rector from 1801 to 1815, converted one of a pair of adjoining houses on Coventry Road into a school for up to 30 girls from poor families who already attended Sunday school, and made the second house available for a schoolmistress. The girls were taught reading, writing, arithmetic, needlework and other work 'suitable to their station'.[191] When Ryder left Lutterworth in 1815 on his appointment as bishop of Gloucester, he conveyed these two properties and a neighbouring house to trustees, with the income from the third property to be used to cover all the costs relating to the school, which became known as Bishop Ryder's school.[192] There were 35 pupils in 1818.[193] The school building reverted to residential use *c*.1833 when a larger 'Bishop Ryder' school was built on the opposite side of Coventry Road, on land given by the earl of Denbigh.[194] The cost of the new building was covered by donations.[195]

Other Schools

Private schools could be short-lived, but in the 19th and early 20th century they played an important role in educating a rising middle class. The masters of the 'church-gates' school and the Sherrier school offered advanced tuition for paying pupils, including older boys.[196] Mr J. Guy's 'School for Young Gentlemen' opened in 1836, and was 'Chiefly for Boarders above Eleven Years of Age', who were taught subjects 'indispensable to trade

188 R.W. Greaves, 'The origins and early history of Alderman Newton's foundation', *Trans. LAHS* 19 (1936–7), 359–61, 366, 369–70.

189 Chinnery (ed.), *Records*, V, 371, 378; *Rpt of Charity Commissioners*, pp. 9–17.

190 Chinnery (ed.), *Records*, V, 509–11; *Rpt of Charity Commissioners*, p. 135.

191 *Leic. Chron.*, 8 Sept. 1855; *Rpt of Charity Commissioners*, p. 138.

192 *Rpt of Charity Commissioners*, p. 138; *ODNB*, s.v. Ryder, Henry (1777–1836), bishop of Lichfield and Coventry, accessed 11 May 2019.

193 *Digest of Parochial Returns*, p. 462.

194 *Abstract of Education Returns*, pp. 19–20; *Rpt of Charity Commissioners*, pp. 138–9; *Leic. Chron.*, 11 Dec. 1875.

195 *Abstract of Education Returns*, p. 19.

196 *St James's Eve. Post*, 1 Mar. 1733; *Leic. Chron.*, 6 Nov. 1847; ROLLR, 1D 41/34/5/251; Z. Crook and B. Simon, 'Private schools in Leicester and the county, 1780–1840', 116, and B. Simon, 'Local grammar schools, 1780–1880', in B. Simon (ed.), *Education in Leicestershire, 1540–1940* (Leicester, 1968).

and business'.[197] Private schools for girls were run by Martha Hand in 1822, Mrs Cherry in 1824, Ann Lord in 1841, Elizabeth Bottrill in 1851, the Misses Bailey in 1861, Letitia Everton in 1870 and Miss Higgs, also in 1870.[198]

Day Schools from 1870

Elementary Schools, 1870–1945

The Education Act of 1870 required sufficient school places to be provided for every child aged between 5 and 13 in schools which met certain criteria. The Sherrier trustees in particular were keen to see that all the town's schools complied, to prevent the imposition of a ratepayer-funded board school that would weaken the Anglican influence within the town. Four things needed to change: places for infants needed to be provided; more places were needed for girls; new admissions policies had to be introduced that did not require prior attendance at a Sunday school; and the headteachers had to be certificated through examination and a period of probation. Additionally, the 'church-gates' school resembled a 'wretchedly dilapidated cottage' that required renovation.[199] The endowments of the 'church-gates' and Ryder schools were too small to effect most of the changes required, but they were funded by separate charities, so any rationalisation or reorganisation required the involvement of the Commissioners for Endowed Schools appointed under the Endowed Schools Act of 1869.[200] Meanwhile, George Binns, the master of Sherrier school, resigned and his son Alfred, who had qualified at Saltley Training College, was appointed in his place,[201] and Harry Ensor, who had recently qualified at Cheltenham Training College, was appointed master of the 'church-gates' school.[202] The two boys' schools merged in 1872, with Alfred Binns as master and Harry Ensor as assistant master.[203] The Sherrier trustees purchased a wooden building from the poor law guardians, originally intended to be a smallpox hospital, and opened it in 1873 as a temporary infants' school.[204]

A draft scheme for further rationalisation and improvement of the schools was drawn up by Lutterworth's rector, the Revd William Wilkinson, and the Revd Edmund Willes of Ashby Magna (a trustee of Sherrier's charity) for discussion between the trustees of all the town's educational charities and those of the Town Estate before the involvement of the commissioners.[205] The rector offered a piece of glebe land which extended from the Sherrier

197 *Northampton Merc.*, 23 Apr. 1836; 17 Mar. 1838.
198 Pigot, *Dir. of Leics.* (1822), 226; *Northampton Merc.*, 26 June 1824; TNA, HO 107/598/14/31; HO 107/2078/376/26; RG 9/2246/56/14; Lutterworth Museum, *Parish Mag.*, Aug. 1870; Nov. 1870.
199 TNA, ED 27/2460.
200 32 & 33 Vic., c. 56.
201 ROLLR, DE 3614/1 (E/MB/B/211/1), mins 8 June 1871, 15 June 1871.
202 ROLLR, DE 3614/1 (E/MB/B/211/1), mins 21 Dec. 1871, 6 June 1872; ROLLR, DE 3614/4 (E/LB/211/1), 24 June 1872.
203 ROLLR, DE 3614/1 (E/MB/B/211/1), mins 21 Dec. 1871, 6 June 1872; ROLLR, DE 3614/4 (E/LB/211/1), min. 24 June 1872.
204 *Leic. Chron.*, 19 June 1873; 27 June 1874; ROLLR, DE 3614/1 (E/MB/B/211/1), mins 1 May, 10 July 1873.
205 ROLLR, DE 3614/1 (E/MB/B/211/1), mins 30 Mar. 1871, 8 June 1871; J.G. Harrod & Co., *Dir. of Derbyshire and Leics.* (1870), 372.

Figure 17 *South elevation of the new Sherrier school of 1876, showing the girls' and infants' schools. The boys'*
school adjoined at right angles to the north east. This image was engraved from the original architect's drawing
by William Bassett Smith, and published by F.W. Bottrill, in 1900.

school (on George Street) to Church Gate, opposite the 'church-gates' school. This provided
the opportunity to erect a single large building for boys, girls and infants.[206] The Town Estate
trustees and the Sherrier trustees each agreed to provide £250 towards building costs.[207]

The Endowed Schools Commissioners set out their scheme in 1874, which was
accepted. The charities of the elder and younger Pooles, Bent, Durrad, Sherrier and
Ryder would merge, and the Ryder school building and a field belonging to Sherrier
school would be sold. The Sherrier school building would be demolished and a
new school built for boys, girls and infants, including an 'upper' division for older
children. Money held by the charity of Richard Elkington of Shawell would also be put
towards the costs.[208] Elkington had left £50 in 1607 to the corporation of Leicester to
provide five one-year loans of £10 to tradesmen in Lutterworth, on terms that were
no longer attractive.[209] Pupils would pay fees ranging from 2*d.* weekly for the youngest
children up to £3 annually for the upper division. Upper-division boys would learn

206 TNA, ED 27/2460; ROLLR, DE 3614/1 (E/MB/B/211/1), mins 21 Dec. 1871.
207 Sumpter, *Brief Historical Review*, 10; TNA, ED 27/2460.
208 TNA, ED 27/2460. Some documents refer to John Elkington, which was a different charity and not
     involved in the scheme.
209 TNA, ED 27/2460; *Rpt of Charity Commissioners*, pp. 20–3; Chinnery (ed.), *Records*, V, 439.

land surveying, navigation, vocal music and Latin or a modern language, and the upper-division girls would study French, music, domestic economy and needlework. Scholarships would be available at both elementary and upper levels.[210]

William Bassett Smith, a London architect, was engaged to design a building with places for 172 boys (including senior pupils), 117 girls and 140 infants.[211] A tender of £2,057 from Law and King, Lutterworth builders, was accepted for the construction.[212] The boys' school was a one-storey building with an entrance on George Street and a separate playground. An adjoining two-storey block contained the infants' school on the ground floor, with an entrance at the west end of Church Gate, and the girls' school on the first floor, with the entrance in a staircase turret (Figure 17).[213] The school was managed by a board of 12 governors, three appointed by the Sherrier charity trustees, three chosen by the Town Estate committee and six elected by the ratepayers in a vestry meeting.[214]

A weekday school was held in the Catholic church from 1881. It closed c.1895, claiming that 'government exactions became too great'.[215]

Secondary Education, 1875–1945

Some residents wanted the upper-division boys to be taught in a separate school, but this proposal was rejected. The commissioners thought the funds were insufficient, and saw no need, as the town and neighbourhood were 'absolutely diminishing in population', fearing that it might 'engender a class jealousy which happily does not exist' in the town.[216] Despite the commissioners' views, the school governors considered four possible sites for a separate upper school in 1875,[217] and the following year, with the approval of the Charity Commission (which had absorbed the work of the Endowed School Commissioners in 1874), the governors purchased 5 a. on Bitteswell Road from the 8th earl of Denbigh for £1,000.[218] William Bassett Smith was again engaged as the architect, and the building tender of Henry Bland & Sons of Leicester was accepted at £4,349. A substantial part of the cost was met from a gift of £3,851 from the estate of Elizabeth Welch of Bath (Som.).[219] She had left the residue of her estate to her brother James Powell, vicar of Bitteswell, and his daughter Mary, with the sum to be 'given in charity' if Mary died without issue. Mary died unmarried in 1875.[220] The new school was officially part of the Sherrier schools but was known colloquially as Lutterworth

210 TNA, ED 27/2460.
211 ROLLR, DE 3614/1 (E/MB/B/211/1), mins 25 Jan., 14 Mar., 28 Mar., 15 May 1872; ES/MB/211/1, min. 3 Oct. 1874; TNA, ED 27/2460, notes 24 May 1872.
212 ROLLR, DE 3614/1 (ES/MB/211/1), mins 11 Sept. 1874, 16 Apr. 1875.
213 F.W. Bottrill, *An Illustrated Handbook of Lutterworth* (Lutterworth, 1900), 11–12.
214 TNA, ED 27/2460; *Leic. Chron.*, 29 Aug. 1874.
215 *Tablet*, 27 July 1929, 22; P. Harris, *Souvenir of Father John Feeley's Silver Jubilee, 1955–1980, and the Centenary of the Parish of Our Lady of Victories and St. Alphonsus, 1880–1980* (Lutterworth, 1980), 9.
216 TNA, ED 27/2460.
217 ROLLR, ES/MB/211/1, min. 10 Sept. 1875.
218 *Leic. Jnl*, 14 Jan. 1881; TNA, ED 27/2464.
219 ROLLR, DE 126/1/28/1–20; *Leic. Jnl*, 14 Jan. 1881.
220 ROLLR, DE 759/7; DE 462/18, pp. 430–7; DE 126/1/28; Irving, *Lutterworth Grammar*, 21–2.

grammar school.[221] It opened in 1881, with 50 places for boarders and 30 for day boys, who paid annual fees of £31 and £6 respectively.[222]

The building costs exceeded the quotation. With pupil numbers lower than expected, the school was under financial pressure from the outset.[223] It closed in 1894, but reopened in 1898, in the hope that more pupils would enrol when the railway opened.[224] Girls were admitted as day scholars in 1902, but pupil numbers were still too low.[225] A new scheme was passed by the Charity Commissioners in 1910, and the land, buildings and other assets passed to Leicestershire Education Authority. Further land was given to the school in 1925 by George Spencer for a playing field.[226] By 1933, pupil numbers had increased to 124,[227] and a new wing was added to the school in 1937.[228]

A 'central school' for 240 children aged 11 to 14 from Lutterworth, Bitteswell and Misterton opened in 1927 at the end of Woodmarket. It was designed by the county architect Ernest Fowler and built by Peter Rourke. The school offered evening classes to older teenagers and adults in mathematics, technical drawing, woodwork and engineering, and 83 people enrolled for these as soon as it opened.[229] Following an extension, the school had 268 pupils in 1934, drawn from 17 contributory schools.[230]

Schools from 1945

The 1944 Education Act introduced free secondary education, and the central school became a secondary modern school. The grammar school became a voluntary controlled Church of England school in 1948.[231] There was a need to extend the grammar school, and in 1965 the county council bought the neighbouring Auburn Place, George Spencer's former house, with its grounds.[232] Under the 'Leicestershire Plan', which introduced comprehensive education across the county, the secondary modern school became Lutterworth High School in 1967, serving all children aged 11 to 14 from Lutterworth and the surrounding villages.[233] The high school gained academy status in 2011 (funded by central government and independent of local authority control), and in 2012 had 728 pupils from a catchment area including 23 villages across south Leicestershire.[234] The upper age limit was increased to 16 over two years from 2015.[235] From 1967 the grammar school welcomed pupils of all abilities aged 14 and over from Lutterworth and Enderby

221 Irving, *Lutterworth Grammar*, 23–4.
222 *Leic. Jnl*, 14 Jan. 1881.
223 TNA, ED 27/2467; ED 27/2468; Irving, *Lutterworth Grammar*, 27–9; *Nuneaton Advertiser*, 9 Apr. 1887; *Leic. Chron.*, 26 Jan. 1889.
224 TNA, ED 27/2471.
225 *Rugby Advertiser*, 22 Nov. 1902; TNA, ED 109/3388.
226 Irving, *Lutterworth Grammar*, 34, 43.
227 TNA, ED 109/3391.
228 Irving, *Lutterworth Grammar*, 45.
229 TNA, ED 21/33526; *Rugby Advertiser*, 4 Nov. 1927.
230 TNA, ED 21/33526, inspection rpt; K.H. Harris, *The First Fifty Years: A Hist. of Lutterworth High School* (Lutterworth, *c*.1977), 5–6 (copy in Lutterworth Museum).
231 Irving, *Lutterworth Grammar*, 56–7.
232 J.S. Dodge, *By Any Other Name: A Brief Account of Lutterworth Grammar School* (Lutterworth, 2008), 10.
233 Dodge, *By Any Other Name*, 10.
234 https://lutterworthhigh.co.uk (accessed 11 May 2020).
235 Ex inf. Helene Chadwick, Lutterworth High School.

high schools.[236] Pupil numbers had risen from 680 in 1967 to 1,700 by the mid 1980s.[237] The school's name was changed in 2006 to Lutterworth College, and academy status was gained in 2012.[238] Teaching was extended to ages 11 to 19 in 2014, when the Sir Frank Whittle Studio School, specialising in engineering, retail, logistics, hospitality and leisure, opened in a separate building for 300 pupils, in conjunction with business partners.[239] The college had a total of 1,194 pupils in 2017.[240] The studio school closed in 2019, as it was unable to attract enough pupils to be viable.[241]

By 1946 the Sherrier school was too small and in poor condition, but national building restrictions prevented any immediate action.[242] A new infants' school opened in 1954–5 on a site off Bitteswell Road, and was extended in 1972.[243] Temporary classrooms accommodated population expansion until 1969, when Wycliffe County Primary School opened for some infants and juniors on Moorbarns Lane. It was extended in 1999, and changed its name to John Wycliffe Primary School.[244] In 2012 it had 270 pupils on the roll.[245] It converted to academy status in 2017.[246] A new junior school to replace the ageing Sherrier school opened next to the infants' school off Bitteswell Road in 1982, and these two adjacent schools formally amalgamated into a single voluntary controlled Church of England primary school.[247] There were 389 pupils on the roll in 2016.[248]

Social Welfare

Poor Relief

St John's hospital was established *c*.1216 to provide food and accommodation for six poor men and hospitality for poor wayfarers. The hospital's master, William Feyse, stated in 1436 that there had been no brethren there for 50 years,[249] and this is supported by the findings from an excavation of part of the site in 2002, which uncovered 22 skeletons, apparently buried before *c*.1400.[250] Cottages belonging to the hospital, probably on the

236 Dodge, *By Any Other Name*, 11; ex inf. Lutterworth College.
237 Irving, *Lutterworth Grammar*, 95; Dodge, *By Any Other Name*, 11, 13.
238 Ex inf. Lutterworth College.
239 *Leics. Merc.*, 4 Sept. 2013.
240 https://files.ofsted.gov.uk/v1/file/2743303 (accessed 20 Jan. 2022).
241 https://www.leicestermercury.co.uk/news/local-news/parents-told-email-lutterworth-school-2441068 (accessed 11 May 2020).
242 CERC, NS/7/1/8135, letter 24 Aug. 1848.
243 *Leics. Merc.*, 17 May 1955; *Hinckley Times*, 12 Dec. 1980.
244 Ex inf. Eileen Durnin, head of infants 1985–2000.
245 https://files.ofsted.gov.uk/v1/file/2075911 (accessed 20 Jan. 2022).
246 https://www.johnwycliffe.leics.sch.uk (accessed 5 Aug. 2020).
247 *Hinckley Times*, 12 Dec. 1980; CERC, NS/7/1/8135, inspection rpt, 1997.
248 https://files.ofsted.gov.uk/v1/file/2614511 (accessed 20 Jan. 2022).
249 *Cal. Papal Reg.* 1427–47, 553.
250 V. Score, 'Excavation on the site of the hospital of St John the Baptist, Mill Farm, Lutterworth', *Trans. LAHS* 84 (2010), 170–1, 176–7.

south side of Church Street, were occupied by five bedeswomen in the early 16th century, who were provided with a small weekly cash sum and an annual gown each winter.[251]

At least 356 Lutterworth children were apprenticed with the agreement of the parish between 1673 and 1856. Their masters followed a wide range of trades, with the three most common being weaving (23 per cent), framework knitting (21 per cent) and shoemaking (16 per cent). Many of the apprenticeships were in Coventry, Hinckley, Leicester, Nuneaton or Rugby, and provided the children with a new legal settlement.[252] An agreement between the overseers and ratepayers that those parishioners who could do so would take a poor child from the parish as an apprentice was broken in 1686 by Lutterworth's rector Henry Meriton, who 'refused to take an apprentice'. Those who had taken apprentices objected. No resolution was reached, and children continued to be placed within the parish.[253]

The parish overseers adopted the 'roundsman' system for the able-bodied poor in the early 19th century, requiring ratepayers to find short-term work for the unemployed. An additional short-term rate was levied in 1822, which could be offset by any wages paid.[254] The system was soon abandoned, and outdoor relief for those unable to earn anything was provided on a scale set by county magistrates, with 2s. 6d. for a man, the same for his wife and 1s. 6d. for each child. This proved unpopular with ratepayers.[255] Outdoor relief from the parish ended following the completion of the Lutterworth Poor Law Union workhouse in 1840.[256]

Charities for the Poor

In addition to the support given to the 'church-gates' school, Margaret Bent's charity also provided an annual distribution to the poor.[257] Sherrier's charity provided an almshouse on the ground floor of the original Sherrier school building. This was demolished when the new school was built in 1874, but the existing almsmen were each given 8s. weekly.[258]

Donations placed in trust, with the income to be used to support Lutterworth's poor, included 40s. annually from George Vernham's estate, in existence before 1673,[259] and interest on £15 left by Theodore Green in 1811.[260] Other gifts were amalgamated in the early 19th century, including £12 from William Allibone, £3 from Rebecca Brewin and £10 from Mary Iliffe, all given before 1708;[261] £10 from Mary Wigley; £5 from the Revd William Welchman; and the dividend paid to creditors from the insolvency of the Lutterworth solicitor Thomas Holled, who had been holding donations totalling £60 from Sarah

251 Warws. RO, CR 2017/E42, f. 1; Goodacre, *Transformation*, 67; above, Lutterworth Parish.
252 ROLLR, DE 2559/89/1–328; J. Farrell, 'Lutterworth pauper children and apprenticeship, 1673–1856', *Leics.* 3 (1983–4), 17–23.
253 ROLLR, QS 6/1/2, p. 97.
254 *Rpt of Poor Law Commission* (Parl. Papers 1834 (44), xxvii), app. B, p. 284; ROLLR, DE 2559/34; Lutterworth Museum, 4D 60/345.
255 *Rpt of Poor Law Commission*, app. B, p. 284.
256 Below, Local Government (Lutterworth Poor Law Union).
257 *Rpt of Charity Commissioners*, pp. 139–40.
258 White, *Hist.* (Sheffield, 1877), 523.
259 *Rpt of Charity Commissioners*, p. 139; ROLLR, DE 2559/99.
260 *Rpt of Charity Commissioners*, p. 141.
261 Nichols, *Antiquities*, 1140.

Charnock, Thomas Wollaston, John Adams and John Thompson.[262] The money purchased properties for the use of the poor in Ely Lane and Bakehouse Lane.[263] Later bequests, with the income to be distributed to the poor, included £20 from Ebenezer Wormleighton in 1821, which was reduced to just £3 through a Chancery suit;[264] the residue of Henry White's estate in 1855, which produced £4 5s. 0d. annually in 1863;[265] £100 from Dr Phillips of Torquay c.1865;[266] £300 from John Smith in 1866;[267] £100 from Charles Watts in 1867;[268] £200 from Martha Smith in 1870;[269] a bequest from Sarah Iliffe in 1877;[270] and £300 from Emma Heap in 1910.[271] These charities were merged under a Charity Commissioners' scheme of 1911 to become Lutterworth United Charities.[272]

Health Care

The Feilding Palmer cottage hospital on Gilmorton Road (Figure 18) was built in 1899 to a design by Townsend & Fordham of Peterborough on a site given by Frances Palmer in memory of her late husband, the Revd Feilding Palmer. Beds for four men and four women were provided in two wards on the ground floor, with an operating theatre, and there were offices and a rest room for the nurses on the upper floor.[273] There was one district nurse attached, who made 2,327 visits in 1909.[274] In 1911 annual subscribers were entitled to one admission of up to four weeks for every guinea subscribed. Other patients paid 2s. 6d. weekly if they were Lutterworth residents, or 5s. weekly if they lived elsewhere, excluding doctors' fees for admission and discharge.[275]

In 1911 James Darlington gave 350 guineas (£367 10s.) towards a new wing, and Lutterworth's rector, Canon Montague Frederick Alderson, added 100 guineas to the fund.[276] Adjacent land was given by George Spencer in 1925, and he later provided £5,000 for a maternity wing, which opened in 1939.[277] In 2019 the building became an urgent care (walk-in) centre for patients across east Leicestershire and Rutland, managed by DHU Healthcare, a community interest company that provided services to the NHS.[278]

---

262 *Rpt of Charity Commissioners*, pp. 140–1; *Digest of Endowed Charities* (Parl. Papers 1867–8 (433)), pp. 678–9.
263 *Rpt of Charity Commissioners*, pp. 140–1.
264 ROLLR, Wills, 1821 T–Z; *Rpt of Charity Commissioners*, p. 141.
265 ROLLR, PR/T/1855/198; White, *Hist.* (Sheffield, 1863), 523.
266 White, *Hist.* (Sheffield, 1863), 758.
267 ROLLR, DE 4336/47; White, *Hist.* (Sheffield, 1877), 523.
268 ROLLR, DE 4336/47; *Staffs. Advertiser*, 30 Mar. 1867; White, *Hist.* (Sheffield, 1877), 523.
269 ROLLR, DE 4336/47; ROLLR, Will register 1870, pp. 606–12.
270 ROLLR, DE 4336/47.
271 *Kelly's Dir. of Leics. and Rutl.* (1916), 564; *Leic. Daily Post*, 9 Sept. 1915.
272 ROLLR, DE 4336/47.
273 *Leic. Chron.*, 15 Apr. 1899; 23 Dec. 1899.
274 ROLLR, DE 783/51/4/1.
275 ROLLR, DE 783/51/5.
276 Ibid.
277 *Leic. Daily Merc.*, 8 June 1939; *Rugby Advertiser*, 1 Feb. 1946.
278 DHU Healthcare Quality Account 2019/2020, https://dhuhealthcare.com/about-us/quality-accounts (accessed 11 July 2021).

Figure 18 *Feilding Palmer Hospital, Gilmorton Road.*

RELIGIOUS HISTORY

THERE WAS ONLY ONE CHURCH in Lutterworth in the Middle Ages, and this may have been built on the site of an early minster. The earliest surviving fabric is from the 13th century. John Wyclif was rector from 1374. He initially pursued an academic life at Oxford, but was forced to leave the university *c.*1381, as some of his views were seen as heretical, and the popular support they appeared to be gathering posed dangers to the church and to society. Wyclif dissented from the doctrine of transubstantiation: that when a priest consecrates the bread and wine for the mass, they become the body and blood of Christ. His belief that salvation was reserved for those predestined by God was orthodox but, by stressing that God alone knew who would be saved, Wyclif was questioning the authority of those of high rank in the church. He withdrew to his parish, where he revised some of his writings and produced new texts. He died in Lutterworth in 1384. In 1428, acting on instructions issued by Pope Martin V, Bishop Fleming ordered Wyclif's bones to be disinterred and burned and their ashes scattered on the waters of the river Swift.[1] Medieval wall paintings were discovered when the church was restored in the 19th century, and have generally been interpreted with reference to Wyclif's life and beliefs.

Any minster church at Lutterworth would have been within the ancient diocese of Leicester. The seat of the bishop moved to Dorchester on Thames (Oxon.) *c.*870,[2] and to Lincoln *c.*1072.[3] Lutterworth remained within the diocese of Lincoln until 1837, when the Leicestershire parishes were transferred to Peterborough diocese,[4] before becoming part of the modern diocese of Leicester in 1926.[5]

The advowson was forfeited to the Crown in 1554, and Lutterworth had a Puritan minister during the latter part of the Civil War and the Interregnum. Although he was ejected in 1660, Presbyterian meetings were licensed in 1672 and evolved into a strong Independent chapel. This became a United Reformed Church in 1972 but closed in 2021. Other strands of Nonconformity also developed in the town, especially Wesleyan Methodism. A Roman Catholic church was built in 1880–1. There were no non-Christian places of worship in the town in 2021.

1   *ODNB*, s.v. Wyclif [Wycliffe], John [called Doctor Evangelicus] (d. 1384), accessed 28 Nov. 2017.
2   A.W. Haddan and W. Stubbs (eds), *Councils and Ecclesiastical Documents relating to Great Britain and Ireland*, III (Oxford, 1871), 129.
3   D.M. Owen, 'Introduction: the English church in eastern England, 1066–1100', in D.M. Owen (ed.), *The Hist. of Lincoln Minster* (Cambridge, 1994), 10.
4   *London Gaz.*, 12 Sept. 1837, 2397–8.
5   *London Gaz.*, 12 Nov. 1926, 7321–2.

Church Origins and Parochial Organisation

The name of the neighbouring parish of Misterton (Minstreton in 1086) means the minster estate or settlement.[6] Minsters were complex early ecclesiastical communities headed by an abbot, abbess or priest, which provided or supervised pastoral care to the laity.[7] The minster that gave Misterton its name was most probably at Lutterworth, where the medieval church stands near the centre of a raised plateau, almost certainly the 'worth' in Lutterworth's place name, which possibly once contained the minster and its precincts.[8] The suffix 'worth' was used in Mercia for important places, including (notably) Tamworth, a Mercian royal centre with a pre-Conquest church which, like Lutterworth, also takes the first part of its place name from a river.[9]

Lutterworth also had early royal connections. In 1066 the manor was held by Earl Ralph, a grandson of Aethelred II.[10] The land at Misterton was divided between three lords in 1086. The part that belonged to the same lord as Lutterworth was rated at two carucates, and this may originally have been Lutterworth minster's endowment.[11] A peculiarity of Misterton in the 13th century and later was its two rectories,[12] which may have been a legacy from the group of clergy that once belonged to the minster church. The earliest documentary evidence for Lutterworth church, however, is the institution of a rector in c.1222, and there is no evidence that it had any dependent chapels.[13] A chapel in Lutterworth's medieval hospital was endowed in the 13th century.[14]

The earliest record of the dedication of the parish church is from 1517, when John Darby asked to be buried in the churchyard of Our Blessed Lady in Lutterworth.[15] The dedication in 2020 was still to St Mary. The benefice was extended in 1949 to include Cotesbach.[16] In 1996 the rector of Lutterworth also became priest-in-charge of Bitteswell, and the benefice became Lutterworth with Cotesbach and Bitteswell in 2001.[17]

Advowson

Nicholas de Verdun presented a certain Simon as rector in 1222.[18] The advowson remained with the manorial lords until 1554, when it was forfeited to the Crown following the execution of Henry Grey, duke of Suffolk. The patronage was retained by

6   B. Cox, *The Place-Names of Leicestershire*, V (Nottingham, 2011), 147.
7   J. Blair, *The Church in Anglo-Saxon Society* (Oxford, 2005), 3.
8   Above, Landscape and Settlement (Settlement before the Market Charter).
9   *VCH Staffs.* XII, 14–16, 125–6; R. Coates, '*Worthy* of great respect', *Jnl of the English Place-name Society*, 44 (2012), 37, 39–41.
10   Above, Landownership (Lutterworth Manor before 1628).
11   *Domesday*, 645.
12   *Tax. Eccl.*, 63.
13   W.P.W. Phillimore (ed.), *The Rolls of Hugh Wells, Bishop of Lincoln 1209–1235*, I (Lincoln Rec. Soc. 3, 1912), 243; II (Lincoln Rec. Soc. 6, 1913), 284; *Tax. Eccl.*, 63; *Valor Eccl.*, 184.
14   *VCH Leics.* II, 43.
15   ROLLR, PR/I/251/320.
16   *London Gaz.*, 1 Nov. 1949, 5201.
17   *Diocese of Leic. Dir.* (1996), 76; Ibid. *Update* (2000/1), 95.
18   Phillimore (ed.), *The Rolls of Hugh Wells*, II, 284.

the Crown until 1949,[19] when the arrangements were varied on the enlargement of the benefice to include Cotesbach. Subsequently, the right of presentation was weighted in favour of Lutterworth as the more populous settlement: the Crown would make the first, third and fourth of every four successive presentations, and the bishop of Leicester (as patron of Cotesbach) would make the second.[20] The bishop's interest was transferred to the Crown in 1957.[21] This changed when Bitteswell was added to the benefice in 2001. Three of every five presentations are made by the Prime Minister (for the Crown, as the Lutterworth interest), one by the Lord Chancellor (for the Crown, being the Cotesbach portion) and one by Christ's Hospital (as patron of Bitteswell).[22]

Church Endowment

Lutterworth was a mid-ranking living c.1255, with a tax assessment of 9 marks (£6).[23] By 1291, its assessment of £20 was the fifth highest assessment of the 40 churches in Guthlaxton deanery.[24] Lutterworth's value was assessed at £25 19s. 11d. in 1535, when 60 per cent of the livings in the county were valued at £10 or less.[25]

The glebe in 1679 comprised two yardlands in the open fields with grazing for 7½ cows and 65 sheep, a close adjoining Moorbarns, seven tenements in Church Street and five tenements to the south of the churchyard.[26] A modus of £3 14s. had been agreed for Moorbarns in commutation of the tithe by at least the 1570s;[27] similarly, 10s. was paid annually c.1700 for Lodge mill.[28]

The annual value of the living was £110 in 1706.[29] Upon enclosure of the open fields in 1792, the rector was awarded 44½ a. for his glebe and 272 a. in lieu of tithes, creating the second largest landholding in the parish.[30] This was mostly laid out in the area between Moorbarns and Coventry Road, where a farmhouse was built, originally named Lutterworth Fields, later Glebe Farm, but with some additional land near the rectory.[31] In 1831 the living was valued at £585, and in 1916 £426.[32] In 1926 Ann Richardson bequeathed to the living a reversionary interest in 152 a. of land at Moorbarns, which was conveyed in 1974, following the death in 1972 of her daughter, Miss E.V. Richardson, the life tenant.[33]

---

19   *Leic. Dioc. Cal.* (1949), 116.
20   *London Gaz.*, 1 Nov. 1949, 5201.
21   *London Gaz.*, 17 Dec. 1957, 7359.
22   *Crockford's Clerical Directory* (2012–13); White, *Hist.* (Sheffield, 1846), 376.
23   Phillimore (ed.), *The Rolls of Hugh Wells*, I, 274.
24   *Tax. Eccl.*, 63.
25   *Valor Eccl.*, 184; J.F. Fuggles, 'The parish clergy in the archdeaconry of Leicester 1520–1540', *Trans. LAHS* 46 (1970–1), 39.
26   ROLLR, 1D 41/2/431.
27   TNA, E 134/12Chas1/East24, mm. 3–3v.
28   ROLLR, 1D 41/2/452.
29   J. Broad (ed.), *Bishop Wake's Summary of Visitation Returns from the Diocese of Lincoln 1706-1715,* II (Oxford, 2012), 856.
30   ROLLR, EN/AX/211/1.
31   ROLLR, DE 2072/149.
32   White, *Hist.* (Sheffield, 1846), 404; *Peterborough Dioc. Cal.* (1916), 155.
33   CERC, CC/OF/NB19/141B.

Rectory House

The rectory house lay to the north of the church. It had five bays in 1606, three of which had upper chambers, and there were two barns, one of five bays and one of three bays.[34] The house had been extended by 1709 to provide six bays with six upper chambers, and another bay had been added to the barns. The homestead contained 5 a.[35] The house was rebuilt for the rector Henry Ryder in 1803 to a design by Samuel Wyatt, of Chelsea (Middx), at a cost of £1,750. The new house was 150 ft. long, with 29 rooms.[36] The building was unsuited to modern clerical living; the central part was demolished in the 1940s to create two houses, and the eastern house was sold with part of the grounds.[37] The remaining rectory was replaced by a smaller house c.1995, built in the grounds, and the western part of the 1803 building was sold.

Religious Life

Religious Life in the Middle Ages

Nicholas de Verdun presented Philip Lovel to the living in 1232. Lovel was required to purge himself of the charge of collusion between himself and his patron, but no further detail was recorded.[38] John Wyclif was presented to the living by Edward III in 1374, during the minority of Henry de Ferrers.[39] Although Wyclif is believed to have lived mostly at Oxford in the 1370s, he was assessed for the clerical poll tax of 1377 at Lutterworth, as one of seven priests. Two of the others were a chaplain and the master of the hospital, but nothing more is known about the other four.[40] The local impact of Wyclif's views in the years following his death in 1384 appear to have been limited. Lollards (a general term for supporters of Wyclif's views) were detected in Leicester, in other parts of the county and at Coventry, but not in Lutterworth.[41] This suggests strong orthodox preaching by John Moorhouse, Wyclif's successor, presented to the living by Henry Ferrers.[42] The disinterment and burning of Wyclif's bones in 1428, and perhaps the iconography within a mural added to the north wall of the church, may have also acted as a local deterrent to the expression of heterodox views.[43] John Horne, a priest who was in Lutterworth church when Wyclif was struck there with his final paralysis,

---

34   Lincs. Arch., DIOC/TER BUNDLE/LEICS/LUTTERWORTH, 1606.
35   Lincs. Arch., DIOC/TER/23, ff. 592–8.
36   ROLLR, DE 6660/1; CERC, ECE/7/1/77948, letters 15 Mar. and 5 June 1937; NHLE, no. 1211070, The Rectory Coventry Road (accessed 9 Aug. 2020).
37   CERC, QAB/7/7/PM19/141.
38   Phillimore (ed.), *The Rolls of Hugh Wells*, II, 316.
39   *Cal. Inq. p.m.* XIII, 68; W.G.D. Fletcher, 'John Wycliffe's presentation to the rectory of Lutterworth', *Trans. LAHS* 8 (1893–8), 184; *ODNB*, Wyclif.
40   A.K. McHardy (ed.), *Clerical Poll Taxes of the Diocese of Lincoln, 1377–1381* (Lincoln Rec. Soc. 81, 1992), 21.
41   J. Crompton, 'Leicestershire Lollards', *Trans. LAHS* 44 (1968–9), 11–44; M. Jurkowski, 'Lollardy in Coventry and the revolt of 1431', in L. Clark (ed.), *The Fifteenth Century*, VI: *Identity and Insurgency in the Late Middle Ages* (Woodbridge, 2006), 145–64.
42   Nichols, *Hist.*, IV, 265, citing bishop's register, Buckingham, II, 199.
43   Below (Wall Paintings).

recounted under oath in 1441 that this had occurred during mass, at the elevation of the host.[44] The timing of this statement is curious, as this was a period when Lollardy was largely quiescent,[45] but it may reflect a strong desire by the church locally to discredit Wyclif's views and reinforce popular belief in the miracle of transubstantiation.

Lutterworth had three religious guilds in the early 16th century. The largest and most important of these stemmed from the gift of Edmund Muryell. In 1478 Muryell conveyed lands and property in Shawell and North Kilworth to endow a guild in honour of the Holy Trinity, the Blessed Virgin Mary, St John the Baptist, St Anthony and St Katherine. A priest was employed to pray for his soul, those of his family and 'all the Brethren and Sistern that shalbe in the same Gild and for all the benefactors to the same'.[46] Later cash bequests to the guild, which was known locally as the 'guild of Lutterworth',[47] included 40s. in 1526 from Thomas Jenkinson,[48] and 20d. in 1528 from Agnes Chapleyn.[49] The lands included in Muryell's initial conveyance were the only endowments declared to the Chantry Commissioners when the guilds were dissolved.[50]

The other two guilds, St Thomas's and St Anne's, made no return to the Chantry Commissioners, and may have had no permanent endowment. John Dannam (d. 1518), Alice Therebarn (d. 1521), John Chapleyn (d. 1524), Robert Smyth (d. 1524) and Thomas Hynde (d. 1534) all left sums ranging from 3s. 4d. to £6 13s. 4d. to St Anne's guild.[51] Chapleyn, the town's bailiff, also left £16 for a priest to sing masses for his soul, and 20s. for two sung trental masses at St Anne's altar.[52] Thomas Jenkinson (d. 1526) left 20s. for two trentals at St Anne's altar,[53] and Thomas Hynde (also Lutterworth's bailiff) left 6s. 8d. for Robert Mason, Lutterworth's parish priest, to sing for his soul and for all Christian souls,[54] and also asked to be buried before St Anne's altar.[55] William Numon (d. 1530) bequeathed 8d. to St Thomas's guild and 12d. to the high light, probably on the rood loft,[56] and John Edmunds (d. 1532) bequeathed 4d. to the rood loft light.[57] A piece of embroidered cloth displayed in the church in 2020 is probably the fabric described to visitors in the 18th century as part of Wyclif's vestments.[58] It may be part of a late

44   G.R. Evans, *John Wyclif* (Oxford, 2007), 210; K.B. McFarlane, *John Wycliffe and the Beginnings of English Nonconformity* (London, 1952), 119–20.

45   R.N. Swanson, *Church and Society in Late Medieval England* (Oxford, 1989), 342–3.

46   Warws. RO, C 2017/D199; *Rpt on the Manuscripts of the late Reginald Rawdon Hastings*, I (London, 1928), 102.

47   M.E.C. Walcott, 'Chantries of Leicestershire and the inventory of Olveston', *Trans. LAHS* 4 (1869–75), 17.

48   ROLLR, PR/I/251, ff. 492–3.

49   ROLLR, PR/I/251, f. 200–200v.

50   A. Hamilton Thompson, 'The chantry certificates for Leicestershire', *Assoc. Archit. Soc. Rpts. & Papers* 30 (1909–10), 513–14, 547–8; below, Local Government (Town Government).

51   ROLLR, PR/I/251, ff. 81 (Dannam), 253v (Therebarn); TNA, PROB 11/21/428 (John Chapleyn); ROLLR, PR/I/251, f. 179–179v (Smyth), 271 (Hynde).

52   TNA, PROB 11/21/428.

53   ROLLR, PR/I/251, ff. 492v–493.

54   TNA, PROB 11/25/278.

55   ROLLR, PR/I/251, f. 271.

56   ROLLR, PR/I/251, ff. 300v–301.

57   ROLLR, PR/I/251, f. 207.

58   J. Throsby, *The Memoirs of the Town and County of Leicester* (Leicester, 1777), II, 113–16; Nichols, *Hist.*, IV, 264.

medieval vestment or altar frontal.[59] Its design bears some resemblance to the Thornton chasuble, suggesting a date of *c*.1510–33.[60]

Bequests of 4*d*. for the great bell by Alice Therebarn in 1521 and 2*d*. for the bells by Agnes Chapleyn in 1527 may have paid for the bells to be rung on the day of burial.[61] John Chapleyn left 6*s*. 8*d*. in 1524 for 'the repayring of the belles',[62] and a similar sum was left by Thomas Jenkinson in 1526, perhaps also for their 'repair'.[63] A Sanctus bell inscribed to St Peter was cast by Newcombe of Leicester in the early 16th century, and is the only surviving pre-Reformation Sanctus bell in Leicestershire.[64]

The eastern end of the north aisle was 'anciently' the Feildings' chapel.[65] The Feildings were said to have 'encreased' the church,[66] perhaps paying for the widening of the aisles in the 14th century. The earliest memorials in this chapel are brasses to John Feilding (d. 1403) and his wife Joan (d. 1418).[67] Armorial glass in the window carrying an inscription to William Feilding and his wife Margery was removed between 1789 and 1810.[68] This was presumably William (fl. 1425), the son of John and Joan, whose wife's name is otherwise unrecorded. Recumbent alabaster effigies of an unidentified couple, the man unusually wearing armour under a civilian cloak, are estimated to date from *c*.1440 to 1450, and are therefore unlikely to be William Feilding (fl. 1329) and his wife Joan Prudhome, as once suggested.[69] It is possible they could be John Feilding (fl. 1433) and his wife Margaret Purefoy, who have no known memorial. There is also a brass plate inscribed in memory of Elizabeth Feilding, who died in 1803.[70] Two brass figures, moved during the 19th century from the west end of the north aisle to the south-east corner of the nave (covered in 2021), are stylistically of the late 15th century, and might possibly have been originally laid with an inscription, now lost but recorded in 1810, to William Feilding (d. 1471) and his wife Agnes, née Seyton. Unrelated to this family, there was also a brass inscription, now lost, to John Reynolds, merchant of the Staple, who died in 1473.[71]

59 M.H. Bloxham, 'Lutterworth church and the Wycliffe relics', *Trans. LAHS* 2 (1860–4), 78–9.

60 http://collections.vam.ac.uk/item/O118444/chasuble-unknown (accessed 18 Dec. 2020).

61 ROLLR, PR/I/251, ff. 253v, 200–200v; E. Duffy, *The Stripping of the Altars: Traditional Religion in England, 1400–1580* (London, 1992), 577–8.

62 TNA, PROB 11/21/428.

63 ROLLR, PR/I/251/492v.

64 Ibid.; G. Dawson, A National Bell Register, http://georgedawson.homestead.com/nbr.html (accessed 24 May 2018).

65 Nichols, *Hist.*, IV, 286–7.

66 Camden, *Britannia*, 517.

67 Nichols, *Hist.*, IV, 265; *A Guide to the Parish Church of St Mary's in Lutterworth* (digital edn, 2011), I, 11, http://www.stmaryslutterworth.org/websiteimages/churchguide2011oct23pt1.pdf (accessed 12 June 2018).

68 Burton, *Description*, 170; Nichols, *Hist.*, IV, 265; Nichols believed this to be to John Feilding and Margaret Purefoy, but mentions no inscription, which might have been broken or removed in the 17th century.

69 Pers. comm., Mark Downing, Church Monuments Society, a specialist in 15th-century effigies. Others have estimated the date as early 15th century (Pevsner, *Leics. and Rutl.*, 300; NHLE, no. 1211040, Church of St Mary Church St (accessed 1 Nov. 2021)), or to the years between 1440 and 1485 (R.H. State, *The Alabaster Carvers* (Ely, 2017), 222).

70 Above, Landownership (Feilding Cadet Estate from 1509).

71 Nichols, *Hist.*, IV, 265, pl. XL, figs 1–5; D.C. Valentine, *Church Brasses of Leicestershire* (Leicester, 1975), 16.

Wall Paintings

Two medieval wall paintings were uncovered during the restoration of the church in 1867–9 and restored alongside the work to the building.[72] A fragment of a third was discovered during conservation work in the 1980s. The earliest of these, on the north wall, facing people as they enter the church, depicts the 'Three Living and Three Dead' (Figure 19), a common subject in medieval art, where three kings out hunting meet three corpses, who remind them of their own mortality.[73] When it was first revealed, only the 'living' could be seen, and the figures were interpreted as people connected to Wyclif's life, with a right-hand border added upon 'restoration' in 1869 to frame the figures.[74] Its true subject was first recognised in the early 20th century, and confirmed when the grinning teeth of the 'dead' were discovered in the 1980s. The composition is now believed to have been painted in the 1330s or early 1340s, making it contemporary with the widening of the aisles, and predating Wyclif's ministry.[75]

A small area of overpainting can be seen on the right-hand figure, depicting a cardinal wearing a red mozetta (cape) and galero (hat), identifying his status, behind a priest wearing eucharistic vestments and looking upwards, with what appears to be a decorated fabric to his right, possibly an altar frontal (Figure 20). This fragment is believed to have been painted in the mid 15th century, and may show the St Gregory mass, a popular legend where a vision of Christ appeared on the altar when Pope Gregory was celebrating mass. If this interpretation is correct, it may have been painted as a restatement of orthodoxy at about the time that Horne swore on oath that Wyclif's collapse occurred at the elevation of the host. It would have acted as a 'permanent' public repudiation of Wyclif's views on transubstantiation.[76] The dating of the image overturns at least part of an earlier suggestion that this painting was added here by Wyclif's supporters c.1384 to show Cardinal Adam Easton and Thomas Brinton, bishop of Rochester (who had condemned Wyclif for heresy), looking up at the skeletons, who were 'defying them to contemplate their own mortality'.[77]

The most prominent painting is a 'doom' over the chancel arch, also of the 15th century, which was uncovered and restored in 1869 (Figure 21).[78] Figures rise from their graves under an image of Christ in glory, but are neither transported to heaven nor dispatched to hell. A figure on the right, the side traditionally reserved for the

72   *Leic. Chron.*, 12 June 1869; M.H. Bloxham, 'Some discoveries made in the progress of the restoration of Lutterworth church', *Trans. LAHS* 3 (1864–9), 361 (Bloxham confuses north and south).

73   M. Gill, 'Adam Easton and the Lutterworth wall paintings revisited', in M. Wending (ed.), *Cardinal Adam Easton (c.1330–1397): Monk, Scholar, Theologian, Diplomat* (Amsterdam, 2020), 108–11.

74   Bloxham, 'Some discoveries', 361; Mrs Thursby, 'A wall painting in Lutterworth church', *Trans. LAHS* 5 (1875–81), 293–5; A.H. Dyson, *Lutterworth: The Story of John Wycliffe's Town* (London, 1913), 42–5; Gill, 'Adam Easton', 107.

75   A.H. Dyson and S.H. Skillington, *Lutterworth Church and its Associations, with a chapter on John Wycliffe* (Leicester, 1916), 14–17; Gill, 'Adam Easton', 108, 110; below (Architectural Development of St Mary's Church).

76   Gill, 'Adam Easton', 102, 108, 112–16.

77   A. Lee, *The Most Ungrateful Englishman: The Life and Times of Adam Easton* (Lydney, 2006), 319–21.

78   *Leic. Chron.*, 12 June 1869; 'Annual summer meeting', *Trans. LAHS* 4 (1869–75), 151.

Figure 19 *The 'Three Living', from an original composition of the 'Three Living and Three Dead', above the north door of St Mary's church. The right-hand border was added in 1869.*

Figure 20 *Fragment from a second image painted over the 'Three Living and Three Dead'.*

Figure 21 *The 'Doom' painting over the chancel arch.*

condemned, wears a bishop's mitre, and it has been suggested that the painting pays 'indirect homage' to Wyclif's views on predestination.[79]

Religious Life after the Reformation

Lutterworth's rector, Baldwin Norton, was deprived of the living in 1562 for refusing to conform to the Elizabethan religious settlement.[80] Robert Sutton was said to have been 'parson of Lutterworth' for six years until 1577, when he stood in the pulpit and 'declared that there was no hope of salvation outside the Roman Church', before fleeing to continental Europe. Sutton was ordained as a Catholic priest in Cambrai in 1578. He later returned to England and was arrested in Staffordshire and executed in 1587.[81]

79　J.P. Hornbeck II, 'Wall paintings in Wyclif's church: evidence of a reformer's legacy?', *Trans. LAHS* 88 (2014), 47–54. Hornbeck erroneously describes the small painting on the north wall as being under (rather than over) the 'Three Living'.

80　*Cal. Pat.* 1560–3, 264; *VCH Leics.* I, 373; H. Gee, *The Elizabethan Clergy and the Settlement of Religion, 1558–1564* (Oxford, 1898), 279.

81　E.H. Burton and J.H. Pollen (eds), *Lives of the English Martyrs*, 2nd ser., I (London, 1914), 301–12.

Nathaniel Tovey was appointed rector in 1630.[82] He heard charges in 1637 against Richard Clayton, the Puritan rector of Shawell, including that Clayton had encouraged a mob to pull down Lutterworth's high cross, proclaiming it a 'prophane thing'.[83] In 1646 the Parliamentary County Committee laid nine articles against Tovey, including being absent for more than six months at royalist garrisons, refusing to use the Puritan *Directory for the Publique Worship of God* for services, refusing to give the sacrament except at the rails, raising the steps in the chancel, 'hindering' other preachers and preaching against Parliament. He was found guilty of the charges and ejected from his living, and his estates in Leicestershire and Worcestershire were sequestered.[84] Several parishioners petitioned for the installation of John Moore, who was appointed, but forcibly prevented from taking up his living.[85] This may be the same John Moore who later preached two lectures at Lutterworth in 1653 against the enclosure of open fields.[86] John St Nicholas was installed as rector. He signed the Leicestershire addresses of 1658 and 1659 which supported attempts to prevent the restoration of the monarchy.[87] During his incumbency a new pulpit was installed, the church windows reglazed, the spire repointed and new lead put on the roof.[88] St Nicholas was ejected in 1660 and replaced by Thomas Pestell the elder, former chaplain to Charles I, who had been deprived of his vicarage of Packington (28 miles north of Lutterworth) during the Civil War.[89]

Henry Meriton became rector of Lutterworth in 1683, and of Peatling Parva in 1685.[90] He added a west gallery to the church in 1684, probably for musicians or singers.[91] Meriton's relationship with his parishioners was marred by his refusal to pay his rates or take an apprentice.[92] It deteriorated further after the loss of the church spire in a storm on Christmas Day 1701.[93] The collapse of the spire caused extensive

82   *ODNB*, s.v. Tovey, Nathaniel (bap. 1597, d. 1658), Church of England clergyman, accessed 26 June 2018.

83   A.P. Moore, 'The metropolitan visitation of Archbishop Laud', *Assoc. Archit. Soc. Rpts. & Papers* 29 (1907–8), 524–6; J. Goodacre, *The Transformation of a Peasant Economy: Townspeople and Villagers in the Lutterworth Area, 1500–1700* (Aldershot, 1994), 9.

84   *Walker Revised*, ed. A.G. Matthews, 246–7; Bodleian Libr., MS Walker, C 5, f. 61; C 11, f. 81r; G. Campbell, 'Nathaniel Tovey: Milton's second tutor', *Milton Quarterly* 21 (1987), 86–7.

85   Nichols, *Hist.*, IV, 264; *Calamy Revised*, ed. A.G. Matthews, 352–3; Campbell, 'Nathaniel Tovey', 87.

86   J. Moore, *The Crying Sin of England* (1653); *ODNB*, s.v. Moore, John (1594/5?–1657), Church of England clergyman and author, accessed 26 June 2018.

87   *Calamy Revised*, ed. A.G. Matthews, 423–4 ; W. Dugdale, *A Short View of the Late Troubles in England* (1681), 471–3.

88   ROLLR, DE 2559/18.

89   *Calamy Revised*, ed. A.G. Matthews, 423–4; *Walker Revised*, ed. A.G. Matthews, 241–2; *Cal. SP Dom.* 1660–1, 52; *ODNB*, s.v. Pestell, Thomas (bap. 1586, d. 1667), Church of England clergyman and poet, accessed 17 Aug. 2021.

90   https://theclergydatabase.org.uk/jsp/search/index.jsp (accessed 3 Jan. 2015); Lambeth Palace Libr., F II/26/46; VG 1/6, f. 56v.

91   ROLLR, 1D 41/41/19; J.H. Gurney, *Address to the Inhabitants of Lutterworth on the Subject of a Proposed Alteration in the Church* (Lutterworth, 1835), 4–5 (copy in Lambeth Palace Libr., ICBS 1900).

92   ROLLR, QS 6/1/2, ff. 97, 99v, 179v, 161v; P.J. Fisher, 'Making their voices heard: Lutterworth's Nonconformists, St Mary's steeple, and a burial controversy', *Trans. LAHS* 94 (2020), 149.

93   The bill and witness statements made to the Court of Chancery state clearly that the spire fell on Christmas Day 1701 (TNA, C 6/345/4, m. 1; C 8/600/5, mm. 1, 3; C 10/379/4, m. 3), and this date is confirmed by entries in the churchwardens' accounts (ROLLR, DE 2559/18). These disprove the assertion made by Nichols a century later, and accepted by subsequent writers, that the spire fell in 1703 (Nichols, *Hist.*, IV, 263).

damage to the tower, bells and church roof, requiring repairs that would cost £1,523.[94]
Insufficient money was raised, and when Meriton spent some donations on beautifying
the chancel, the cost of which was his personal responsibility, a suit was brought against
him by Joshua Ferrand (an innkeeper) and Thomas Winterton (a mercer) on behalf of
the town's inhabitants for misapplying funds.[95] They may have acted on behalf of the
town's Nonconformists, to prevent a church rate being set. Meriton raised a counter-
suit against Ferrand and Winterton, claiming they had collected £800 towards repairs,
but diverted funds to their own businesses.[96] Concurrently, causes were also brought in
the archdeacon's court by Meriton against Ferrand and Winterton for non-attendance
at church, and by Ferrand against Meriton for neglect of duty, including allegations
that Meriton refused to bury at least nine parishioners who attended Nonconformist
worship.[97] The outcome of these causes does not survive, but all the witnesses confirmed
the burial allegations. The Chancery suits were devolved to local magistrates for
arbitration, but the costs awarded to Meriton remained unsettled at his death in 1711.[98]
Daniel Defoe visited Lutterworth in the 1720s, and noted that 'The Church was lately
beautified, and paved with a costly Pavement of chequered Stone; and the Pews are new,
and everything in it both in Church and Chancel, except the Pulpit'.[99] This work had
probably been ordered by Meriton.

Henry Ryder was appointed rector in 1801. Probably a high churchman on his
appointment, he had become an evangelical by 1811. He held a weekly lecture in a
Lutterworth factory, 'and the room was always crowded for the occasion'.[100] This was
presumably William Buszard's cotton factory on Bitteswell Road.[101] Ryder also founded
a girls' school in the town.[102] He left Lutterworth in 1815 upon his appointment as
bishop of Gloucester.[103]

Joseph Hansom was appointed as architect to the church in 1835, to create additional
seats and to move the pulpit from its position on the north side of the church to stand
in front of the chancel arch.[104] A short south gallery had been added to the church in
1807, and Hansom extended this and added a matching gallery on the north, creating
330 new seats, 280 of which were for children.[105] The cost of £610 was met by donations
and a grant of £120 from the Incorporated Church Building Society. The font stood
at the base of the tower, with a vestry to its north and 'lumber room' to the south, and

94   ROLLR, DE 2559/18; B. Carne (ed.), *Parish Accounts of Lydiard Tregoze*, https://www.thelydiardarchives.
     org.uk/item/report-no-3, p. 14 (accessed 22 Jan. 2022).
95   TNA, C 6/345/4; C 8/600/5; C 6/345/84.
96   TNA, C 10/379/4.
97   ROLLR, 1D 41/4/L/085–8; 1D 41/4/L/089–91.
98   TNA, C 11/1731/34; DE 2094/1; Fisher, 'Making their voices heard', 143–64.
99   D. Defoe, *A Tour thro' the Whole Island of Great Britain* (London, 4th edn, 1748), II, 423.
100 *ODNB*, s.v. Ryder, Henry (1777–1836), bishop of Lichfield and Coventry, accessed 12 May 2019; G.C.B.
     Davies, *The First Evangelical Bishop: Some Aspects of the Life of Henry Ryder* (London, 1958), 4–5, 11;
     W.J. Baker, 'Henry Ryder of Gloucester, 1815–1824: England's first evangelical bishop', *Trans. Bristol and
     Gloucestershire Archaeology Society* 89 (1970), 132–3.
101 Above, Economic Hist. (Manufacturing).
102 Above, Social Hist. (Education).
103 *ODNB*, s.v. Ryder, Henry.
104 St Mary's church, plan prior to changes; Lambeth Palace Libr., ICBS 1900/3, 15–16, 28–9.
105 ROLLR, 1D 41/41/19; 1D 41/41/202; Lambeth Palace Libr., ICBS 1900/8, 15–16.

there was a pipe organ in the west gallery.[106] A marble mural monument to Wyclif, by Richard Westmacott the younger, was installed on the north wall of the chancel, with an inscription by Charles le Bas, one of Wyclif's biographers.[107] Curate John Gurney realised with concern in 1838 that there were now insufficient private pews, as 'Little shop keepers and persons among the best class of the poor' aspired to have their own seat, which the Nonconformist chapels would provide.[108]

The glass in the east window of the church, by Clayton & Bell, was given by the Revd Feilding Palmer in 1884 in memory of his parents Edward Feilding and Sarah Palmer.[109] A new font was given by the family of the late John Goodacre in 1890, replacing one given by Lord Denbigh in 1704.[110] Two new bells, cast by Taylors of Loughborough, were given in 1894 by Thomas Blackwell, when the opportunity was taken to rehang the other six bells in a new frame.[111]

A rearrangement at the west end of the church c.2000 created a coffee area at the back of the south aisle and a creche and toilets at the rear of the north aisle, with stairs to an office on a mezzanine floor.[112] The church in 2018 had a growing congregation and described its services as 'Mostly informal [with a] limited use of liturgy/robing'.[113] The church was open to visitors every morning in 2019, and was a member of the Major Parish Churches Network, a group of c.300 churches across England identified by the Church Buildings Council as being physically large and historically or architecturally important, and as making a significant contribution to the local community beyond the role of a typical parish church. The group provides mutual support to its members and assists with the development of conservation and liturgical plans to inform any future building changes.[114]

Architectural Development of St Mary's Church

St Mary's church comprises a chancel with an organ chamber and vestry to its north, a nave of four bays with clerestory of five bays, a west tower, north and south aisles that extend as far west as the west wall of the tower, and a south porch (Figure 22). The fabric is fieldstone with dressed stone buttresses, and the top stage of the tower is dressed stone.

The earliest parts of the church are the chancel, the lower stages of the tower, and the north and south nave arcades, which had all been built by the late 13th century. The west wall of the tower contains a single lancet window, as does the south wall of the chancel, and evidence was found for two lancet windows in the east wall of the chancel when the church was restored in 1867–9. The piscina in the chancel is also of the 13th century, as

106 Lambeth Palace Libr., ICBS 1900/23–4, 28–9, 32–3; ICBS MB 7, p. 207.

107 Lincs. Arch., COR.B. 5/5/3/2/5–6; C.W. Le Bas, *The Life of Wiclif* (London, 1832); Pevsner, *Leics. and Rutl.*, 300.

108 Lambeth Palace Libr., ICBS 1900/34–7.

109 Pevsner, *Leics. and Rutl.*, 300.

110 ROLLR, DE 4336/1.

111 *Leic. Chron.*, 19 Jan. 1895.

112 *A Guide to the Parish Church of St Mary's in Lutterworth* (digital edn, 2011), I, 6.

113 https://lutterworthchurch.org/wp-content/uploads/2018/02/Lutterworth-Cotesbach-Bitteswell-Curacy-Profile-2018.pdf (accessed 8 Dec. 2020).

114 https://www.churchofengland.org/resources/diocesan-resources/strategic-planning-church-buildings/major-parish-churches (accessed 11 Aug. 2021).

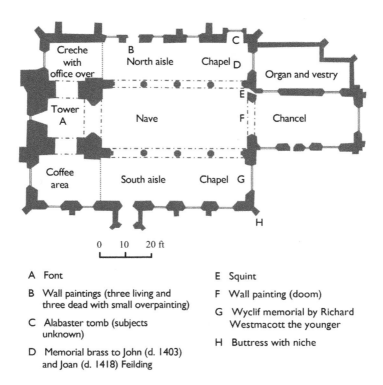

A Font

B Wall paintings (three living and
   three dead with small overpainting)

C Alabaster tomb (subjects
   unknown)

D Memorial brass to John (d. 1403)
   and Joan (d. 1418) Feilding

E Squint

F Wall painting (doom)

G Wyclif memorial by Richard
   Westmacott the younger

H Buttress with niche

Figure 22 *Plan of St Mary's church.*

are the three arches from the tower to the nave and its aisles, indicating that the aisles extended as far as the west side of the tower when they were built.[115]

The north and south aisles were widened in the early to mid 14th century, with the south aisle built slightly wider than the north. The 14th-century tie-beam roofs survive in both aisles. A five-bay clerestory was added in the 14th century, with crenellated parapet, and the nave roof is largely of the 14th century, with carved roof bosses.[116] The chapel at the east end of the south aisle was also created at about this time, probably originally as a chantry chapel. The east window of this aisle is of four lights with splayed cill, to admit the maximum light to the altar; a piscina sits under an ogee arch; and the window immediately to the right of the piscina has flowing curvilinear tracery. On the exterior, the corner buttress contains a niche, perhaps for a statue. This chapel apparently predates the establishment of the main Lutterworth guild, although it is likely that it was used by this guild. There was a rood loft by at least 1532,[117] and evidence for a rood stair survives on the south side of the chancel arch.

115 Pevsner, *Leics. and Rutl.*, 298; NHLE, no. 1211040, Church of St Mary Church St (accessed 13 June 2018).

116 NHLE, no. 1211040, Church of St. Mary Church St (accessed 13 June 2018).

117 ROLLR, PR/I/251/207.

Figure 23 *St Mary's church, west elevation. The top section of the tower was added in 1761, following damage caused by the loss of the spire in a storm in 1701.*

The church had a spire, which fell in 1701 and was never replaced.[118] It was said to bear the arms of Lord Ferrers of Groby,[119] and was possibly built or rebuilt in 1414 to increase the visibility of the church when the charter was obtained for an annual fair.[120] The same arms appear on the east wall of the chancel.[121] Attempts to rebuild the spire

118 Fisher, 'Making their voices heard', 150–5.
119 Burton, *Description*, 170.
120 *Cal. Pat.* 1413–16, 181.
121 Burton, *Description*, 170.

failed through lack of money in 1701 and again in 1759,[122] but the top stage of the tower was rebuilt in 1761, at a cost of £365.[123] Its dressed stone and heavy pinnacles provide a harsh contrast to the fieldstone of the lower stages (Figure 23).

Restoration of the Fabric

Following the fall of a corbel in 1866, a committee sought plans for the restoration of the church from the London architect William Bassett Smith, and three of the leading church architects of the Gothic Revival, William Butterfield, John Loughborough Pearson and George Gilbert Scott. Scott's proposals were accepted.[124] A subscription of £4,260 was soon raised towards the estimated cost of £7,000.[125] The north aisle was extended east, providing room for the organ and vestry, the galleries were removed, and the wall paintings discovered. The Wyclif memorial was resited at the east end of the south aisle to provide access to the new vestry from the chancel.[126] Gifts given to the church at the completion of the restoration in 1869 included a window in the north aisle by Burlison & Grylls, who also restored the wall paintings.[127] The south porch was rebuilt in 1881, to a design provided by Scott in 1866, and includes a carved head and face of Wyclif over the door.[128]

Protestant Nonconformity

No illegal religious meetings were recorded in Lutterworth in 1669,[129] and only six dissenters were recorded in the parish in 1676.[130] Two Quakers interrupted church worship in 1682, but they may not have been residents.[131] Six 'recusants' were noted in 1687, who were possibly Protestant dissenters, not Roman Catholics.[132] The relative strengths of each Nonconformist meeting were recorded in 1709, 1829 and 1851. Rector Henry Meriton, who by 1709 was refusing to bury Nonconformists,[133] reported four families of 'Anabaptists', between 26 and 36 families of Independents and one Quaker in the parish, but no 'Papist'.[134] In 1829, 700 people were meeting for worship in the Independent chapel, and there was a meeting of ten 'Huntingtonian Calvinists' and another of 70 Wesleyan Methodists.[135] Only two returns were made to the religious census of 1851, when the Independent chapel was attended by 229 people in the morning and 363 in the evening, and the Wesleyan Methodist chapel had 40 worshippers in the morning and 60 in the evening.[136] Some of those attending the chapels probably lived in neighbouring villages.

122 Fisher, 'Making their voices heard', 143–64; ROLLR, QS 3/177/58/M/22; QS 5/1/3, f. 44.
123 ROLLR, DE 2094/2.
124 ROLLR, DE 895/1; DE 4336/39.
125 Northants. RO, ML 1116, pp. 513–15.
126 Bloxham, 'Some discoveries', 360; *Leic. Chron.*, 27 June 1868; 12 June 1869.
127 *Leic. Chron.*, 12 June 1869.
128 Pevsner, *Leics. and Rutl.*, 300; Northants. RO, ML 601; *Rugby Advertiser*, 3 Dec. 1881.
129 R.H. Evans, 'Nonconformists in Leicestershire in 1669', *Trans. LAHS* 25 (1949), 135.
130 A. Whiteman (ed.), *The Compton Census of 1676: A Critical Edition* (Oxford, 1986), 336.
131 Nichols, *Hist.*, IV, 264.
132 *Cal. SP Dom.* 1686–7, 379.
133 ROLLR, 1D/41/4/L089–91; Fisher, 'Making their voices heard', 158–62.
134 Broad, *Bishop Wake's Summary*, II, 857.
135 ROLLR, QS 95/2/1/21.
136 TNA, HO 129/408/27; HO 129/408/28.

The registrations of James Robinson's house in 1819[137] and of his factory later that year,[138] Thomas Storer's house in 1720,[139] John Jennens' house in 1733,[140] Joseph Freeman's house in 1740,[141] and Ann Cox's house, also in 1740,[142] cannot be matched to any congregation or denomination. Other registrations are considered below.

Presbyterians, Independents, Congregationalists and the United Reformed Church

Dissenting worship was permitted in 1672, and a licence was issued that year for Presbyterian meetings to be held in John Winterton's house.[143] Such meetings became proscribed in 1673, but Nonconformists began to meet again in 1689, after the Toleration Act was passed.[144] The group were almost certainly Presbyterian and may have been led by Joseph Lee, the ejected rector of Cotesbach, who preached for a time in an old barn in Lutterworth before 'falling into weakness'.[145] By 1692 the congregation was paying £28 annually for Peter Dowley to be their minister.[146] He was said to have attracted 460 hearers to his meetings, including 69 owners of property.[147] Lutterworth's rector, Henry Meriton, referred to this congregation as Independents, and recorded that they met on one weekday each month and twice each Sunday.[148] Meriton's successor, George Anderson, described the same congregation in 1721 as Presbyterians, and said that their number included up to 300 people from neighbouring villages.[149] These meetings may have moved round the homes and outbuildings of several of their number, or the group may have fractured because of slightly different beliefs, as licences for dissenting worship were issued for John Andrews's house in 1720, and the houses of Richard Winterton in 1723 and John Winterton in 1724, possibly sons of the John Winterton licensed to hold Presbyterian worship in 1672.[150]

Peter Dowley died in 1731 and was succeeded as minister by his son John. Shortly afterwards the congregation divided, and a group known as the 'Little Meeting' began to meet separately under the Revd A. Kidman.[151] The 'Little Meeting' registered a new building of three bays for worship in 1741, on John Andrews's land in Ely Lane.[152] The congregations reunited *c.*1776 and agreed that Thomas Grundy should be their pastor.[153] A large chapel was built in Worship Street in 1777 (later George Street), on

137 ROLLR, 1D 41/44/378.
138 ROLLR, 1D 41/44/399; no more is known about this factory.
139 ROLLR, QS 44/1/1, rot. 4v.
140 ROLLR, QS 44/1/1, rot. 2.
141 ROLLR, QS 44/1/1, rot. 2v.
142 Ibid.
143 *Cal. SP Dom.* 1672, 402.
144 ROLLR, N/C/211/1, f. 1.
145 A. Gordon, *Freedom after Ejection: A Review (1690–1692) of Presbyterian and Congregational Nonconformity in England and Wales* (Manchester, 1917), 68; *Calamy Revised* (ed. A.G. Matthews), 320.
146 Gordon, *Freedom*, 68.
147 Dr Williams's Libr., John Evans' List of Dissenting Congregations, MS 34.4, f. 64.
148 Broad, *Bishop Wake's Summary*, 857.
149 Lincolnshire Arch., Gibson 12, f. 466.
150 ROLLR, QS 44/1/1, rot. 3, 4v; *Cal. SP Dom.* 1672, 402.
151 *Leic. Chron.*, 12 May 1877; Bruce, Gates and Gates, *Brief Hist.*, 5.
152 Bruce, Gates and Gates, *Brief Hist.*, 5; ROLLR, QS 44/1/1, rot. 2v.
153 *Leic. Chron.*, 12 May 1877.

Figure 24 *Lutterworth Independent chapel (on the left), c.1800. The farmhouse on the right was demolished in the early 19th century and replaced by a Sunday school room and manse.*

the site of their meeting place of 1689, and was registered as an 'Independent' chapel (Figure 24).[154] This is believed to have been rebuilt in the early 19th century in a similar style, with the datestone of 1777 retained. The walls are of red brick, with pilasters on each side at the front and a hipped roof. There is evidence that there were originally two doors on the west front, but these have been replaced by windows and a single central door.[155] The registrations for worship of William Crispin's house in 1804, the houses of John Rainbow and William Booker in 1808, and Richard Hurley's outbuilding in 1808 may indicate the period of rebuilding when the chapel could not be used. Each of these registrations included some names in common, and John Rainbow was a trustee for the Independent church. The registration of Joseph Miles's house in 1822 was also connected to the same group of people.[156]

The chapel was restored in 1877, when the old 'high-backed pews', windows and 'leaky' roof were replaced, and an organ and heating added. The total cost was £938, raised by subscriptions, a bazaar and a musical evening.[157] By 1883, this had become the Congregational church.[158] It became part of the Association of Congregational Churches of Lutterworth, Gilmorton and Walcote in 1944, which had five deacons and 56 members.[159] Ullesthorpe had been added to the group by 1966. As a result of the national union between the Congregational and Presbyterian churches in 1972, it became

---

154 Bruce, Gates and Gates, *Brief Hist.*, 4–5; ROLLR, QS 44/1/2; TNA, HO 129/408/28.
155 RCHM, *An Inventory of Nonconformist Chapels and Meeting-houses in Central England* (London, 1986), 129; NHLE, no. 1211075, United Reform Church George St (accessed 13 June 2018).
156 ROLLR, 1D 41/44/163, 198, 202, 204, 481.
157 *Leic. Chron.*, 24 Mar. 1877; 12 May 1877.
158 *Leic. Chron.*, 17 Nov. 1883.
159 Bruce, Gates and Gates, *Brief Hist.*, 28.

Lutterworth United Reformed Church.[160] Alterations to the church in 1997 provided a kitchen, toilets and new stairs.[161] The congregation dwindled in the early 21st century, and by 2012 it had lost its permanent minister.[162] Numbers continued to fall, and the church closed in 2021. The grade II listed building, owned by the East Midlands Synod of the URC, was put on the market, its fittings and contents were made available to other churches and local funds were given to various charities. Following a final thanksgiving event, the former members ceased meeting together for worship.[163]

Baptist and Calvinist Churches

Thomas Morris of Lutterworth became a deacon of the early Baptist church at Sutton in the Elms in about 1650, and was a signatory of the General Baptist Confession of 1651.[164] John Kitchen of Lutterworth, a Baptist, was preaching illegally at Leire and Whetstone in 1669,[165] and in 1672 was licensed to hold worship in Lutterworth and Shilton (Warws.).[166] Arnesby Baptist church had eight members from Lutterworth in 1705.[167] In 1709 rector Henry Meriton reported that an 'Anabaptist' named Perry, a mechanic, led occasional services in Lutterworth that were attended by about 30 'hearers'. This congregation no longer met in 1712.[168]

A Particular Baptist congregation began to meet for prayers in 1816, and were recorded as ten Huntingtonian Calvinists in 1829.[169] A house in Ely Lane, occupied by Mary and Ann Wright, was registered for worship in 1829 by Joseph Dunkly, John Wright and Benjamin Lea.[170] Lea had been associated with the Independent chapel, but was excommunicated from that church in 1830.[171] In 1837 Lea and Wright registered a property in Greyhound Lane (later Chapel Street) for worship, owned by Martha Paddy and Mary Ann Oliver.[172] The following year, Richard de Fraine was invited to the pastorate.[173] A 'small, neat' and plain Particular Baptist church was built adjacent to the Greyhound Lane property in 1839 and registered for worship, with the neighbouring building converted to a schoolroom and vestry.[174] The church held three services each Sunday in 1899.[175] The chapel closed shortly after the death of its pastor, John Woodfield,

160 *Lutterworth Independent*, Dec. 1979, 10.
161 Bruce, Gates and Gates, *Brief Hist.*, 41.
162 Ex inf. Irene Moore, church leader, 10 May 2012.
163 Ex inf., Revd Timothy Huc, 25 Aug. 2021; https://urc.org.uk/images/General-Assemblies/Assembly2021/GA_Report_Church_closures_-_Final.pdf (accessed 12 Aug. 2021).
164 Anon., 'Sutton-in-the-Elms and Arnesby', *Trans. of the Baptist Historical Society* (1909), 181, 183.
165 Evans, 'Nonconformists', 134–5.
166 *Cal. SP Dom.* 1672, 462, 676.
167 A. Betteridge, 'Early Baptists in Leicestershire and Rutland (IV): Particular Baptists; later developments', *Baptist Quarterly* 26 (1976), 217.
168 Broad, *Bishop Wake's Summary*, 857.
169 R.F. Chambers, *The Strict Baptist Chapels of England*, IV (1963), 78; ROLLR, QS 95/2/1/21.
170 ROLLR, QS 95/2/1/21; 1D 41/44/610.
171 Bruce, Gates and Gates, *Brief Hist.*, 11.
172 ROLLR, 1D 41/44/662.
173 Chambers, *Strict Baptist*, 78.
174 ROLLR, 1D 41/44/673; White, *Hist.* (Sheffield, 1846), 404; Chambers, *Strict Baptist*, 78–9.
175 *Kelly's Dir. of Leics. and Rutl.* (1899), 286.

in 1940.[176] The building was sold to Lutterworth Rugby Club in 1954.[177] It became the home of Lutterworth Christian Fellowship Church in 1977.[178]

Wesleyan Methodists

Wesleyan Methodists are believed to have met in Lutterworth from the 1770s.[179] The first Wesleyan chapel was built for 150 worshippers in 1815 at the north-eastern end of Baker Street, at a cost of £500.[180] It transferred from the Hinckley to the Rugby circuit when Lutterworth railway station opened in 1899.[181] Services were held that year on Sunday afternoons and evenings, and on Friday evenings.[182] Thomas Champness, who founded the *Joyful News* publication and directed its profits towards the training of Methodist ministers, moved to Lutterworth in 1903.[183] By 1905, 'largely through his efforts', a new Wesleyan Methodist church with seating for 270 people was built at the junction of Coventry Road and Bitteswell Road, adjacent to the Wyclif memorial (Figure 1).[184] The church, built in red brick with Bath stone dressings, included a porch, a short tower with a small stone spire and a large cross wing for the Sunday school, and was designed by Albert Lambert of Nottingham. Almost the entire cost of £3,400 had been raised by the time it opened.[185] Champness died just six months later.[186] An extension to the church, for social use, was added in 1925, and a new entrance foyer was built in 1980 to mark the seventy-fifth anniversary of the building.[187] The spire deteriorated and was demolished in 1989.[188] A further extension was added to the front of the church in 2005.[189] As the only Methodist church in Lutterworth, this church was little affected by the reunification of the main streams of Methodism in 1932 other than by a change of the denomination name to the Methodist Church.

Primitive Methodists

A group of *c.*30 Primitive Methodists and labourers walked from Leicester to Lutterworth on a Sunday morning in 1839 to hold a camp meeting. They 'sang through the town' in two companies and set up banners 'near the spot on which good Wickliff's bones were burned, and near the brook into which his ashes were cast'. They were joined by many inhabitants, and concluded the day with a missionary meeting.[190] By 1846, a small building in Greyhound Lane had been converted into a Primitive Methodist

---

176 Chambers, *Strict Baptist*, 79.
177 *Rugby Advertiser*, 3 Sept. 1954; Ex inf. Colin Hudson, secretary of Lutterworth Rugby Football Club, 2011.
178 Below (Other Protestant Denominations).
179 K.H. Harris, *Two Hundred Years of Methodism in Lutterworth* (Leicester, 2004), 1.
180 TNA, HO 129/408/27; White, *Hist.* (Sheffield, 1846), 404; OS Map 25", Leics. LVIII.16 (1904 edn).
181 K.H. Harris, *Two Hundred Years*, 1.
182 *Kelly's Dir. of Leics. and Rutl.* (1899), 285–6.
183 *The Times*, 31 Oct. 1905; tablet in Wycliffe Memorial Methodist Church.
184 *Kelly's Dir. of Leics. and Rutl.* (1916), 564; *Northampton Merc.*, 10 Nov. 1905.
185 *Midland Mail*, 29 Apr. 1905.
186 *Coventry Eve. Telegraph*, 31 Oct. 1905.
187 *Rugby Advertiser*, 27 Mar. 1925; *Lutterworth Independent*, May 1978, 3; K.H. Harris, *Two Hundred Years*, 41.
188 K.H. Harris, *Two Hundred Years*, 56.
189 Ibid. 67.
190 T. Morgan, 'Rise and progress of Primitive Methodism in Leicester and its vicinity', *Primitive Methodist Magazine* (1842), 91–7.

chapel.[191] The building closed as a place of worship in 1878 and was sold, with the proceeds given to the Primitive Methodist church in Rugby.[192]

Other Protestant Denominations

Salvation Army members from Rugby began to hold services in Lutterworth in 1886.[193] They rented the former People's Club on Coventry Road from 1887, and moved to Oxford Street (later Bank Street) in 1895, but ceased meeting between 1903 and 1910.[194] The Jehovah's Witnesses had opened a kingdom hall on Lower Leicester Road by 1962.[195] They continued to meet in 2020.[196]

Lutterworth Pentecostal Church, a Christian Fellowship church belonging to the Fellowship of Assemblies of God, began to meet in 1976 and bought the former Baptist chapel in Chapel Street in 1977.[197] In 2018 they held two services on Sundays and two weekday services each week. Lutterworth Community Church was formed in 1981 by Brian and Jean Hickford and Chris and Wendy Byrne. It became part of the East Midlands Christian Fellowships group, but the church closed in 2019 because the congregation had reduced and was no longer sustainable.[198]

Modern Roman Catholicism

Viscount Feilding (the future 8th earl of Denbigh) converted to Catholicism in 1850.[199] A mass centre was opened in 1873 in a converted room over a coach house at the Denbigh Arms.[200] In 1880 the 8th earl provided 4 a. of land on the east side of Bitteswell Road for a church and presbytery, with a substantial donation towards the building costs, and the 5th Baron Braye (Alfred Verney-Cave) offered to support a priest who would also serve Lord Braye's private chapel at Stanford Hall (5 miles south of Lutterworth).[201] Raising the remaining funds proved challenging, and only a presbytery and a dual-purpose single-cell school/chapel were built, with £700 debt outstanding when the chapel opened in 1881.[202] The architect was C.G. Wray of London,[203] although it was said that the plans were drawn by Alfred Hazeland, who had trained as an architect prior to

191 White, *Hist.* (Sheffield, 1846), 404.

192 K.H. Harris, *Two Hundred Years*, 7.

193 *Northampton Merc.*, 15 May 1886; *Nuneaton Advertiser*, 6 Nov. 1886.

194 *Northampton Merc.*, 19 Mar. 1887; *Rugby Advertiser*, 15 June 1895; 7 Nov. 1903; 22 Jan. 1910.

195 Lutterworth RDC, *The Rural District of Lutterworth Official Guide* (London, 1961), 15.

196 https://apps.jw.org/ui/E/meeting-search.html#/weekly-meetings/search/E/Lutterworth (accessed 30 Dec. 2020).

197 *Lutterworth Independent*, Feb. 1977, 5; *Coventry Eve. Telegraph*, 5 June 1978.

198 http://www.lccweb.org.uk/index.php?option=com_content&view=article&id=86&Itemid=64 (accessed 17 Apr. 2012); East Midlands Christian Fellowships, Rpt and accounts 2019, https://register-of-charities. charitycommission.gov.uk (accessed 22 Jan. 2022).

199 *The Times*, 27 Nov. 1939.

200 *Tablet*, 12 Apr. 1873, 18; 6 Sept. 1873, 16; 28 Aug. 1875, 14; 20 Aug. 1881, 37; D. Sweeney, *Centenary Book: A Short Hist. of the Diocese of Nottingham* (Newport, 1950), 45.

201 *Tablet*, 20 Aug. 1881, 37; *Kelly's Dir. of Leics. and Rutl.* (1899), 285; Sweeney, *Centenary Book*, 45.

202 *Tablet*, 10 Sept. 1881.

203 *Leicester Jnl*, 12 Aug. 1881; https://taking-stock.org.uk/building/lutterworth-leicester-our-lady-of-victories-and-st-alphonsus (accessed 12 July 2021).

Figure 25 *The Catholic Church of Our Immaculate Lady of Victories and St Alphonsus, east elevation. The central roof cross marks the liturgical east end of the original church (which points towards the north west).*

joining the priesthood.[204] Hazeland became the chapel's first priest. The chapel could seat 100 people and was dedicated to Our Immaculate Lady of Victories and St Alphonsus.[205] Daily services were held in 1899, with three services each Sunday.[206] Later extensions in red brick almost surround the original building (Figure 25) and provided a much larger church for a congregation that numbered *c.*250 in 1983.[207] The altar contains a relic of the Blessed Robert Sutton, former rector of Lutterworth, which was transferred from Stonyhurst College (Lancs.) and placed there on the four-hundredth anniversary of Sutton's martyrdom in 1987.[208] In 2021 the church shared a priest with St Pius X church in Narborough.[209]

A convent of St Clare was established in a disused bank in 1912, with a chaplain and two novices.[210] It closed in 1925, with the small community 'distributed among other houses of the Order', probably in France.[211]

204 P. Harris, *Souvenir of Father John Feeley's Silver Jubilee*, 9.
205 *Tablet*, 20 Aug. 1881, 37.
206 *Kelly's Dir. of Leics. and Rutl.* (1899), 286.
207 Ex inf. Kate Chapman, member of the congregation.
208 *Leic. Merc.*, 25 July 1987.
209 https://www.ourladyofvictories.co.uk; https://stpiusxnarborough.org (accessed 11 Aug. 2021).
210 *Tablet*, 19 Oct. 1912, 7.
211 *Tablet*, 14 Nov. 1925, 26; Ex inf. Sister M. Bede, OSC archivist, 20 Jan. 2012.

LOCAL GOVERNMENT

BURGAGE PLOTS WERE CREATED IN the 13th century, but there is no evidence that the burgesses were granted a charter of liberties. Lutterworth's institutional structure resembled that of a village until the mid 19th century, with manor courts and a vestry, but with one important addition: by the 16th century, certain lands and properties were owned by a trust, which was able to collect the rents and spend these in ways that benefited the town. The trust's early history is obscure, but it appears to have evolved from one of the town's medieval religious guilds, later becoming known as the Town Estate.

The assizes of the justices itinerant were held in Lutterworth during the 1340s, the only venue in Leicestershire known to have hosted them apart from Leicester itself.[1] Only two medieval court rolls survive for the Guthlaxton hundred courts, both from between 1458 and 1464, and both were held in Lutterworth.[2] Lutterworth became the centre of a poor law union in 1835, and of a rural district council in 1894. Local government changes in 1974 reduced the number of district councils in Leicestershire, and Lutterworth was brought within the expanded area of the Harborough District Council, based in Market Harborough.

Manorial Government

The manor court was said to be held with the privileges pertaining to the Crown (*regale*) in 1279, although the almost contemporary hundred rolls mention only the assize of bread and ale and view of frankpledge.[3] The courts were clearly busy,[4] but details of the income survive for very few years. This fluctuated widely for reasons that are not clear, from extremes of 25s. in 1322[5] to £8 13s. 6d. in 1339.[6] More usual years may be the yield of 57s. 7d. from the two views of frankpledge in 1359,[7] and the 51s. 10d. recorded in 1512–13 (3 per cent of the manorial income).[8] In 1445 the pleas and perquisites of the courts and the view of frankpledge were said to be worth nothing beyond the fee and

1   TNA, JUST 1/1400, m. 164.
2   TNA, SC 2/183/69–70.
3   Nichols, *Hist.*, IV, 247–8; Bodleian Libr., MS Rawl. B 350, f. 23; *Rot. Hund.* I, 239; M. Hagger, *The Fortunes of a Norman Family: the de Verduns in England, Ireland and Wales, 1066–1216* (Dublin, 2001), 127.
4   TNA, E 101/258/2.
5   TNA, SC/1146/17.
6   G.A. Holmes, *The Estates of the Higher Nobility in Fourteenth-century England* (Cambridge, 1957), 147, citing TNA, SC 11/801.
7   TNA, SC 6/908/33.
8   TNA, SC 6/HENVIII/1824.

expenses of the steward.[9] There were three tithings in 1562, for the town, Moorbarns and the village of Catthorpe.[10]

The manor had two ovens, worth 10s. in 1316 and 1360,[11] although one oven, worth 6s. 5d., was repaired with stone and thatch and then leased for 40s. in 1322.[12] The smaller of the two ovens had fallen out of use by 1648, and the other could bake only half of the town's requirement. More than 16 households had their own private ovens by 1659.[13]

Two bread weighers and two ale tasters were appointed in 1657. In 1734 the bread weighers also weighed butter, and pairs of constables, ale tasters, flesh and fish tasters, leather sealers, headboroughs, pinders, neatherds and townmasters were also chosen by the manor court. The number of constables had increased to four by 1751. A town crier was also elected in 1857, as was a pinder, despite the open fields having been enclosed.[14]

Almost the only presentments made in the 19th century were for nuisances, including steps and bow windows that projected beyond the building line, and cellar windows. Penalties for infringements ranged from 1d. to 3s.[15] Some retailers may have regarded this as a small annual cost for the benefit of a bow window to display their stock. The manor court also acted as a quasi-planning authority. A special court met in 1802 to inspect the alterations made by George Smith, a wine merchant, to his property in Church Street, and to consider further proposed alterations. The jurors specified in detail how far the building could be extended, and ordered Smith to pay an annual fee of 3s. for the privilege of encroaching upon the street.[16]

Town Government

The Town Estate

The town was never incorporated, but from the 16th century the community achieved an element of self-governance through a trust that owned property and applied the rents for the benefit of residents. The origins of the trust, which became known as the Town Estate, almost certainly lie in Edmund Muryell's endowment of a chantry in 1478, which appointed 12 feoffees to hold the assets of the guild, and stipulated that rents from landholdings were to be kept in the 'Com[m]on box' of the town until they were sufficient to employ a priest.[17] In 1509 five cottages, several shops and more than 10 a. of land in Lutterworth were held to the use of the town (*ad usu[m] ville*), probably by the guild, in addition to any assets elsewhere.[18] Prior to its dissolution at the Reformation,

9   *Cal. Inq. p.m.* XXVI, 195–6.
10   TNA, SC 2/183/83.
11   *Cal. Inq. p.m.* VI, 36 (1316); TNA, C 135/152/5 (1360).
12   TNA, SC 6/1146/17.
13   TNA, E 134/1658–9/Hil16, mm. 5–6; Goodacre, *Transformation*, 167–8.
14   Warws. RO, CR 2017/M34, M35/4, M35/9, M37/3.
15   Warws. RO, CR 2017/M/36/17–23, M37/1–2, M37/11.
16   Warws. RO, CR 2017/M35/56.
17   Warws. RO, CR 2017/D199; above, Religious Hist. (Religious Life before 1547). Melton Mowbray presents a similar example of guild assets becoming town assets: D. Pockley, 'The origins and early records of the Melton Mowbray Town Estate', *Trans. LAHS* 45 (1969–70), 20–38.
18   Warws. RO, CR 2017/E42.

the guild declared lands in Shawell and North Kilworth to the Chantry Commissioners, and these were sold by the Crown in 1549.[19] Other landholdings appear to have been concealed. Gifts of lands and tenements by Richard Palmer, Roger Smith and Alice Smith in 1484–5, Edward Wells in 1489–90, John Hutt in 1495–6, William Cocks in 1497–8 and William Pawley in 1505–6 were later recorded as belonging to the town, but had probably originally been given to the guild.[20] Freehold land in the town valued at 11s. 10d. in 1518, and owned by the master of the guild, was held by the 'Master of the Towne' in 1536.[21]

The potential for disagreement between the manorial court and the Town Estate was minimised by the election of the townmasters at the manor court and through the distinct interests of each body. The manor court regulated the fields and dealt with matters of law and order, while the Town Estate channelled its income towards maintaining and improving roads, bridges and pavements, which was arguably of greater interest to the mercantile community. In 1540 'every man in the town' was 'compelled' to pay his share of the cost of keeping the bridges and pavements in repair.[22] Additional gifts for the repair or maintenance of Bransford bridge, Spital bridge and the town's pavements were made by several townspeople, including William Pawley in 1507, Sir William Feilding in 1518, John Paybody in 1520, John Chapleyn in 1524, John Wheatley in 1563 and Francis Peake in 1579.[23] A new feoffment for the Town Estate was made in 1710, restating that two townmasters should be chosen annually at the manor court and should present accounts annually, and requiring leases to be granted for no more than 21 years and to be approved at a meeting of the inhabitants.[24] By the 18th century, the Town Estate income was benefiting the full community. Expenditure included the construction of almshouses and a workhouse in 1721 in Hartshall Lane (later George Street),[25] the demolition and rebuilding of the schoolhouse in 1781, and the building of a new workhouse in 1801.[26] By 1839, when annual income was £241 18s., all the principal streets had been made up with the 'best materials', and the footways were paved or flagged and had kerb stones.[27]

The town's need for additional school places led to the agreement of a new scheme in 1871.[28] The assets were vested in the official trustee for charity land, and the office of townmaster lapsed. The new trustees comprised the rector, the churchwardens, any magistrate resident in Lutterworth and nine others chosen at a vestry meeting from among those who paid annual rates of at least £25. The income was to be used to maintain public buildings and to assist with the education or health-care needs of the poorer classes, with up to £40 to be spent annually on lighting the streets.[29] The following

19   A. Hamilton Thompson, 'The chantry certificates for Leicestershire', *Assoc. Archit. Soc. Rpts. & Papers* 30 (1909–10), 513–14, 547–8; *Cal. Pat. Edward VI*, II, 185, 188.
20   ROLLR, DE 4336/33/1. The list was displayed in the church in 1790: Nichols, *Antiquities*, 1139–40.
21   TNA, WARD 2/6/241/22, ff. 2, 5.
22   TNA, PROB 11/31/690.
23   ROLLR, Will Register 1515–26, f. 374–374v (Paybody); PR/I/255/86 (Wheatley); TNA, PROB 11/15/491 (Palley); 11/21/428 (Chapleyn); 11/62/73 (Peake); Nichols, *Antiquities*, 1140 (Feilding).
24   Nichols, *Hist.*, IV, 254–6; *Rpt of Charity Commissioners* (Parl. Papers 1839 [163], xv), pp. 129–32.
25   ROLLR, DE 2559/102.
26   ROLLR, DE 914/1.
27   *Rpt of Charity Commissioners*, pp. 131–3.
28   Above, Social Hist. (Education).
29   *Leic. Chron.*, 30 Nov. 1872.

year, the trustees provided £250 towards new schools.[30] From 1894, the churchwardens were replaced as trustees by two people chosen by the parish council. Later expenditure included street-name signs in 1895, donations towards the fire brigade in 1901 and 1913, and street alterations in 1916 to create room for a war memorial.[31] The Town Estate purchased the market tolls in 1923.[32]

A further revision of the charity's objects in 1972 gave the Town Estate the power to make grants and gifts of furniture, fuel and clothing to individual residents in need.[33] The number of trustees was reduced to nine: the rector, three chosen by the parish council and five co-opted by the other trustees.[34] The charity subsequently changed its name to Lutterworth Town Estates. Its income in 2019 was £71,224, mostly derived from rent on its portfolio of properties, with a book value of £1,361,285.[35]

Town Hall

The earl of Denbigh agreed to let a triangular site on sloping ground alongside High Street in 1834 for a 'market place and town hall'.[36] A committee of eight was formed which agreed to buy the site from Lord Denbigh for 400 guineas (£420).[37] Joseph Hansom, the architect of Birmingham town hall and designer of the hansom cab, produced plans for a building in the Greek Revival style, with an open market hall at ground level and a large hall (set diagonally to maximise its length) and small committee room above.[38] The upper floor exterior included a full-width pediment with four Ionic columns.[39] The building cost £1,200, but subscriptions initially failed to reach the amount required. The trustees of the Town Estate borrowed at least £330 towards the cost, which they had repaid by 1839.[40] The building opened in 1836 and was managed by the townmasters. The upper floor was used for public meetings, occasional balls and, until 1906, fortnightly petty sessions and a monthly county court (Figure 26).[41]

The ground floor was enclosed during a refurbishment in 1907 (Figure 27).[42] A separate charity was established in 1983 under a scheme by which one third of the surplus income of the Town Estates charity would pass to the Town Hall Charity each

---

30   Above, Social Hist. (Education).
31   *Nuneaton Advertiser*, 12 Jan. 1895; J. Sumpter, *A Brief Historical Review of the Charity known as the Lutterworth Town Estate Trust* (Lutterworth, c.1926), 7.
32   Above, Economic Hist. (Trades and Services).
33   *Coventry Eve. Telegraph*, 17 Mar. 1972.
34   *Leicester Merc.*, 17 Mar. 1972.
35   Rpt and Financial Statements 2019, https://beta.charitycommission.gov.uk/charity-details/?regid=217609&subid=0 (accessed 31 Mar. 2020).
36   Lincs. Arch., COR.B. 5/5/3/2/1.
37   Lutterworth Museum, Resolutions from public meeting 25 Mar. 1835; F.W. Bottrill, *An Illustrated Handbook of Lutterworth* (Lutterworth, 1900), 11.
38   Lutterworth Museum, signed plans dated June and July 1835; P. Harris, *Architectural Achievement*, 17–51, 79–83.
39   Pevsner, *Leics. and Rutl.*, 301; NHLE, no. 1211129, Town Hall High St (accessed 31 Mar. 2020).
40   P. Harris, *Architectural Achievement*, 95; ROLLR, DE 914/1; White, *Hist.* (Sheffield, 1846), 401.
41   White, *Hist.* (Sheffield, 1877), 522; P. Harris, *Architectural Achievement*, 95–6; *Morning Post*, 8 Feb. 1873; *Leic. Jnl*, 21 Feb. 1890; *Leic. Daily Post*, 9 Mar. 1906.
42   P. Harris, *Architectural Achievement*, 96.

Figure 26 *Town hall, main upper room, in 2015. The Royal Arms on the right reference the room's use as a magistrates' and county court until 1906.*

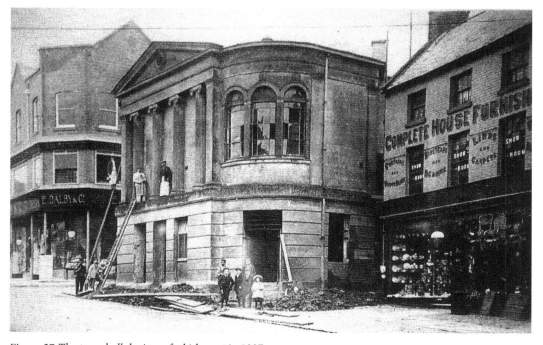

Figure 27 *The town hall during refurbishment in 1907.*

year. Modernisations costing c.£45,000 were completed in 1986.[43] A wider door and the addition of a new lift in 2021 improved accessibility.[44]

Parish Government before 1894

Lutterworth was notably successful in obtaining annual contributions towards the cost of poor relief in the 17th century from the owners of land in neighbouring depopulated parishes.[45] An agreement of 1693 shared the remaining cost between the occupiers of land in the parish and the owners of properties in the town 'according to the intrinsique value of their holdings'.[46]

A workhouse was established in 1721, and the parish paid a fixed sum to a contractor to feed and clothe its residents. The poor rate was cut by one quarter, but there were problems with the contractor. The parish decided to erect a more suitable building in 1724, and appointed one of its residents to look after the other inhabitants. The workhouse contained 20 paupers in 1724, with costs offset by work undertaken, including spinning and 'winding quills' (winding yarn on bobbins for weavers).[47]

The cost of poor relief rose from £309 10s. in 1777 to £1,017 in 1803.[48] The workhouse was partially rebuilt by the townmasters in 1801–2, and several wealthier residents provided a total of £133 towards the cost.[49] It was enlarged in 1810–12, when the parishes of Bruntingthorpe, North Kilworth and South Kilworth agreed to share the building for their non-able-bodied poor.[50] Kilby, Peatling Parva, Shearsby, Swinford and Walton (in Knaptoft) joined this union in 1819.[51] The workhouse had between 20 and 30 inmates in 1834 who were 'mostly women and children and infirm persons'.[52] The town also owned five houses on Bakehouse Lane and 13 on Ely Lane and Webbs Yard, off Ely Lane, which it used 'for the habitation and employment of the poor'.[53]

43   *Lutterworth Independent*, Mar. 1983, July 1983, Nov. 1983; http://www.lutterworthtownhall.org.uk/ trustees.htm; Lutterworth Town Hall Charity, rpt and accounts 2017, https://beta.charitycommission. gov.uk/charity-details/?regid=515314&subid=0 (both accessed 31 Mar. 2020); P. Harris, *Architectural Achievement*, 97.
44   *Rugby Advertiser*, 21 Apr. 2021.
45   Above, Social Hist. (Social Character).
46   ROLLR, QS 6/1/2/11, f. 157.
47   Anon., *An Account of Several Workhouses for Employing and Maintaining the Poor* (1725), 153–4.
48   *Rpt. of Committee to Inspect and Consider Poor Returns* (Parl. Papers 1776–7), p. 384; *Abstract of Poor Rate Returns* (Parl. Papers 1803–4 (175), xiii), p. 264.
49   ROLLR, DE 914/1; *Rpt of Charity Commissioners*, p. 132.
50   ROLLR, DE 1463/6, mins 31 Oct. 1810, 24 Oct. 1812.
51   Lutterworth Museum, 4D 60/342.
52   *Rpt of Poor Law Commission* (Parl. Papers 1834 (44), xxvii), app. B, p. 292.
53   ROLLR, DE 1463/6, mins 25 Jan. 1803, 3 Mar. 1837; *Rpt of Charity Commissioners*, pp. 140–1; above, Social Hist. (Social Welfare).

Lutterworth Poor Law Union

Lutterworth Poor Law Union was formed in 1835, comprising 30 parishes in Leicestershire, Northamptonshire and Warwickshire.[54] Lutterworth had two of the 31 guardians. The union workhouse, for 200 inmates, was built on Woodmarket in 1839–40 and cost £5,000. The architects were George Gilbert Scott and William Bonython Moffatt.[55] The construction met with local protests and two bricklayers were assaulted while at work in 1839 by two stocking makers, for working on 'the Bastille'.[56] A meeting of ratepayers in 1840 approved the sale of the parish cottages in Ely Lane, Webbs Yard and Bakehouse Lane.[57] From the net proceeds of £582 8s. 3d., the Poor Law Commissioners agreed that £110 could be used to repay the money that had been borrowed to purchase two of the cottages, and £337 7s. 3d. used to repay the parish share of the cost of building the union workhouse.[58] The remainder was retained by the poor law union.[59]

The union workhouse became a public assistance institution in 1929 and a care home for the elderly, known as Woodmarket House, in 1948. The buildings were demolished c.1970, and a privately owned modern care home was built on the site.[60]

Local Government after 1894

Lutterworth Parish Council

Lutterworth's first parish council, elected in 1894, had eight members.[61] The first chairman was Lupton Topham Topham of Lutterworth House, a barrister.[62] A wealthy and active Town Estate provided many of the facilities the town required, but the elected council provided a different perspective on the town's needs and access to government borrowing. Two of the council's early and important achievements were the provision of allotment gardens and (through the parochial committee, which comprised the parish councillors and Lutterworth's two district councillors) a recommendation to the rural district council in 1913 to provide working-class housing.[63]

The parish council chose to redesignate itself as a town council in 1974, with a mayor rather than a chair.[64] There were 13 town councillors in 1975.[65] This number had increased to 16 by 2020, when Lutterworth was divided into four wards. Committees dealt

54 Youngs, *Admin. Units*, II, 693.
55 http://www.workhouses.org.uk/Lutterworth (accessed 2 Apr. 2020).
56 *Northampton Merc.*, 17 Aug. 1839.
57 ROLLR, DE 1463/6, mins 3 Mar. 1837, 20 Mar. 1840, 14 May 1841; *Leic. Chron.*, 9 May 1840.
58 ROLLR, DE 1379/37/2; DE 1463/6, min. 14 May 1841.
59 *Digest of Endowed Charities* (Parl. Papers 1867–8 (433)), pp. 678–9.
60 http://www.workhouses.org.uk/Lutterworth (accessed 2 Apr. 2020); https://www.cqc.org.uk/location/1-370431463#accordion-1 (accessed 15 Aug. 2021).
61 *Nuneaton Advertiser*, 22 Dec. 1894.
62 *Rugby Advertiser*, 27 Apr. 1895; TNA, RG 13/2951/16/24.
63 Above, Landscape and Settlement (Settlement); *Leic. Chron.*, 19 Jan. 1895; 27 Apr. 1895.
64 *Coventry Eve. Telegraph*, 10 June 1974; 12 June 1974.
65 *Lutterworth Independent*, July 1975.

with allotments, recreation areas, public conveniences and town events. The council also made recommendations to the district council on planning applications and highways.[66]

District Councils

Lutterworth Rural District Council was formed in 1894 and comprised the Leicestershire parishes in Lutterworth Poor Law Union, with the exception of Wigston Parva and the addition of Westrill and Starmore.[67] At the first election for the town's two representatives, Lutterworth's existing guardians of the poor (William Footman and Richard Sansome) were defeated, and Lupton Topham Topham was elected with Arthur Bannister, the former proprietor of the steam brewery.[68] Both were 'ardent Conservatives'.[69] Council meetings were originally held in the board room at the workhouse.[70] The rural district council moved to premises in The Narrows in 1931, before purchasing the much larger Lutterworth Hall on Woodmarket in 1939.[71]

Harborough District Council was created in 1974 by merging the rural districts of Market Harborough, Lutterworth and Billesdon, and the urban district of Market Harborough.[72] The new council met in Market Harborough, and Lutterworth Hall was sold in 1979.[73] Lutterworth was represented by four councillors in 2019 for two reconstituted wards, Lutterworth East and Lutterworth West.[74]

The A5 Partnership

Harborough District Council is a member of the A5 Partnership, together with other county and district councils from Leicestershire, Northamptonshire, Staffordshire and Warwickshire; four local enterprise partnerships (voluntary partnerships between local government and businesses) in Leicestershire, Staffordshire, Warwickshire and Birmingham; East Midlands Councils (a regional forum for local government); and National Highways (formerly Highways England). Together they are responsible for agreeing a consistent local government strategy to support economic growth within a 62-mile corridor of land along the Northamptonshire to Staffordshire section of Watling Street. The first strategy document was issued in 2011, and a later plan was agreed for 2018 to 2031.[75] The contribution of district council members to this forum is clearly important to Lutterworth, given the impact of the Magna Park logistics estate (adjacent to the A5) on local employment and the level of traffic on Lutterworth's southern bypass.

66   https://www.lutterworth.org.uk/committees.html (accessed 6 Apr. 2020).
67   Youngs, *Admin. Units*, II, 693, 695.
68   *Leic. Chron.*, 8 Dec. 1894; 22 Dec. 1894.
69   *Rugby Advertiser*, 10 Feb. 1928; 5 Dec. 1908.
70   *Kelly's Dir. of Leics. and Rutl.* (1899), 286.
71   *Rugby Advertiser*, 27 Feb. 1931; 12 May 1939; *Leic. Daily Merc.*, 16 June 1939; 8 Sept. 1939; T. Bailey, *Lutterworth in Wartime: The Impact of World War Two on a Rural Area of England* (Lutterworth, 2014), 36.
72   Youngs, *Admin. Units*, II, 696.
73   *Coventry Eve. Telegraph*, 2 Nov. 1979.
74   https://www.harborough.gov.uk/homepage/104/district_council_election_results_-_may_2019 (accessed 6 Apr. 2020).
75   A5 Partnership, *The A5: Draft: A Strategy for Growth, 2018–2031*, 160, 209, 211.

Public Services

Water and Sewerage

Twenty pump reeves were appointed for ten street pumps in 1731, with duties probably including keeping the roads free of dust in the summer and washing the streets at the end of every market and fair.[76] The town was solely dependent on *c.*100 private wells and 15 public pumps in 1896. A meeting of ratepayers was called that year to consider asking the RDC to supply piped water, but it concluded that it was 'too soon to consider the question'.[77]

The Lutterworth Freehold Land Society Ltd was formed in 1898, with Lord Denbigh as president and Marston Buszard (d. 1921) and Lupton Topham Topham as vice presidents.[78] It purchased building land on New Street and Leicester Road to help people who wished to own their own home, but within a year the company had largely turned away from its original purpose and acquired the powers to lay pipes and supply water. In 1899 it built a waterworks and water tower on Bitteswell Road, fed by a new well, 40 ft. deep, and changed its name to Lutterworth Freehold Land, Building and Water Supply Co. Ltd.[79] The company sought to sell the waterworks to the parish council in 1910, but as the council would have no power to raise a water rate, it set the matter before the RDC.[80] Before anything could be agreed, the waterworks company went into liquidation.[81] Negotiations continued, but were delayed by the First World War.[82] The business assets were purchased by the RDC for £3,400 in 1920.

The water supply proved insufficient for population growth, and George Spencer sank a new well and pump in 1929, which he donated to the RDC for the use of the town.[83] A new water scheme in 1939 diverted water from local springs to underground tanks in Misterton, from where it was pumped to the water tower and piped from there by gravity feed.[84] Following the amalgamation of water companies in the late 1940s and 1950s, Lutterworth's water was drawn from Stanford reservoir and treatment works.[85]

The Town Estate had laid sewers in part of the town by 1839.[86] The town did not adopt the Public Health Act of 1848, but a nuisances committee of seven people was established in 1855.[87] Following a number of deaths from 'fever' in 1856, the committee recommended laying sewers in Bakehouse Lane and Ely Lane. The Town Estate could afford to pay no more than one third of the cost, and ratepayers refused to cover the

---

76   Warws. RO, CR 2017/M35/2.

77   *Rugby Advertiser*, 26 Dec. 1896.

78   *Leic. Chron.*, 5 Mar. 1898.

79   ROLLR, DE 2072/149; *Rugby Advertiser*, 17 Dec. 1898; 21 Jan. 1899; 17 June 1899; *Kelly's Dir. of Leics. and Rutl.* (1912), 554.

80   *Rugby Advertiser*, 5 Feb. 1910.

81   *London Gaz.*, 27 Dec. 1910, 9675.

82   *Leic. Daily Post*, 17 Oct. 1913; *Rugby Advertiser*, 16 Oct. 1915; 25 July 1919.

83   *Rugby Advertiser*, 6 Dec. 1929.

84   *Rugby Advertiser*, 5 Sept. 1935; *Leic. Daily Post*, 16 June 1939; W.W. Baum, *The Water Supplies of Leicestershire* (Leicester, 1949), 101.

85   Lutterworth RDC, *Handbook*.

86   *Rpt of Charity Commissioners*, pp. 131–3.

87   ROLLR, DE 4336/33/1, 14 Dec. 1855; *Northampton Merc.*, 6 Sept. 1856.

remainder, obtaining legal opinion that laying sewers was beyond the committee's powers.[88] Most of Lutterworth appears to have had sewers by 1876, but it is not clear from surviving records when they were laid.[89] The first sewage works was built by the RDC off Moorbarns Lane in 1901. This was extended in 1935 and replaced by larger works to the south west in 1971.[90]

Cemetery

Lutterworth never had a burial board. St Mary's churchyard was extended when required, reaching 4 a. (1.6 ha.) in the 1980s, a legacy of the large glebe.[91] Population growth in the late 20th century made further provision necessary, and Lutterworth Town Council acquired land and opened Leaders Farm cemetery (1.2 ha.) on the junction of Coventry Road and Brookfield Way c.2013.[92]

Gas and Electricity

A meeting of inhabitants in 1850 heard from gas engineers from four towns, and the ratepayers present agreed that Lutterworth should be lit by gas. The Lutterworth Gas Light & Coke Co. was formed that year, and purchased land to the east of the town for a gas works. Gas street lights were installed in 1851, when the Town Estate agreed to contribute £20 annually towards the cost, with the balance paid by a rate on the town's houses.[93] The gas business was incorporated as a limited company in 1907.[94] The gas works were enlarged in 1929.[95] They were demolished c.1970, following conversion of the supply to natural gas.[96]

The Leicestershire and Warwickshire Electric Supply Co. was authorised to supply electricity to homes and businesses in Lutterworth and surrounding villages in 1926. A supply had been laid along the main roads by 1927.[97]

88   ROLLR, DE 4336/33/1, 30 Dec. 1856; *Leic. Jnl*, 28 Nov. 1856; 12 Dec. 1856; 19 Dec. 1856; 2 Jan. 1857; 16 Jan. 1857.
89   ROLLR, DE 1379/413, pp. 135, 137, 148, 156.
90   *Rugby Advertiser*, 27 July 1901; 9 Aug. 1935; *Coventry Eve. Telegraph*, 15 July 1971.
91   *Leic. Chron.*, 27 June 1868; *Leic. Jnl*, 16 Apr. 1869; *Leic. Chron.*, 27 May 1899; St Mary's church burial register, 1909, 1939.
92   *Leic. Merc.*, 19 Mar. 1991; https://www.bbc.co.uk/news/uk-england-leicestershire-15611604; https://www.lutterworth.org.uk/leaders-farm-cemetery.html; https://pa2.harborough.gov.uk/online-applications/applicationDetails.do?activeTab=summary&keyVal=M610P9HWGJ000 (both accessed 2 Apr. 2020).
93   *Leics. Merc.*, 28 Sept. 1850; 29 Mar. 1851; Warws. RO, CR 2017/D170, ff. 87–8; ROLLR, DE 4336/33/1.
94   *Rugby Advertiser*, 15 June 1907.
95   *Rugby Advertiser*, 12 July 1929.
96   *Coventry Eve. Telegraph*, 14 Oct. 1970.
97   *Rugby Advertiser*, 5 Feb. 1926; 5 Nov. 1926; 16 Sept. 1927.

Figure 28 *Lutterworth Police Station, built in 1842, closed in 2013 (south elevation).*

Law and Order

Constables' accounts include expenditure in the 1650s on a cuck-stool (ducking stool) with wheel, a whipping post and a cage (lock-up).[98] A night watch was agreed in 1789 and 'places of confinement' were built in 1812.[99] These were probably the underground cells within the gaol, which stood at the junction of Regent Street and Stoney Hollow.[100]

Lutterworth police station was built in 1842 on the junction of Leicester Road and Gilmorton Road at a cost of £731 (Figure 28). It had two cells, a walled yard, an office and a superintendent's house.[101] The superintendent's post was downgraded to inspector in 1922.[102] Lutterworth division then had two sergeants and seven constables, with the constables and one of the sergeants living in eight different villages. With the aim of

98 ROLLR, DE 2559/24, e.g. entries 3 Apr. 1654, 20 May 1657, 10 June 657, 25 June 1657 (cuck-stool); 8 Apr. 1657 (whipping post); 2 Oct. 1655, 21 Feb. 1659 (cage).

99 ROLLR, DE 1463/6, mins 7 Oct. 1789, 31 Jan. 1812.

100 A. Amos, *Lutterworth Police Station: Celebrating 150 Years of Existence, 1843–1993* (Dunton Bassett, 1993), 1.

101 Pevsner, *Leics. and Rutl.*, 302; NHLE, no. 1228055, Magistrates' Court, Police Station, Superintendent's House Gilmorton Road (accessed 5 Apr. 2020); *Leic. Jnl*, 30 June 1843.

102 ROLLR, DE 3831/24, p. 59.

reducing divisional costs, the Home Office gave agreement in 1930 for the sergeant in Lutterworth to be provided with a car, for three village constables to be provided with motorcycles with sidecars to enable them to patrol larger areas, and for the other officers to be replaced by police boxes. When the change took effect in 1931, Lutterworth became the first county police division in England to use a motor patrol system.[103] Lutterworth police station closed in 2013.[104]

Lutterworth hosted petty sessions and a county court from the 18th century until 1906, and magistrates' courts until 1998. The magistrates' court moved from the town hall to a new building adjacent to the police station in 1905–6.[105] The courtroom closed in 1998.[106]

Fire Services

The lower floor of the 'church-gates' school housed the parish fire engine in 1838.[107] The parish council took over the management of the fire brigade in 1895, and introduced a scale of charges for sending an engine outside the town (including to farms within the parish).[108] With only a short hose, the equipment was inadequate for large blazes.[109] County councils became responsible for fire services from 1948.[110] Lutterworth fire station initially moved to premises adjacent to the RDC offices at Lutterworth Hall, and subsequently to Gilmorton Road c.1979. In 2020 the station was part of Leicestershire Fire and Rescue Service, and had a mix of salaried and on-call employees.

103 *Rugby Advertiser*, 14 Nov. 1930; Amos, *Lutterworth Police*, 5–6.
104 Ex inf. Leicestershire police archivist, 2020.
105 *Leic. Daily Post*, 9 Mar. 1906.
106 G. Smith, *Around Lutterworth: A Second Selection* (Stroud, 2002), 43.
107 *Rpt of Charity Commissioners*, p. 133.
108 *Rugby Advertiser*, 4 May 1895; 17 Aug. 1895.
109 *Yorkshire Post*, 6 Feb. 1936.
110 Fire Services Act, 1947.

APPENDIX

Lutterworth's Street Names

The names of the many of the streets in the oldest part of Lutterworth have changed over the centuries, and some names have changed more than once. The street names given in the text are those mentioned in the original sources. The modern name for those that have changed is listed below.

Former name	Name in 2022
Back Lane	Bank Street
Bakehouse Lane	Baker Street
Beast Market	Market Street
Ely Lane	Station Road
Greyhound Lane	Chapel Street
Hartshall Lane	George Street
Neats Market	Market Street
Oxford Street	Bank Street
Shotts Lane	Misterton Way
Small Lane	Bank Street
Snellsgate	Misterton Way
Worship Street	George Street

ABBREVIATIONS

a.	acres
Assoc. Archit. Soc. Rpts. & Papers	*Associated Architectural Societies, Reports and Papers*
Bk of Fees	*Liber Feodorum. The book of fees, commonly called Testa de Nevill* (1920)
Burton, *Description*	W. Burton, *The Description of Leicestershire* (King's Lynn, 2nd edn, 1777)
Cal. Chart.	*Calendar of the Charter Rolls*
Cal. Close	*Calendar of the Close Rolls*
Cal. Inq. p.m.	*Calendar of Inquisitions Post Mortem*
Cal. Papal Reg.	*Calendar of the Papal Registers*
Cal. Pat.	*Calendar of the Patent Rolls*
Cal. SP Dom.	*Calendar of State Papers, Domestic*
Calamy Revised, ed. A.G. Matthews	A.G. Matthews (ed.), *Calamy Revised: Being a Revision of Edmund Calamy's Account of the Ministers and Others Ejected and Silenced, 1660–2* (Oxford, 1934)
Camden, *Britannia*	W. Camden (trans. P. Holland), *Britain, or a chorographicall description of the most flourishing kingdomes, England, Scotland, and Ireland, and the islands adjoyning, out of the depth of antiquitie* (1637)
CARC	Coventry Archives Research Centre
CERC	Church of England Record Centre
Chron.	*Chronicle*
CJ	*Journals of the House of Commons*
Co.	Company
Complete Peerage	V. Gibbs, H.A. Doubleday and Lord Howard de Walden (eds), *The Complete Peerage of England, Scotland, Ireland, Great Britain and the United Kingdom* (London, 1910–38)
Cott.	Cottage
Dioc.	Diocese

Dir.	*Directory*
Domesday	A. Williams and G.H. Martin (eds), *Domesday Book: A Complete Translation* (London, 2002)
Edn	*Edition*
Eve.	*Evening*
Fenwick (ed.), *Poll Taxes*	C.C. Fenwick (ed.), *Poll Taxes of 1377, 1379 and 1381*, pt 1 (British Academy Records of Social and Economic Hist. n.s. 27, 1998); pt 2 (n.s. 29, 2001)
Gaz.	*Gazette/Gazetteer*
HER	Historic Environment Record
Hist.	History
Hist. Parl. Commons	*The History of Parliament: The House of Commons* (History of Parliament Trust)
Ho.	House
Jnl	*Journal*
L&I Soc.	List and Index Society
L&NWR	London and North Western Railway
L&P Henry VIII	*Letters and Papers of Henry VIII*
Leic.	Leicester
Leics.	Leicestershire
Leics. CC	Leicestershire County Council
Leics. & Rutl. HER	Historic Environment Record for Leicestershire and Rutland
Libr.	Library
Lincs. Arch.	Lincolnshire Archives
LJ	*Journals of the House of Lords*
Merc.	*Mercury*
Min./mins	Minute/minutes
Nat. Comm. Dir.	*National Commercial Directory*
NHLE	National Heritage List for England http://www.historicengland.org.uk/listing/the-list
Nichols, *Antiquities*	J. Nichols, *Antiquities in Leicestershire, being the 8th volume of the Bibliotheca Topographica Britannica* (London, 1790)
Nichols, *Hist.*	J. Nichols, *The History and Antiquities of the County of Leicester*, 4 volumes (London, 1795–1815)
ODNB	*Oxford Dictionary of National Biography*
OS	Ordnance Survey

Parl. Papers	Parliamentary Papers
PAS	Portable Antiquities Scheme
Pevsner, *Leics. and Rutl.*	N. Pevsner (rev. E. Williamson), *The Buildings of England: Leicestershire and Rutland*, 2nd edn (Harmondsworth, 1984)
RCHM	Royal Commission on the Historical Monuments of England
RDC	Rural District Council
Rec. Soc.	Record Society
RO	Record Office
ROLLR	Record Office for Leicestershire, Leicester and Rutland
Rot. Chart.	*Rotuli Chartarum in Turri Londinensi asservati* (Record Commission, 1837)
Rot. Hund.	*Rotuli Hundredorum* (Record Commission, 1812 and 1818)
Rot. Lit. Claus.	*Rotuli Literarum Clausarum* (Record Commission, 1833–44)
Rpt	Report
RSA	Rural Sanitary Authority
St	Street
Tax. Eccl.	*Taxatio Ecclesiastica Anglie et Wallie ... circa AD 1291* (Record Commission, 1801)
TNA	The National Archives
Trans. LAHS	*Transactions of the Leicestershire Archaeological and Historical Society*
Univ.	University
Valor Eccl.	*Valor Ecclesiasticus, temp. Hen. VIII* (Record Commission, 1810–34)
VCH	Victoria History of the Counties of England
Walker Revised, ed. A.G. Matthews	A.G. Matthews (ed.), *Walker Revised: Being a revision of John Walker's Sufferings of the Clergy During the Grand Rebellion, 1642–60* (Oxford, 1948)
Warws.	Warwickshire
White, *Hist.*	W. White, *History, Gazetteer and Directory of Leicestershire and Rutland*
Yorks. N.R.	Yorkshire, North Riding
Yorks. W.R.	Yorkshire, West Riding
Youngs, *Admin. Units*	F.A. Youngs, *Guide to the Local Administrative Units of England* (London, 1991)

GLOSSARY

The following technical terms may require explanation. Fuller information on local history topics is available in D. Hey, *The Oxford Companion to Family and Local History* (Oxford, 2010), or online at the VCH website (http://www.victoriacountyhistory.ac.uk). The most convenient glossary of architectural terms is *Pevsner's Architectural Glossary*, 2nd edn (New Haven and London, 2010), which is also available for mobile devices.

Advowson: the right to nominate a candidate to the bishop for appointment as rector or vicar of a church. This right was a form of property that was often attached to a manor but that could be bought and sold.

Amercement: a fine imposed by a manorial court for an offence.

Attainder: an order made by a judge or Act of Parliament by which the real and personal estate of a convicted individual was forfeited and could not be inherited.

Bailiwick: A district or place under the jurisdiction of a bailiff, who manages the land on behalf of the land owner.

Bordar: a smallholder, farming land recently brought into cultivation on the edge of a settlement.

Brief: an appeal issued under the royal seal seeking donations for a deserving cause, addressed to the ministers and churchwardens of parishes, which had to be read out from the pulpit and a collection taken. The money, and the document endorsed with the amount collected, had to be given to a travelling collector.

Burgage: a plot of land fronting a market place or main street in a town, characteristically long and thin in shape, occupied by a burgess (q.v.), usually for a money rent (burgage tenure).

Burgess: a citizen of a borough, often a member of its governing body or a resident of an unincorporated town occupying a burgage (q.v.) plot in the commercial heart of the town.

Carucate: a unit of taxation and originally the amount of land that a team of eight oxen could plough in a year. The acreage varied from place to place but was often about 120 a.

Chantry: masses celebrated for the souls of the founder and anyone nominated by the founder, or for the souls of members of a guild or fraternity.

Commons: areas of land governed by agreements made at the manorial court, giving specified rights (e.g. of grazing a certain number of animals or of collecting furze) to certain people (e.g. the occupiers of ancient cottages).

Demesne: in the Middle Ages, land farmed directly by a lord of the manor rather than granted to tenants. Although usually leased out from the later Middle Ages, demesne lands often remained distinct from the rest of a parish's land.

Dower: The part of an estate, generally one-third, which passed by common law to a widow on the death of her husband for her lifetime or earlier remarriage.

Dredge: mixed barley and oats.

Enclosure: the process whereby open fields (q.v.) were divided into closes and redistributed among the various tenants and landholders. From the 18th century, enclosure was usually by an Act of Parliament obtained by the dominant landowners; earlier, it was more commonly done by private agreement or by a powerful lord acting on his own initiative.

Feoffees: trustees appointed to manage land or other assets for the benefit of others.

Glebe: land belonging to the church to support a priest.

Hearth tax: tax levied twice a year between 1662 and 1688, assessed on the number of hearths or fireplaces in a house.

Husbandman: a farmer who generally held his land by copyhold or leasehold tenure.

Ionic: in Classical architecture, a type of column with specific features, including a scroll-shaped embellishment at the top.

Iron Age: a period from 800 BC to AD 42, divided into the early Iron Age (800–100 BC) and the late Iron Age (100 BC–AD 42).

Knight's fee or service: an amount of land capable of providing enough money to support a knight for a set period of time – almost invariably 40 days – when required, though some fees demanded other kinds of military service, such as an archer or a warhorse. Such obligations became monetary or in kind, and by the 13th century, as estates were divided up, smaller estates could be held as fractions of a knight's fee.

Legal settlement: a term relating to the application of the Poor Relief Act of 1662 (sometimes known as the Settlement Act), which defined the parish to which a person belonged and which was obliged to provide that person with poor relief when necessary. A legal settlement in a parish could be obtained in a number of ways, including by birth, marriage and apprenticeship, and could change several times over a person's life. The Act was replaced in 1834 by the Poor Law (Amendment) Act.

Legumes: a family of plants usually grown for human or animal consumption as part of a crop rotation, which includes peas and beans and also clover.

Ley: individual arable strips in open fields (q.v.) that have been converted to grass for one or more seasons.

Lollards: a pejorative name given to followers of the beliefs of John Wyclif, who rejected the authority of priests.

Manor: a piece of landed property with tenants regulated by a private (manor) court. Originally held by feudal tenure (see knight's fee), manors descended through a succession of heirs but could also be given away or sold.

Mark: a monetary unit used in accounting equal to two thirds of a pound, i.e. 13s. 4d.

Maslin: mixed wheat and rye.

Mercer: a shopkeeper who sold fabrics and often other imported goods.

Messuage: a house with its surrounding land and outbuildings.

Open (common) fields: communal agrarian organisation under which an individual's farmland was held in strips scattered between two or more large fields, intermingled with the strips of other tenants. Management of the fields, and usually common meadows and pasture, was regulated through the manor court or other communal assembly.

Pays: A distinctive area of countryside which was, until modern times, farmed or exploited in a particular way and had other common social or economic features.

Pilaster: a flat Classical column projecting from a wall.

Pinder: a manorial officer in charge of the pound, where stray animals were kept.

Pioneer crop: a crop selected for its ability to improve the quality of land that has not been sown for many years, ahead of crop production.

Presbyterian: the Presbyterian Church rejected government by bishops and was governed by a body of ministers and lay people who were equal in rank.

Probate inventory: a list and valuation of the moveable goods and livestock owned by a person when they died.

Rectory: (1) a church living served by a rector, who generally received the church's whole income; (2) the church's property or endowment, consisting of tithes, offerings and usually some land or glebe.

Roman: a period of British history from AD 42 to 410, divided into the early Roman (AD 42–250) and the late Roman (AD 250–410).

Rustication: a type of decoration used in Classical architecture involving cutting back just the horizontal, just the vertical or all the edges of blocks of stone used for the face of a building to make them more prominent.

Soke: in the Domesday Book, a soke was a dependent, free territory covering several settlements where the land was held by free peasants.

Sokeman: a type of free peasant.

Stapler: a merchant who was a member of the Company of the Staple at Calais, which controlled the export of wool to continental Europe in late medieval England.

Stint: the number of animals a tenant was allowed to graze on common pastures, as agreed and enforced through the manor court.

Sub-infeudation: the granting of land held by a feudal tenant to a sub-tenant.

Terrier: register of the lands belonging to a landowner, originally including a list of tenants, their holdings and the rents paid, and later consisting of a description of the acreage and boundaries of the property.

Tithe: a tax of one tenth of the produce of the land, which originally went to the church. It could be divided into great tithes (corn and hay), which went to the rector, and small tithes (livestock, wool and other crops), which supported a vicar.

Tithing: a system where groups of ten households were responsible to the manor court for the good conduct of each of their members.

Turnpike: a road administered by a trust, which covered the cost of maintenance by charging tolls.

Vestry: (1) a room in a church where clerical vestments are stored; (2) an assembly of leading parishioners and ratepayers which is responsible for poor relief and other secular matters as well as for church affairs.

Villani: see Villein

Villein: in the Middle Ages, a peasant tenant who technically belonged to the lord, suffered legal handicaps and usually owed labour services on the lord's demesne as well as rent. Villeinage gradually declined during the later Middle Ages. The earlier villani, mentioned in the Domesday Book, enjoyed freer status.

Virgate: a standard holding of arable land in the Middle Ages of a quarter of a carucate (q.v.), generally 15 to 40 acres, depending on the quality of the land. A virgate usually generated surplus crops for sale at market; those with fractions of a virgate probably needed to work part-time for better-off neighbours. Also called a yardland.

Worsted: a high-quality woollen yarn made from long fibres, and the fabric made from this yarn.

Yardland: see Virgate.

This history of Lutterworth has been written using a wide range of primary source material, both printed and manuscript. This list includes the main sources used, which is best consulted in conjunction with the footnotes and the list of Abbreviations.

The National Archives, the Record Office for Leicestershire, Leicester and Rutland, and the other repositories mentioned here have online catalogues and research guides, although the online catalogues may not include all their holdings.

Manuscript Sources

The National Archives (TNA) at Kew holds the records of national government from the late 12th century onwards, with some earlier material. Calendars (brief abstracts) of some of the administrative records of government in the Middle Ages and the early modern period have been published, and are also used in this history. The main classes of manuscript documents used are:

BT 31	Board of Trade, files of dissolved companies
C 1, C 5, C 6, C 8, C 10, C 11	Court of Chancery Pleadings
C 66	Patent Rolls
C 134, C 135, C 142	Inquisitions Post Mortem
C 241	Certificates of Statute Merchant and Statute Staple
CP 40	Court of Chancery Pleadings and Proceedings, Richard II to Philip and Mary
E 41	Treasury of Receipt, Ancient Deeds
E 101	King's Remembrancer, Marshalsey of the Household, Estreats
E 134	King's Remembrancer, Depositions taken by Commission
E 179	Exchequer Taxation Records, 1190–1690
E 182	King's Remembrancer, Accounts of Land and Assessed Taxes
E 315	Court of Augmentations, Grants
ED 21	Ministry of Education, Public Elementary School Files, 1857–1946

ED 27	Secondary Education, Endowment Files
ED 109	Board of Education, HM Inspectorate Reports on Secondary Institutions
HO 107	Home Office, Census Enumerators' Returns, 1841, 1851
HO 129	Home Office, Ecclesiastical Census, 1851
IR 18	Tithe Files, 1836–70
IR 23	Land Tax Redemption Office, Quotas and Assessments
IR 58	Board of Inland Revenue, Valuation Office, Field Books
IR 130	Board of Inland Revenue, Valuation Office, Record Sheet Plans
JUST 1/1400	Rolls for the Justices in Eyre, of Assize, of Oyer and Terminer, and of the Peace
LR 2	Office of the Auditors of Land Revenue, Surveys and Rentals
LR 15	Office of the Auditors of Land Revenue, Enrolment Books
MAF 32	National Farm Survey Farm Records, 1941–3
MAF 68	Agricultural Returns, 1866–1988
PROB 4	Prerogative Court of Canterbury, Probate Inventories
PROB 11	Prerogative Court of Canterbury, Wills
RG 9–14	Registrar General, Census Enumerators' Returns, 1861–1911
SC 6	Special Collections, Ministers' and Receivers' Accounts
SC 11	Special Collections, Rentals and Surveys
STAC 8	Court of Star Chamber Proceedings, James I
WARD 2	Court of Wards and Liveries, Deeds and Evidences
WO 30/48	War Office. Returns of Inns and Alehouses for Billeting, 1686

The British Library

| Add. Ch. 73016 | Deeds 1597 |
| Add. Roll 66077 | Accounts of the estates of William, Lord Ferrers 1361–2 |

MS Catalogue of Lord Frederick Campbell's Charter

Dr Williams's Library

| MS 34.4 | John Evans' List of Dissenting Congregations |

Lambeth Palace Library holds central records of the Church of England (including documents previously held at the Church of England Records Centre). The classes of records used include:

CC/OF/NB	Church Commissioners, Benefice Files
ECE 7/1	Ecclesiastical Commissioners for England, Benefice Files
F II	Faculty Office, Fiats
ICBS 1900	Incorporated Church Building Society, Files
ICBS MB	Incorporated Church Building Society, Minute Books
NS 7/1	National Society, School Files
QAB 7/7	Governors of the Bounty of Queen Anne, Parsonage Measures Files

Principal Probate Registry

Wills proved from 1858

Record Office for Leicestershire, Leicester and Rutland in Wigston, Leicestershire, holds records of county administration, records of the diocese of Leicester (from 1926), some earlier archidiaconal records and numerous parish, school, family and business records. The principal classes of documents used in this history are:

1D 41/2	Leicester Archdeaconry, Glebe terriers
1D 41/4/L085-91	Leicester Archdeaconry Court, Proceedings and Cause Papers
1D 41/18	Leicester Archdeaconry, Church Inspections and Archdeacons' Visitations
1D 41/34	Leicester Archdeaconry, Subscriptions of curates and schoolmasters
1D 41/41	Leicester Archdeaconry, Faculties
1D 41/44	Registrations of meeting houses
5D 33/189	Farnham Bequest, MS notes of George Farnham
18D 67/2520	Sale Particulars, Misterton Estate
35'29/378–82	Particulars of Moorbarns and Rental of Feilding Estate in Lutterworth
245'50	Leicester Archdeaconry, Visitations
DE 115/1	Prior's Map of Leicestershire
DE 126, DE 3614	Sherrier School Records

DE 203	Enclosure Commissioners' Minutes
DE 617/13	Leicestershire Constabulary, Lutterworth District, Police Constable's Journal
DE 783/25–6	Plans of Farms and Estates in Lutterworth
DE 783/29	Sales Particulars, Land at Moorbarns
DE 783/51–2	Feilding Palmer Cottage Hospital, Annual Reports and Building Plans
DE 895/1	Report by George Gilbert Scott on St Mary's Church, 1866
DE 914/1–2	Town Masters' Accounts 1761–1872
DE 1012	Deeds
DE 1379/37	Lutterworth Board of Guardians, Sale of Parish Property
DE 1379/413–15	Lutterworth RSA, Minutes 1872–94
DE 1379/446–9	Lutterworth RDC, General Committee Minutes 1900–33
DE 1379/450	Lutterworth RDC, Committee for Working Class Housing Minutes 1919–21
DE 1379/451–2	Lutterworth RDC, Central Committee Minutes 1921–37
DE 1379/453	Lutterworth RDC, Housing Committee Minutes 1934–49
DE 1379/457, DE 2107/9	Lutterworth Parochial Committee Minutes 1915–27, 1947–9
DE 1463/6, DE 4336/33	Vestry Minutes 1789–1960
DE 2015	Greenwood's Map of Leicestershire
DE 2072/149	Board of Inland Revenue, Valuation Office, Schedules
DE 2094, DE 4336	Parish Registers
DE 2559/18–21	Churchwardens' Accounts, 1639–1894
DE 2559/24–5	Constables' Accounts, 1651–1707, 1809–32
DE 2559/35–47	Overseers of the Poor, Accounts, 1673–1829
DE 2559/89	Apprenticeship Indentures
DE 2559/99	Sessions Order
DE 2559/102	Town Masters' Accounts, 1707–26
DE 2559/104	Deed of Exchange
DE 2559/124	Census of Heads of Households and Occupations, 1821
DE 3799	Business and Personal Papers of the Pettit Family

DE 3831/121	Leicestershire Constabulary, Police Journal
DE 4336/39	Committee for Restoration of St Mary's Church, Minutes
DE 4336/47	Scheme for Lutterworth Charities
DE 6660/1	Memorandum of Agreement, Parsonage House
EN/AX/211/1	Copy of Enclosure Allotments
EN/MB/211/1	Enclosure Commissioners' Minutes
Leicester Archdeaconry Probate Records	Admons and wills; Probate inventories (PR/I); Probate records (PR/T); Wills, 1563–1858; Wills and inventories, 1500–1603; Wills from 1858 (DE 462); Will registers, 1515–33
Ma/L/4C	Map of Leicestershire, Charles Smith, 1801
Ma/L/35	Map of Leicestershire and Warwickshire, Christopher Saxton, 1576
Misc. 239	Enclosure map
N/C/211/1	Lutterworth Independent Chapel Covenant and Members
Ordnance Survey maps	
QS 3/177/58/M/22; QS 5/1/3	Quarter Sessions Requests for Briefs
QS 6/1/2	Quarter Sessions Order Book 1678–1700
QS 36/2/1, 5, 7, 10	Quarter Sessions Alehouse Recognisance Books
QS 44	Quarter Sessions Licences for Dissenters' Meeting Houses
QS 62	Quarter Sessions Land Tax Assessments
QS 95	Quarter Sessions Returns of Dissenters
Ti/155	Tithe maps and Apportionments

Cotesbach Educational Trust, Cotesbach

The Trust holds the Marriott family archive, which includes documents relating to the purchase of Moorbarns. These include:

CEA 1/1/166–7, CEA 1/1/182	Deeds and plans
CEA 1/1/185, CEA 1/1/720	Sales documents

Lutterworth Museum

4D 60/342	Letter from County Magistrates to Peatling Magna parish about sharing Lutterworth's workhouse, under the 1782 Poor Relief (Gilbert's) Act
4D 60/395	Lutterworth Town Estate Charges for Market Stalls

Box 77	Miscellaneous, cinema programme
Box 92	Miscellaneous, records of some Lutterworth businesses, the station and sidings and RDC handbook
Box 129	Miscellaneous, details of Town Hall Charity and the first council houses

Photograph Collection

Harborough District Buildings Records relating to Lutterworth

Plans by Joseph Hansom for Town Hall, 1835

Printed Resolutions of Meeting held in 1835 to discuss provision of Town Hall

List of Subscribers to Town Hall Fund

Various original local newspapers and periodicals

Leicestershire and Rutland Historic Environment Record

Details are available online at https://www.heritagegateway.org.uk/gateway/chr. Supporting papers are held by Leics. CC at County Hall, Glenfield.

Bodleian Library, Oxford

MS Rawlinson B 350	MS notes of William Burton
MS Walker C11	MS notes of John Walker

Buckinghamshire Record Office

D 104-51-2	Indenture, Lodge Mills

Coventry Archives and Research Centre

BA/B/16/361/1; BA/D/4	Deeds relating to Lutterworth 1349–1498

Gloucestershire Archives

747 BA 2933	Letters about collection of briefs

Lichfield Record Office

Wills, administrations and inventories

Lincolnshire Archives holds records relating to the diocese of Lincoln, which included Lutterworth until 1837. The most important classes used are:

Bishop's Registers (Wills)	
COR B 5	Bishops' correspondence
DIOC/TER	Glebe terriers
M/F 1/45–46, M/F 1/50–51	Visitation Records of Bishop Gibson

Northamptonshire Record Office holds records relating to the diocese of Peterborough, which included Lutterworth between 1837 and 1926, and records of county administration and county families. The records used are:

Boxes X920–6	Diocese of Peterborough, Visitation Returns
ML 587, ML 594, ML 597, ML 601	Diocese of Peterborough, Visitation Returns
ML 1116, ML 1118, ML 1120	Diocese of Peterborough, Faculties and Licences
QS 2A	Northamptonshire Quarter Sessions, Turnpike Plans
Temple (Stowe) 7/2	Temple Family of Stowe, Estate Papers

Warwickshire Record Office

CR 26/1/9/39	Deeds Moorbarns
CR 2017	Family and Estate Papers, Feilding Family, Earls of Denbigh
DRB 81/23–24	Parish Registers
MR 13	Court Rolls of the Manor of Atherstone

Printed Sources

The most important printed sources, including calendars of major classes of records in The National Archives and parliamentary papers, are included in the list of Abbreviations. The Lincoln Record Society has published many original records of the ancient diocese of Lincoln which contain information about Lutterworth. Transcripts of some other original documents have been published by the *Associated Architectural Societies, Reports and Papers* and within the *Transactions of Leicestershire Archaeological and Historical Society*.

Good collections of Leicestershire trade directories and 20th-century telephone directories are held at ROLLR. National newspapers and local newspapers have also been used extensively in this research, some within the collections held at ROLLR and others digitised by the British Newspaper Archive.

Books and Articles

John Nichols's *History and Antiquities of the County of Leicester* (London, 1795–1815) remains an important secondary source for the history of the county. The Lutterworth entry is in volume IV, part 1 (1807). This largely incorporates the earlier entry for Lutterworth in William Burton's *Description of Leicestershire*, 2nd edn (King's Lynn, 1777).

The main sources used for architectural history are N. Pevsner (rev. E. Williamson), *The Buildings of England: Leicestershire and Rutland*, 2nd edn (Harmondsworth, 1984), and the various listings of properties on the National Heritage List for England.

INDEX

CPSIA information can be obtained
at www.ICGtesting.com
Printed in the USA
JSHW041257210123
36516JS00005B/70